Unconventional AIRCRAFT

SECOND EDITION

Peter M. Bowers

TAB BOOKS
Blue Ridge Summit, PA

SECOND EDITION
FIRST PRINTING

Copyright © 1990 by **TAB BOOKS.** First edition copyright © 1984 by **TAB BOOKS**.

Printed in the United States of America

Library of Congress Cataloging-in-Publication Data

Bowers, Peter M.
      Unconventional aircraft / by Peter M. Bowers. — 2nd ed.
          p.   cm.
      ISBN 0-8306-8450-6 — ISBN 0-8306-2450-3 (pbk.)
      1. Airplanes.   I. Title.
   TL671.B59   1990
   629.133—dc20   89-48466
                                                              CIP

TAB BOOKS offers software for sale. For information and a catalog, please contact TAB Software Department, Blue Ridge Summit, PA 17294-0850.

Questions regarding the content of this book should be addressed to:

      Reader Inquiry Branch
      TAB BOOKS
      Blue Ridge Summit, PA 17294-0214

Acquisitions Editor: Jeff Worsinger
Technical Editor: Norval G. Kennedy
Production: Katherine Brown
Cover Design: Lori E. Schlosser

Contents

About the Cover

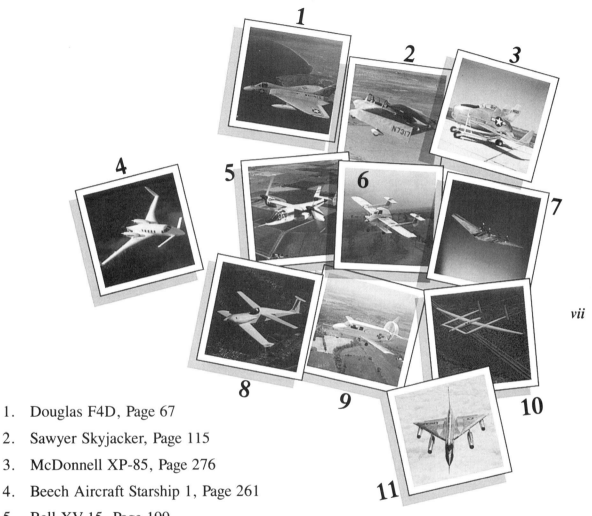

vii

Introduction

Defining an "unconventional aircraft" is like asking someone "How high is up?" It's largely a matter of individual interpretation—one man's "conventional configuration" can easily be another man's "freak."

In the early years of aircraft development—roughly to 1914, when the performance requirements of World War I forced relative standardization of the basic aircraft configuration—there were no standards by which to determine "conventionality" or the lack of it. Many different inventors were taking different approaches to the primary problems of flight.

When viewed in light of today's practices, many of these early efforts seem to be freaks. Some proved to have merit and warranted further development; others were unworkable and were dropped. However, subsequent state-of-the-art changes in other areas resulted in the resurrection and actual use of some features that were failures when they first appeared.

The "standard" airplane that we know today—with the main lifting surfaces in front, the empennage, or tail surfaces behind, and the people and cargo in a box-like interconnecting structure called the fuselage—was pretty well firmed up by 1909. Relatively minor variations to this basic configuration have been made continually right up to the present to meet special requirements.

Other configurations such as tailless, canard (the "tail" ahead of the wing), direct lift, and different powerplant and accessory arrangements were believed by their proponents to have specific advantages that justified their continued development. Some of these dropped from the scene when their inherent disadvantages overcame their alleged advantages and were largely forgotten. Other people reinvented some of these in later years—sometimes only to fail again, but in other cases to succeed because the feature was now compatible with or made workable by the prevailing state-of-the-art.

This book is not intended to be a catalog of odd aircraft. Rather, it presents related groupings of what by *today's* standards can be considered separate categories of unconventional configurations—canards, delta wings, tailless, etc.—and explains the reasoning behind them. Some aircraft qualify for inclusion under two or more categories but are placed according to their most prominent feature. Gliders and airplanes are freely mixed in appropriate presentations. Some of the aircraft are best remembered for some characteristics other than the basic configuration in which they appear. For example, the Messerschmitt 163 is more famous for being the first rocket-powered interceptor than the first tailless design built in quantity.

The fact that some basic configurations (such as canard and tailless) are presented in chronological order does not necessarily establish an order of technical progression or imply that the detail of one was derived from a preceding presentation.

The book also illustrates minor variations of standard features that make particular aircraft models distinctive and shows some specialized uses of aircraft outside the normal channels of military operations, transportation, and sport. Some designs that defy logical categorization are grouped in a separate "What Is It?" chapter.

I apologize in advance to those readers who will be disappointed because their "Favorite Freak"—uh..."unconventional aircraft"—has been omitted. There are simply too many to include in a book of this size and price. Also, aircraft specifications and performance figures have been minimized. Some are not included because none are available for those particular designs, most details of which survive only in photos. This book emphasizes the *configurations* of the aircraft and the reasons for them. The figures given are to establish the size and operational regime of the aircraft, not to make detailed comparisons between designs that are actually not comparable.

Acknowledgments

I wish to acknowledge the assistance of the following people in providing data, photographs, and other assistance during the compilation of this book: James H. and James R. Dilonardo, Joseph P. Juptner, and Jim Larsen, photos; Anne Piersall, typing; Art Shultz, drawings; Dave Sclair, Publisher of the *Western Flyer* newspaper; Victor D. Seely of the Museum of Flight; Jay Spenser of the National Air and Space Museum; and John Underwood, photos and data. Also numerous unnamed correspondents and fellow collectors who have added to the Bowers archives over the past 50 years.

1
CHAPTER

Canard Aircraft

SINCE THE FIRST SUCCESSFUL AIRPLANE—THE WRIGHT brothers' 1903 Flyer—was built in the configuration that we know today as a *canard,* it is the logical design with which to begin a book about what we now consider to be unconventional aircraft configurations.

A MISNOMER

First off, the term *canard* is a misnomer. In the generally accepted aeronautical sense, it means an aircraft with the horizontal "tail" surfaces—the stabilizer and elevators—ahead of the wing or wings instead of behind. The term can logically be applied to airships as well as to airplanes and gliders. In fact, the early Zeppelins did have forward-located horizontal control surfaces in addition to their conventional tails (FIG. 1-1). In general, the term implies the forward location of the *primary* control, not an auxiliary. The word *canard* is French for duck, and the reference to the bird is because the duck's wing is at the rear of its body, as viewed in flight—not that the tail is ahead of the wing. A canard is also a joke, or an absurdity, so in this day of solidly "conventional" aircraft, the term is doubly applicable to canard aircraft.

In many cases, canard aircraft can be considered as tandem-wing designs with relatively small forward wings. In such cases, the forward surfaces, which usually consist of a fixed surface corresponding to the stabilizer, plus elevators, carry a significant portion of the flight load.

In recent years, the term has been applied to auxiliary surfaces added to the front of otherwise conventional airplanes (along with some delta-wing types) for trimming action or airflow control, rather than for primary control or partial load-carrying as on a true canard airplane.

TWO TYPES

There are two basically different types of canard aircraft. First, there is the classic or true canard, which this author prefers to call a "two-surface canard," meaning that there are only two sets of flying surfaces and that the entire pitch control, or stabilizer/elevator function, is performed entirely by the surfaces (monoplane or biplane) ahead of the main wing, which can be a single unit or a set of biplane or even triplane surfaces.

The other is what the author calls a "three-surface canard" while others call it a "hybrid canard." These can also be called double-ended, in that they have an additional horizontal surface, either fixed or moveable,

Fig. 1-1. The early Zeppelins can be called canard aircraft in that they had elevators forward as well as aft. The quadruplane surfaces seen on the nose of LZ-7 Deutschland in 1910 are duplicated at the rear. The nonmoveable stabilizers are rigidly attached to the rear of the hull.

1

some distance aft of the wing that performs either a sta-bilizer, elevator, or lift function, or all three.

These two canard configurations will be discussed separately and later in this chapter, with the classic "two-surface" first.

WHY THE CANARD?

Before they started, the Wright Brothers had plenty of previous man-built aircraft to follow—and, of course, the bird—so why did they put the tail out in front? For one, they recognized the function of the "horizontal rudder" in changing the flight attitude, or *pitch,* of the aircraft and figured that it would be more effective ahead than behind. In this they were correct, but were not aware of the disadvantages at the time.

Their other prime reason was their initial flying site. They were operating on sand, and therefore could not use wheels. Their gliders and the 1903 Flyer sat level on skids and very close to the ground. The broth-ers also recognized the need to "rotate" the aircraft to obtain a higher angle of attack during takeoff and land-ing, and such a low-slung machine would drag a "tail" that was out behind. They did have a vertical rudder behind the wings—and yes, it did drag on rotation, but they allowed for that. The booms that supported the rudder were pivoted and the bracing wire ran only from the top forward to the rear lower points. As the rudder dragged, the booms pivoted upward with no effect on control because the rudder was not being deflected across the airstream.

ADVANTAGES

In modern usage, the primary advantage of the canard layout is improved maneuverability, which keeps the military interested in continued development. The better maneuverability of the canard has also been very helpful in improving the heretofore sluggish per-formance of some of the recent ultralight recreational designs.

Another advantage claimed for the canard aircraft is that it can be made "stallproof." The lightly-loaded forward wing will stall before the main wing that car-ries most of the load will stall. This allows the nose to drop slightly, thereby increasing the airspeed and allowing the aircraft to continue normal flight without stalling the main wing.

DISADVANTAGES

The primary disadvantage of the canard design is that it is inherently unstable in pitch, or movement about the lateral axis of the aircraft. Instead of damping out a displacement about this axis as does a horizontal tail behind (like the feathers on an arrow), the airstream acts on the forward surface to increase the displace-ment. In his writings. Orville Wright declared that the pitch stability of a canard was a direct function of pilot skill.

Early experience showed that if the forward sur-face carried any significant load at all, it figured promi-nently in the balance setup. Stalling the forward sur-face removed that much of the two-point support, like kicking the legs out from under one end of a table—the other legs continue to support the opposite end, so the table itself drops at the unsupported end. The "stallproof" idea was quickly dropped and canards vanished for all practical purposes until serious experi-mentation got under way early in the World War II search for performance improvement. Nothing came of this at that time, either.

There have been some very successful canards in recent years, however, that do take advantage of the acknowledged benefits of the configuration for special-purpose operations. However, they have gimmicks to keep the forward surface from stalling, either by limit-ing the angle of attack, using blown flaps on the canards, using an airfoil with different lift characteris-tics, or using it only as a trimming surface with no essential load on an established design such as a delta-wing or swept-back tailless. Some modern aerody-namic missiles are canards, but they operate with computers and automatic pilots that detect any dis-placement and make corrections before the displace-ment can develop into a major divergence.

For anything with pre-1960's technology and pilot-ing, however, the canard was a disaster. It is significant that as soon as the Wrights adopted wheels that held their planes higher off the ground and permitted rolling starts (late in 1909), they got rid of the canard and put the elevators in back with the rudder.

The most numerous canard designs in use today are in the field of ultralights, which, as a class, go a long way back toward the Wright Brothers' kind of fly-ing: very limited speed range, limited maneuverability, and no significant payload. There have probably been

2

more canards built for this specific activity in the 1980-1988 time frame than all the other canards produced back to the year 1901. However, canard designs are now appearing in larger high-performance aircraft like turboprop business designs and small transports.

TWO-SURFACE CANARDS

A characteristic of nearly all the early two-surface canards was that the forward moveable surface was what would be called today a "flying tail," in that the entire surface moved to perform the elevator function; there was no fixed stabilizer ahead of a hinged elevator. In the years following World War I, the few new canard designs that appeared had fixed forward stabilizers rigidly attached to the fuselage, with full-span elevators hinged to the stabilizer.

The Wright Flyers

The first successful powered man-carrying flying machine was the Wright Brothers' 1903 Flyer. They retained the same configuration into 1909 (FIG. 1-2),

then put the elevators behind the wing as most other builders were then doing.

Note that the biplane elevators of this 1908 Wright Model A did not have fixed horizontal stabilizers ahead of them. The surfaces were pivoted at a point well behind the leading edge to divide and balance the air load so that the full load would not be transmitted to the pilot's hand. As it was, the surface tended to swerve under changing loads or gusts on the aircraft instead of remaining stable as similar surfaces preceded by a fixed stabilizer would do. Later canard designs by others reduced this sensitivity by adding a fixed horizontal stabilizer ahead of the canard elevators.

Note that the canard on the Wright design functions primarily as a control surface and does not contribute much to the total lift. The pilot and engine are both located on the wing, which means that the center of gravity of the machine is close to or actually behind the leading edge of the wing—not ahead of it, as it would be if the canard were carrying a load proportional to it size.

The Wright's design did not improve significantly after 1909; the Brothers ceased to be inventors and

3

Fig. 1-2. Wright Brother's Model A of 1908, a refinement of their original canard airplane of 1903.

devoted their main energy to litigation—suing other aircraft builders for infringing their patents. They retained wing-warping for lateral control and chain drive from one central engine to two outboard propellers. Wilbur Wright died of typhoid in 1912. After dabbling with tractor designs inspired by others, Orville sold the company in 1915.

Specifications, 1908 Wright Model A: Powerplant, Wright 30-hp; span 36 feet 4 inches; wing area 415 square feet; gross weight 1,200 pounds; top speed 44 mph.

Santos-Dumont 14bis

The first recorded airplane flight in Europe (they spelled it "aeroplane") was made on October 26, 1906, by Alberto Santos-Dumont, a Brazilian living in Paris. He was already famous as a flier because of the small airships he had built and flown around Paris since 1899. The designation of his canard aeroplane was 14bis, derived from the fact that its first trip off the ground was made while suspended from his No. 14 airship.

Powered by a 24-hp water-cooled pusher engine, the 14bis made a few straight-ahead hops, with a maximum duration of 21.4 seconds and a distance of 750 feet. The design was a true canard, with the forward surface carrying some load (FIG. 1-3). There was no lateral (roll control) system; the designer relied on generous dihedral for lateral stability as had the earlier Langley Aerodrome (see Chapter 2). The pilot was located well ahead of the wing and 24-hp pusher

4

Fig. 1-3. Alberto Santos-Dumont in his canard 14bis, the first airplane to fly in Europe.

engine, soon increased to 50, and stood upright as he had in his airships. Santos-Dumont quickly recognized the inherent disadvantages of the canard design, his next aeroplane, the famous Demoiselle of 1908, pioneered what was to become the classic "tractor" configuration.

Specifications: Powerplant, Antoinette 24-hp (later, 50-hp); span 36 feet 9 inches; area 560 square feet; gross weight 661 pounds; maximum speed 25 mph.

Vaniman Triplane

A French builder, Melvin Vaniman, built an ambitious triplane and tried it in October 1908 (FIG. 1-4). This had many shortcomings, having been built before Wilbur Wright's famous August-December demonstrations that showed French and other European designers the importance of three-axis control and efficient propellers. The Vaniman was influenced by earlier Wright details in having the engine right alongside the pilot on the lower wing, with an extension shaft driving a single propeller behind the wing. An elevator in the form of an unloaded canard was ahead of the wing, as was the rudder that used a separate set of booms. At first, the Vaniman had no provision for lateral control, but even after projecting wingtip ailerons were added, the triplane was unable to fly.

Fig. 1-5. The French Fabre canard monoplane of 1910 was the first airplane to take off from water.

Fabre Hydroplane

This unique design, built by Frenchman Henri Fabre in 1910, is more famous for being the first heavier-than-air flying machine to take off from water under its own power than for being a canard. This historic flight was made on March 28, 1910 (FIG. 1-5). It did not come down on the water, and the performance was not repeated. It proved, however, that airplanes could be flown from water as well as land. The American Glenn Curtiss began continuous public seaplane operations on January 26, 1911.

The Fabre machine was a true canard with significant loading of the forward surfaces. Note the location of the variable weight—the pilot—between the wing and the canards. The elevator is a separate surface on top, with direct control from the pilot through a stick and push-pull rod. The fixed forward surface has almost enough span to reclassify the design as a tandem-wing.

Note the seven-cylinder Gnome rotary engine aft of the wing and the extensive use of vertical fin area on the fuselage and wing. The flat-bottom floats have barely enough displacement to support the weight of the machine when afloat; it is doubtful whether they could keep it afloat during a rough landing or the extensive taxiing that must have been anticipated because the rear floats were fitted with water rudders that look surprisingly like those in use today.

Specifications: Powerplant, Gnome rotary 50-hp; span 45 feet 11 inches; wing area 183 square feet; gross weight 1,047 pounds; top speed 55 mph.

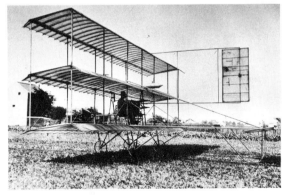

Fig. 1-4. The French Vaniman triplane canard of 1908 also had a canard rudder carried on a separate structure from the elevator.

5

1910 Deperdussin

This French Deperdussin canard was displayed at the 1910 French Aero Show, but there is no information relative to subsequent flights.

The canard had a fixed stabilizer with movable elevators on torque tubes mounted on the tips of the stabilizer instead of being hinged behind it. Also, a fixed vertical fin and movable rudder were carried at the front of the machine instead of at the rear as on most other canard designs (FIG. 1-6).

The engine was located in the fuselage ahead of the pilot, with an extension shaft running aft along the bottom to pulleys that drove two propellers through belts or chains. These were actually the unique feature of this particular Deperdussin design. This was the first known use of coaxial propellers rotating in different directions to neutralize torque reaction and to permit a smaller propeller diameter for a given power, thereby permitting a shorter landing gear. Prop-behind-the-tail pushers have a special problem here in that the tail has to be high off the ground just to ensure adequate propeller clearance.

1912 Voisin

The advantages of the tractor design over the canard were solidly established by 1912, but some die-hard designers kept trying. FIGURE 1-7 shows a French Voisin seaplane flying in one of the popular seaplane races and air shows held at Monaco in 1912.

The canard surface included a fixed stabilizer that contributed significantly to the lift (note the high angle of incidence), with hinged elevators behind it. The rudder was forward, but there was no vertical fin associated with it. The vertical surfaces between the wings were fixed fins to provide directional stability. The pilot was seated ahead of the wing while the engine was inside the fuselage, ahead of the trailing edge of the wing and driving the pusher propeller through an extension shaft.

A major drawback to seaplanes with pusher engines then and now is the problem of spray kicked up by the floats going through the propeller.

Specifications: Powerplant, Renault 80-hp; span 44 feet 3 1/2 inches; wing area 376 square feet; gross weight 1,212 pounds; maximum speed 62 mph.

6

Fig. 1-6. The French Deperdussin of 1911 was not only a canard, it featured the first known application of coaxial propellers.

Fig. 1-7. The French Voisin canard seaplane of 1912 featured an odd arrangement of four flat-bottomed pontoons.

Bleriot 1912 Canard

In spite of the rapid ascendancy of the tractor-type airplane as pioneered by the French builders Louis Bleriot and Alberto Santos-Dumont, some stubbornly continued to work on canard designs practically up to World War I. Bleriot himself, with a highly successful monoplane in production (see Chapter 7) continued to experiment with canards, building two different canard monoplanes in 1911 and 1912. While neither got beyond the prototype stage, they are nevertheless interesting examples of his thoughts of the time, particularly the 1912 model (FIG. 1-8).

Platz Sailboat Glider

Perhaps the most unusual canard design of them all was the flexible-wing Platz glider of 1923. Rheinhold Platz was the chief designer of the German Fokker firm in 1917 and 1918 and for the relocated Dutch firm after World War I. When sport gliding became popular in Europe in the early 1920s, he developed this super-simple device.

It had only two rigid parts, the longitudinal beams that formed the fuselage and the single wing spar. The surfaces were like the main sails and jibs of two small sailboats joined at 180 degrees on the waterline. Platz' use of single-surface flexible cloth for lifting surfaces preceded the famous Rogallo Wing by nearly 40 years, but nothing came of it at the time. With only two

Fig. 1-8. The French Bleriot Model XXXIII of 1912 (Bleriot used Roman numerals) was one of the last of the original true canards and carried its elevator on a single boom ahead of the fuselage and mounted the rudder on a unique structure that bypassed the wing and pusher engine.

Fig. 1-9. The spans of the fore and aft surfaces of the 1923 Platz glider were equal, but because of the area differential and control functions, it should be regarded as a canard rather than a tandem-wing.

Fig. 1-10. The most publicized canard since pre-World War I days was the short-lived German Focke-Wulf 19a Ente of 1927.

beams, the whole thing could be rolled up and carried over the pilot's shoulder while he rode home on a bicycle!

The control system was unlike anything seen before or since. The pilot held the ends of the canard booms, which were lifting surfaces, in his two hands (FIG. 1-9). Once trimmed for level flight, he lowered both hands to increase lift and thereby raised the nose, and pushed upward with both hands to lower the nose. To initiate a left turn, he would push up slightly with his left hand and pull down similarly with his right to provide differential aileron action.

Platz' glider did fly, but how well and for how long is not known. Other than historical references, nothing has been heard of it since it was briefly described in some 1923 publications.

Focke-Wulf Ente

Extensive publicity made the German Focke-Wulf FW 19a Ente of 1927 the best-known canard design of the 1920s and for many years thereafter. *Ente,* by the way, is the German word for duck, and also joke or hoax. The product of a major aircraft manufacturing firm, it was a true canard, with significant lift from the forward surface and the variable passenger load in a cabin on the center of gravity, which was well ahead of the wing (FIG. 1-10).

In an attempt to make the elevators more effective, they were mounted slightly below the stabilizer on external hinges to obtain better airflow over them through a slot effect. As with many other canards before it, the FW 19a had a very large vertical fin and rudder combination due to its relatively short distance from the center of gravity compared to conventional tractor designs or canards, such as the Deperdussin and Voisin (which had "unstable" rudders at the very front). Even then, the Ente needed additional fin area in line with the wing.

The "Ente" flew successfully but crashed in September 1927 after a very short career. A second "Ente" was then built and flew successfully for several years. Its major contribution to aviation can be considered its re-introduction of the tricycle landing gear; a design feature that had been abandoned at the start of World War I.

Specifications: Powerplant, two Siemens SH-14 of 100-hp each; span 32 feet $9^{1}/_{2}$ inches; gross weight 3,638 pounds; maximum speed 88 mph.

Raab-Katzenstein Sportplane

The German firm of Raab-Katzenstein combined glider technology with some of the FW 19a's concepts with this tricycle-geared single-seat canard pusher (FIG. 1-11). There was a fixed stabilizer forward, with hinged elevators, but the fins and rudders were between the wings instead of behind them. Note the skid structure extending behind the main wheels to keep the propeller

Fig. 1-12. The Gee Bee Ascender of 1930 was built from the major components of a standard American Aeronca C-2 lightplane.

Fig. 1-11. The single-seat German Raab-Katzenstein canard sportplane of the mid-1920s.

from contacting the ground if the plane tipped backward or landed at a high angle of attack.

By canard standards, the R-K was conventional. Its unique feature was the use of integral booster rockets to speed up the takeoff, after which it cruised on normal engine power. The rocket-assisted takeoff technique was perfected during World War II and has been in wide use ever since.

Gee-Bee Ascender

An example of quick adaptation of some standard airplane components to an unconventional experimental design is presented by the Gee-Bee Ascender of 1931 (FIG. 1-12). It used the long wire-braced wing (36 feet) and 30-hp two-cylinder engine of a production single-seat Aeronca C-2 lightplane, which was virtually a powered glider.

The Ascender, so named because of its apparent direction of flight, was the creation of the Granville Brothers, who had a small airplane factory on the airport at Springfield, Massachusetts. They were soon to become famous as the builders of the stubby record-smashing Gee-Bee (for Granville Brothers) racing planes.

The Ascender was a pure experiment, but showed some innovations, particularly in powerplant placement. Again, as it had on the FW-19a and the Raab-Katzenstein, the level attitude of the fuselage proved to a natural for tricycle landing gear several years before

that arrangement made its significant comeback. Note the similarity to the FW-19a in the need for a very large vertical fin at the rear of the fuselage, because of its short distance from the center of gravity.

Ambrosini SS-4

The all-metal SS-4 of 1939 (FIG. 1-13) was the second canard effort of the Italian firm of Societe Aeronautica Italiana A. Ambrosini & Sons of Passignano—Ambrosini, for short. Their first canard was a little 38-hp sportplane, the SS-3, which was named *Anitra*—Italian for duck.

With a 960-hp Isetta-Fraschini engine, the unnamed SS-4, based on SS-3 aerodynamics, was the most powerful canard airplane to date. It was designed

9

Fig. 1-13. The Italian Ambrosini SS-4 fighter was the highest-performance and the most versatile canard built from the time of the Wright Brothers to World War II.

as a slick fighter, with retractable tricycle landing gear and a formidable battery of one 30mm cannon and two 20mm cannons. It was also the highest-performance canard so far, with a top speed of 355 mph and also the longest-lived. It survived two years of testing, but crashed in 1940 following a powerplant failure.

The canard carried part of the load and consisted of a fixed stabilizer and conventional elevators. The problem of a short moment arm for the vertical fin and rudder was resolved by using two of each, located halfway out on each slightly swept-back wing, a configuration that was to be used on some later canard designs and even some tailless types.

Because of the prevailing World War II situation and the time required to advance from a flying prototype to the delivery of production models, a second prototype SS-4 was cancelled as the firm devoted all of its effort to conventional models already in production.

The overall flight performance and characteristics of the SS-4 were never to be matched by another propeller-driven canard.

10 The Curtiss CW-24B Flying Mockup

In 1940, the U.S. Army encouraged aircraft manufacturers to develop new fighter planes of greatly improved performance through the use of unconventional configurations. The giant Curtiss-Wright (C-W) Corporation of Buffalo, New York, was one of the respondents with its Model CW-24, but took a cautious and unique approach to the problem. The airplane was designed and built at C-W's St. Louis Division in St. Louis, Missouri.

Instead of building what was to be the final design right away, C-W built a lightweight full-scale wood-and-fabric flying mockup, the CW-24B (FIG. 1-14) was shipped to the Army test base at Muroc Dry Lake, California, for flight testing; too little was known about the "new" configuration to try it on the factory field in St. Louis.

Powered by an air-cooled 275-hp Menasco engine, the CW-24B featured a fixed tricycle landing gear but did not carry part of the load on the canard; this was a trimming surface only. Actually, because of its swept wing, the CW-24B could be regarded as a swept-wing

Fig. 1-14. Curtiss-Wright investigated canard designs cautiously by building this lightweight CW-24B mockup of a proposed high-powered fighter in 1941.

tailless design with the elevators on the nose instead of combined with the ailerons as *elevons* (see Chapter 3).

After a successful test program involving 169 flights, during which various changes were made in the amount and distribution of vertical fin area, the CW-24B was sent to the National Advisory Committee for Aeronautics (NACA) for test in their full-scale wind tunnel at Langley Field, Virginia.

Curtiss XP-55 Ascender

After successful tests of the CW-24B, the U.S. Army was convinced that its basic configuration was suitable for a new fighter design and awarded Curtiss a contract for three of the CW-24 models, which were given the Army designation of XP-55 (X for Experimental, P-55 for Pursuit Model No. 55).*

The XP-55 (FIG. 1-15) was designed to use the new 2,200-hp Pratt & Whitney X-1800 engine. Because this was not available when promised, all three XP-55s were redesigned to take the older and well-proven 1,275-hp Allison V-1710 engine then being used on the Lockheed P-38 and Curtiss P-40 pursuits, both prewar designs. The failure of the X-1800 and other new-model engines to be ready on schedule also imposed serious handicaps on several other new and unconventional fighter designs.

---

*The U.S. Army designated its fighters as P-for-Pursuit from 1924. This was changed to F-for-Fighter in 1948 while retaining the same number. Had they survived in service, the XP-55s would have become XF-55s.

Fig. 1-15. After testing of the CW-24B proved that the Curtiss-Wright canard design was workable, the Army awarded a contract for three XP-55 Ascender fighters.

The first XP-55 flew on July 19, 1943, but crashed in November when it fell into an inverted flat spin after a stall and would not recover. The pilot escaped by parachute after the plane fell 16,000 feet. He benefited from a special feature of the plane; because of the danger of the pilot going through the pusher propeller when leaving the cockpit via parachute, an explosive charge was installed to blow the propeller off in such emergencies.

The second XP-55 was too far along to be conveniently modified as a result of No. 1's experiences, so it was flown under restrictions, including prohibition of stalls below 20,000 feet. The third XP-55 had increased wingspan and elevator travel. It was also the only one of the three fitted with armament, four .50-caliber machine guns. Flight testing began in April 1944, and No. 3 proved to be the heaviest canard built so far. While it was 35 mph faster than the Italian SS-4, it did not have that design's docile characteristics.

The third XP-55 crashed May 27, 1945, while doing a slow roll at a military air show. The second is now preserved by the National Air and Space Museum.

Specifications: Powerplant, Allison V-1710-95 of 1,275 hp; span 40 feet 7 inches; wing area 209 square feet; gross weight 7,710 pounds; maximum speed 390 mph at 19,300 ft.

Miles Mockups

The urgencies of war open up channels of research that are otherwise largely ignored, in the hope of coming up with a superior feature that will pay off. In 1940, Britain's Royal Navy was having problems landing high-performance conventional fighters on aircraft carrier decks. Several manufacturers were funded to work on the problem. Miles Aircraft, a small firm that built trainers, had ideas for a canard design, but the authorities turned it down.

Undaunted, the firm went ahead on its own to develop a low-cost manned mockup of its concept. It worked, but not well enough to overcome the problem. It did, however, greatly disturb officialdom in that the firm used controlled wartime materials on an unauthorized project. The government did eventually buy and test it, however, but did not authorize development of the actual fighter.

The Miles M.35 was a single-seater with fixed forward stabilizer fitted with elevators (FIG. 1-16). Ailerons were in the main wing, which had a span of 20 feet, and a single 130-hp Gypsy Major engine was at the rear of the fuselage. Wing area was 135 square feet. There was a central fixed fin with a bumper wheel at the bottom to keep the propeller off of the ground, but the regular vertical fins and rudders were at the wingtips in the manner of many proven tailless designs. For simplicity, the tricycle landing gear was fixed. Gross weight was 1,850 pounds. The most unusual feature, compared to previous canards, was the seating of the pilot in the extreme nose, where he would have unexcelled visibility for the tricky carrier landings.

Miles also developed a more advanced twin-engine model, the M.39, along similar aerodynamic lines (FIG. 1-17). With twin-tractor 140-hp Gypsy Major 2C engines, it was sort of a return to the FW-19a concept but with later technical and aerodynamic improvements. Again, the M-39 mockup got official government testing but no authorization for a final design.

Specifications: Wing span 37 feet 6 inches; maximum speed 164 mph.

11

Fig. 1-16. The British Miles M.35 had tricycle gear, but had an extra wheel aft to keep the pusher propeller from hitting the ground on an over-rotated takeoff or landing.

Fig. 1-17. The Miles M.39B had two tractor engines and fully retractable tricycle landing gear.

Kyushu J7W-1 Shinden

The Japanese got aboard the canard bandwagon late in World War II. This was an original design of a naval officer, Captain Michinori Tsuruma, who visualized it as a jet. However, he had to settle for a 2,130-hp Mitsubishi Ha 43-42 radial engine driving a unique six-bladed pusher propeller on an extension shaft (FIG. 1-18). On paper, the Shinden (Japanese for "Magnificent Lightning") looked so good that the Navy ordered 1,800 of them from the Kyushu Hikoki firm before the prototype flew. Armament was to have been four 30mm cannon.

First flight of the Shinden was on August 3, 1945, shortly before the war ended. The single prototype survived to be evaluated by the Allies and is now in storage at the National Air and Space Museum.

Specifications: Wing span 36 feet 5 inches; gross weight 10,584 pounds; maximum speed 466 mph.

North American X-10

After World War II, the U.S. Army Air Forces (U.S. Air Force since 1947) instituted an X-for-Experimental series of pure research aircraft, both manned and unmanned. One of these, the rocket powered X-1, was the first airplane to break the sound barrier. Some designs in the X-series were prototypes for what could become production items, but others were pure experimentals.

One built primarily as a test vehicle for the systems of a more sophisticated aircraft was the unmanned North American X-10 of 1953-59 (FIG. 1-19). This was a delta-wing type with canard elevators forward, which were for trim only in the manner of the CW-24B /XP-55. Power was supplied by two Westinghouse J-40 jet engines. A novelty at the time was the use of out-

Fig. 1-18. The Japanese Kyushu Shinden of 1945 was designed for a jet engine but had to make do with a buried reciprocating engine that drove a unique six-bladed propeller.

Fig. 1-19. The North American X-10 research missile had angled fins and rudders that were nearly 20 years ahead of their time.

13

wardly-canted vertical fins and rudders in a style to be used by the F-14 and F-15 fighters of today. The X-10 could take off under its own power from retractable tricycle landing gear.

Approximately 11 X-10s were built, and at least four were evaluated as guided interceptor missiles. After rejection as such and completion of the original systems testing, the surviving X-10s were used as high-altitude targets for the Boeing BOMARC IM-99 unmanned interceptor missile. The essential layout of the X-10 was to reappear a few years later in the pair of XB-70 manned bombers that were built for the Air Force.

SAAB Viggin

Jet propulsion made a workable configuration of the delta-wing (see Chapter 4). After it became an accepted standard, it began to take on variations, notably adding canard surfaces as on the X-10. Another canard-combined-with-delta design is the Swedish Vig-gin (Thunderbolt) supersonic fighter, introduced in 1967 by Svenska Aeroplane Abtiebolaget (SAAB) and still in production.

Unlike the X-10, the Viggin has a loaded canard, with fixed stabilizer and elevators. Its acceptance as a standard military airplane made it the most-produced canard model until the configuration caught on in a big way in the ultralight sportplane movement of the late 1970s.

FIGURE 1-20 shows an interesting detail. Because the elevators are ahead of the center of gravity and attached to a horizontal stabilizer, "down" elevator displacement is used to raise the nose of the airplane. On canard elevators that are not fitted to a stabilizer (as on the X-10 or the Wright Flyer), the entire surface is pointed upward to raise the nose. However, only that portion of the surface ahead of the pivot point is actually raised; the greater portion behind the pivot is lowered, just as though it was hinged on a fixed stabilizer.

Specifications: Powerplant, 16,203 pound thrust Volvo RM8B; span 34 feet 9^1/$_2$ inches; wing area 495

14

Fig. 1-20. The Swedish SAAB Viggin was the first design with a loaded canard to be placed in series production since before World War I.

square feet; gross weight 37,478 pounds; maximum speed Mach 2 at altitude.

Recreational Canards

The success of the SAAB Viggin reawakened interest in canards in other areas of the aeronautical community, particularly the homebuilt and ultralight fields. Some of these worked very well because of their light weight and low speed, being in effect powered hang gliders. Others of higher performance succeeded through the application of the very latest airfoils and aerodynamics, new structural procedures that permitted super-smooth surfaces, and extensive use of computers as design tools. Four examples are presented here.

Rutan VariViggin Clearly inspired by the Viggin, Burt Rutan's wooden VariViggin appeared in 1967 as a tandem two-seat amateur-built sport plane that was different only in being a canard (FIG. 1-21). Citing the poor records of past canards, other designers predicted

a similar lack of success for the VariViggin (named for the Viggin, with the "Vari" indicating variable geometry; Rutan tried several different wing forms on it), but they did not take Rutan's engineering expertise into account. The VariViggin was notably successful and plans for homebuilders were soon on the market. Some 900 sets of plans have been sold.

Basically, the VariViggin is a delta-wing design with a loaded canard consisting of fixed horizontal stabilizer with elevators. It has tricycle landing gear, of course. Powerplant is a 150-hp Lycoming O-320; span of initial version 19 feet, later increased to 23 feet 8 1/2 inches; original wing area 119 square feet; gross weight 1,700 pounds; and high speed 163 mph.

Rutan VariEze The success of the VariViggin inspired Rutan to develop a more advanced canard two-seater for the homebuilt market. This featured simplified wood-and-foam construction that made building easy, hence the name VariEze. In general appearance, the VariEze and the very similar Long-EZ owe much more to the XP-55 than to the Viggin, even though it

Fig. 1-21. Burt Rutan's VariViggin of 1967 was inspired by the Swedish Viggin and triggered the current boom in canard designs for homebuilts and ultralights.

features a loaded canard (FIG. 1-22). The rudders are incorporated in winglets at the wingtips; Rutan led the industry in adding these devices, which improve wing efficiency. An oddity of the design, which first flew in May 1975, was that only the nosewheel of the tricycle landing gear was retractable. This feature is used to lower the fuselage when the plane is on the ground to simplify crew access.

The first VariEze was powered with a 63-hp converted Volkswagen automobile engine and set a closed-course distance record in its weight class, under-500-kilograms (1,250 lbs), 1,628 miles. In the interest of higher performance, the 100-hp Continental O-200 became the standard powerplant. Over 400 VariEzes are known to have been completed at this writing, making it one of the most popular two-seater homebuilts.

An improved and enlarged Long-EZ has since come on the market, powered by a 115-hp Lycoming O-235 engine. This, too, is a record-breaker, having made a straight-line nonstop unrefueled flight over 4,000 statute miles.

VariEze specifications, with a O-200 engine: Wing span 22 feet 2½ inches; wing area 53.6 square feet; gross weight 1,050 pounds, cruising speed 195 mph.

Pterodactyl Ptraveller Tailless designs were quite numerous in the hang glider movement at the time pilots seeking more versatility began to install small (10 to 20-hp) two-stroke cycle engines in the established hang glider designs. The early examples were simply cases of finding a suitable location for the engine and developing and installing a mount for it.

The novelty of a powered hang glider had enormous appeal, and soon developed into a full-scale boom in ultralights, as the powered versions were called. Most of the standard glider designs were quickly adapted to power, and many new designs were developed from the start as ultralight airplanes.

Representative of a popular hang glider that was fitted with an engine and then modified further to improve its performance is the Pterodactyl (FIG. 1-23). This was originally a tailless with a moderately swept wing, but became even more popular after power was

Fig. 1-22. A pair of Rutan Long-EZs, of which there are now many homebuilt examples. Note the long one-piece canopies and the nonretracting main landing gear.

added. Four Pterodactyls were used to make the first coast-to-coast crossing of the U.S. in ultralights in 1979.

An improved version is the Pterodactyl Ptraveller, which retains the basic wing but adds a flat canard surface mounted on two aluminum booms to improve maneuverability. The canard surface is not loaded and has no standard airfoil section.

Fig. 1-23. The Pterodactyl Ptraveller is a good example of a tailless hang glider that was adapted to power. A flat canard surface was added to improve controllability.

Ptraveller specifications: Powerplant 30-hp Cayuna; span 33 feet; gross weight 450 pounds; maximum speed 55 mph.

Goldwing Goldwing is an example of a canard design developed from scratch as an ultralight airplane as opposed to being adapted from a hang glider. It has a full and enclosed fuselage and a full cantilever double-surface wing that does away with the maze of wires used on most hang gliders and related ultralight airplanes (FIG. 1-24). Because of this extensive refinement, the Goldwing has higher performance for a given power than most of its contemporaries.

Goldwing specifications: Powerplant 30-hp Cayuna; span 30 feet, gross weight 480 pounds; top speed 70 mph.

Beech Starship 1

The first major manufacturer of commercial airplanes to adopt the modern canard configuration was the Beech Aircraft Corporation of Wichita, Kansas. It entered the field cautiously, however, by having Burt

Fig. 1-24. The Goldwing was designed from scratch as an airplane after the ultralight boom was started by adding small engines to existing hang gliders.

17

Fig. 1-25. The Beech Aircraft Corporation Starship of 1987 was developed from earlier Rutan designs and is the first modern canard intended for commercial use. This is the third prototype.

Rutan's Scaled Composites Company (later acquired as a Beech subsidiary) build an 85-percent-scale prototype that flew in August 1983. This drew heavily on the planform of the well-proved Rutan VariEze. The wing contained elevons and Fowler flaps, and two turboprop engines were installed as pushers in nacelles above the wing.

The Starship canard was notably different from others. It featured a variable sweep, from four degrees forward to 30 degrees aft, this sweep being linked to flap movement to offset resultant pitch and trim changes. Elevators were also fitted to the canard.

The production Model 2000 Starship (FIG. 1-25), an 8- to 11- place executive transport, is a milestone airplane apart from being the first commercial canard. It is the industry's first production effort for a relatively large airplane using honeycomb graphite/epoxy as primary structure throughout. The first of six pre-production Starship 1's flew on February 15, 1986, and deliveries to customers commenced in 1989.

Specifications: Powerplants two 1,200-hp Pratt & Whitney PT-6A-67; wing span 54 feet, 4³/4 inches; length 45 feet 1 inch; wing area 280.9 square feet, gross weight 14,000 pounds; high speed 405 mph.

THREE-SURFACE CANARDS

The three-surface canard preceded the Wright Brothers by nearly a decade, most notably in the unsuccessful creations of the British inventor Hiram Maxim in 1894. Serious French designers like Bleriot and Voisin were using the three-surface arrangement by 1905.

The leading American practitioner was Glenn Curtiss, who started airplane design work with Alexander Graham Bell's Aerial Experiment Association (A.E.A.) in 1907 and later continued on his own. The first three A.E.A. airplanes, all of which flew, were three-surface canards with a fixed horizontal stabilizer behind the wing and elevators ahead. Many other designs of the pre-World War I years were also three-surface canards as noted elsewhere in this book.

In post World War II years, small canard surfaces, either fixed or moveable, have been added to the noses of some existing conventional designs for such special purposes as smoothing out airflow along the fuselage, or added to the tail surfaces to improve control at lower-than-normal airspeeds.

Three-surface canards are appearing frequently on many of the new designs of the middle and late 1980s. Like the true canard itself, the three-surface canard seems to be one of those abandoned configurations whose time has come again. Some of the oldest and the newest three-surface canards follow.

Lejeune Double Canard

The French Louis Lejeune No. 1 of 1909 (FIG. 1-26) was unorthodox on several counts, notably the bicycle landing gear that qualifies it for Chapter 8. It is also a notably different three-surface canard, with *two* sets of biplane forward surfaces carried on pairs of bamboo booms projecting forward from the outer wing struts and braced with wires. Lateral control was by wing-

Fig. 1-26. The French LeJeune No. 1 of 1909 featured bicycle landing gear and two sets of canard elevators mounted ahead of the wingtips.

18

warping. With only a 15-hp Buchet engine, it is doubtful that Lejeune No. 1 ever flew.

Curtiss-Herring Reims Racer

After dissolution of the A.E.A., Glenn Curtiss continued airplane development on his own, and teamed with another pioneer, Augustus Herring, to establish a manufacturing firm, the Herring-Curtiss Company, in 1909. The first products were major improvements of the late A.E.A. designs, powered with Curtiss-built engines and having elevators ahead of the wings and a fixed stabilizer and moveable rudder behind. Curtiss attained instant worldwide fame by winning the major event at the world's first Aviation Meeting, the Gordon Bennett Cup at Reims, France, in August 1909 (FIG. 1-27).

Curtiss soon broke off the Herring partnership and continued to build three-surface canard pusher biplanes on his own—the first builder to produce a standard advertised model in significant numbers. As this Model D was refined, elevators were added to the rear stabilizer while the forward elevators were retained. As a revenue-producing sideline, Curtiss organized the Curtiss Exhibition Company, in which selected Curtiss pilots flew Curtiss airplanes at public gatherings for fancy fees.

One of the Curtiss pilots was the noted Lincoln Beachey. One day late in 1910 he damaged the canard elevator of his Curtiss Model D just before a scheduled

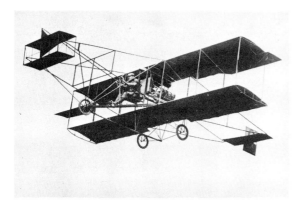

Fig. 1-27. Glenn Curtiss in the three-surface canard pusher with which he won the 1909 Gordon Bennett race. The elevators are forward, the fixed stabilizer is aft.

exhibition flight. Not wanting to delay the show by taking time to repair the elevator, he figured that the rear elevator would be able to do the job alone and simply removed the forward unit. The Model D worked even better than ever, and Beachey was able to convince Curtiss that the forward elevator was unnecessary. Over the next year Curtiss gradually eliminated the forward elevator from new designs, and many Model D's in the field had the forward elevators removed while retaining the boom structure that supported them because the booms still supported other parts of the airplane. Existing and subsequent Curtiss pushers without forward elevators were soon nicknamed "Headless Curtisses." Curtiss' removal of the forward surfaces from three-surface canards inspired their removal from other designs, and the feature had all but vanished from new designs by the outbreak of World War I.

Specifications: 1909 Reims Racer: Powerplant, one 51-hp Curtiss V-8; overall span, 33 feet 4 inches (wings alone, 26 feet 7 inches) gross weight 700 pounds; top speed around a 20-kilometer closed course (12.43 miles) 46 mph.

Modified Voisin

After the French pilot Henri Farman extensively modified the tandem-wing biplane with canard that he had Gabriel Voisin build for him (and in which he won a 50,000-Franc prize making the first one-kilometer circular flight by a European-built airplane) Voisin adapted Farman's improvements for subsequent production and built bona-fide three-surface canards by greatly reducing the span of the rear wing. Although this shortened unit was now a tail rather than a wing, it still had camber like the wing and contributed significant lift (FIG. 1-28). There were no rear elevators, so pitch control was through the monoplane canard surface.

This had a much shorter center of gravity moment arm than the Curtiss, and required a much greater degree of movement to perform its function. This shortened moment and reduced effectiveness foretold the eventual demise of the three-surface canard.

By 1909 the Voisin configuration had been pretty well standardized in production, and seven Voisins appeared in the famous 1909 Reims meeting. The noted British historian Charles H. Gibbs-Smith listed the Voisin as one of the six outstanding designs of 1909.

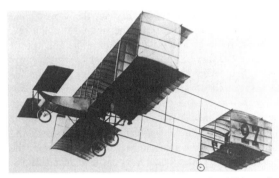

Fig. 1-28. The 1909 French Voisin had a fixed lifting tail on a long moment arm and a canard elevator on a very short moment arm.

Specifications: Powerplant one 50-hp Antoinette; wing span 32 feet 9½ inches; combined wing and lifting-tail area 521.5 square feet, top speed 55 mph.

Farman Longhorn

20   Henri Farman went into business for himself after modifying his 1907 Voisin and became one of the leading French manufacturers right up to World War II. Things got a bit confusing when his brother Maurice formed a company of his own in 1909 and built very similar airplanes. The brothers combined their firms in 1912, after which some were designed by Henri and others by Maurice, and were so designated for a few years before standardizing on F-for-Farman model numbers.

Both brothers had been building three-surface canards and continued into 1913. By this time the rear canard had been fitted with elevators and the front elevator was becoming redundant. The Farmans then followed Curtiss' example and deleted the forward elevator from the 1913 S.11 model. However, it was retained for the 1912 S.7 model that was still in production (FIG. 1-29).

Both models were licensed to British manufacturers, who built many of each for the Royal Flying Corps and the Royal Naval Air Service. Because of its forward-elevator support structure, the British nicknamed the S.7 the Farman "Longhorn" while the S.11 became the "Shorthorn."

The European arms race that preceded World War

I kept the obsolescent S.7 in production beyond its prime, and gave it the distinction of being the last three-surface canard to be produced in quantity. It served as a first-line reconnaissance and bombing airplane well into 1915 and as a trainer for even longer. Some examples were even forced down behind the German lines and captured.

Specifications: Powerplant 70-hp Renault or 75-hp Rolls-Royce "Hawk"; wing span 51 feet; gross weight 1,887 pounds, top speed 59 mph.

The reappearance of the three-surface canard in the post World War II years preceded the revival of the two-surface canard, but even then it was not a feature of a new design. Rather, it was an addition made during modification of a well-established production airplane, the four-place Cessna 182 (FIG. 1-30).

Three-Surface Revival

The Wren Aircraft Corporation of Ft. Worth, Texas, made extensive modifications to the Cessna, particularly to the wing, to improve its low-speed performance, increase lift, and give it short-takeoff-and-landing (STOL) capability. The canard was added to the nose immediately behind the propeller. Fitted with elevators that are coupled to the tail elevator, the configuration improves pitch control during low-speed flight. The canard also increases total lift by offsetting much of the down-load on the horizontal tail required to trim out the nose-down pitching moment.

Fig. 1-29. The Farman S.7 Longhorn of 1912 was one of the last three-surface canards in large-scale production. This example was forced down intact behind the German lines early in World War I. Note German insignia.

Fig. 1-30. The Wren is a standard Cessna 182 that became a three-surface canard when modified for extended slow-flight performance. Note the small added canard on the nose.

First flown in January 1963, the Wren modification to the Cessna is still being made at a new plant in Buckeye, Arizona.

Piaggio Avanti

A contemporary and competitor of the Beech Starship, the all-metal Italian Piaggio Avanti marks the first application, or revival, of the three-surface canard to new modern designs (FIG. 1-31). Twin turboprop engines are mounted as pushers on a straight wing and conventional swept tail surfaces are mounted a very short distance behind.

Piaggio does not call the fixed forward surface, which contributes significantly to lift but does not control pitch, a canard. This surface is fitted with slotted flaps that are coupled to the main wing flaps and deflect with them to offset changes in trim.

It is noteworthy that the distance of the forward surface, or foreplane, from the wing is nearly double the distance from the wing to the horizontal tail, just about reversing the distances of the 1909 Voisin.

Specifications: Powerplants two 850-hp Pratt & Whitney PT-6A-66; Wing span 45 feet 5 inches; length 46 feet 1 1/4 inches; wing area 169.64 square feet; gross weight 10,510 pounds; high speed 460 mph at 27,000 feet.

Rutan Voyager

No discussion of canard aircraft of any type could ever be complete without mention of the most famous individual canard since the 1903 Wright Flyer—the Rutan "Voyager" (FIG. 1-32). Between December 14 and 23, 1986, this tandem-engine two-seater, crewed by Dick Rutan and Jeana Yeager, made the first unrefueled non-stop flight around the world, covering 26,678 miles in 216 hours.

Its totally unique configuration is a prime example of form dictated by function, the plane being designed for only one specific mission. Aside from its record performance, Voyager is a significant design on several other counts. It is the first airplane of significant size to be built with high strength-to-weight-ratio graphite. This weight-saving material, combined with other special design features, permitted the unprecedented gross-weight to empty-weight ratio of 3.6 to 1; many

Fig. 1-31. The Italian Piaggio Avanti of 1986 is essentially a conventional straight-wing airplane with a very short tail moment arm and a trimming canard on a very long moment arm.

Fig. 1-32. The unique pod-and-boom Rutan Voyager made the first nonstop, nonrefuelled flight around the world. While it has two engines, it is not a true twin: the engines are not alike.

conventional airplanes do well to attain a ratio of 1.6 to 1.

Efficient cruise performance was obtained by the extremely high wing aspect ratio of 33 to 1, which exceeds even that of many high-performance sailplanes. Finally, Voyager is a remarkable example of successful small private enterprise. It was designed by two inspired and highly knowledgeable people, put together virtually as a homebuilt by small crew in a minimally-equipped shop, used much donated equipment and materials, and was paid for largely by nickles-and-dimes contributions from many small supporters, mainly in the homebuilt sport aircraft movement.

"Voyager" has now been put on permanent display in the National Air and Space Museum in Washington, D.C.

Specifications: Powerplants, one 130-hp air-cooled Continental O-240 tractor, one 110-hp water-cooled Continental IOL-200 pusher; wing span 110 feet; empty weight equipped, 2,683 pounds; gross weight for world flight, 9,694 pounds; cruising speed 81-150 mph (variable with fuel weight), world flight average 122 mph.

2
CHAPTER

Tandem-Wing Aircraft

MOST OF THE WORLD'S TANDEM-WING AIRCRAFT HAVE been those with two sets of wings mounted at opposite ends of the fuselage or other central framework, with each supporting an approximately equal portion of the total load. A very few have been "triple tandems" with a third set of wings in the middle. Some flew, but none have been notably successful.

ADVANTAGES

Part of the thinking behind the tandem is that there is more lifting area available in two sets of full-size wings than in a single set of wings and a small tail on an aircraft of the same span and length.

One of the first things that the inventors of the early flying machines learned was the importance of light wing loading—the *pounds* of aircraft carried by each *square foot* of wing area. Average personal aircraft like the Cessna 152 today have wing loadings on the order of 10 to 14 pounds per square foot. The turn-of-the-century designers were working down around 1.25 to 1.50 pounds per square foot and even then doing all they could to shave off ounces. With the feeble power-plants of the day, any excess weight was a severe handicap.

One way of reducing wing loading is to increase the wing area. With the light structures of the old days, the area increased at a greater rate than the weight with an increase in size, so expanding what would ordinarily be a horizontal tail surface into a full-size lifting wing was easy to do. A given wing area could also be accommodated in a shorter-span tandem monoplane without introducing the structural complexities and interference drag of the biplane arrangement.

DISADVANTAGES

This logic conveniently overlooks the fact that there is also more airframe weight involved, more aerodynamic drag as well as lift, more inertia, and more power required to move the greater mass.

The earlier designs, built with old-fashioned airfoil sections that had large travel of the center of pressure (CP, or point of lift) with the changes in angle of attack that resulted from changes in speed, had a serious longitudinal trim problem. Ordinarily, as speed increases and angle of attack decreases, the CP of most airfoils moves aft. Since both wing sets are lifting equally, the center of gravity (CG) of the aircraft must be halfway between them instead of very near the CP of a main wing as it is on a conventional design. As the CP of both wing sets moves aft, the moment, or distance of the forward-wing CP relative to the CG *decreases* while the moment between the rear-wing CP and the CG *increases*. This inequality of moments is more than the trimming surfaces (tabs or the elevators) can handle, so the aircraft pitches down. Aircraft with a very limited speed range, such as ultralights and gliders, or latter-day designs utilizing airfoils with zero CP travel, do not have this particular problem but are not yet able to show enough advantages to overcome the inherent disadvantages.

Another problem is the greater inertia in pitch, or movement about the lateral axis. On conventional designs, this axis is relatively close to the center of the single wing, and the pitch inertia is limited essentially to the mass of the fuselage. On a tandem, the pitch axis is midway between both sets of wings; in addition to pitching the fuselage up, for example, the entire mass

24

of the forward wing has to be lifted above the pivot point and the rear wing moved below it. That's a lot of extra mass to move; it requires greater control force application and has the aerodynamic disadvantage of adding greatly to the trim drag.

If and when large tandem airplanes are built, still another problem will appear. Traditionally, transport planes carry all their fuel in their wing. Since this is close to or coincides with the airplane center of gravity, there is little or no trim change problem as the fuel is consumed. A tandem-wing transport would logically carry fuel in both wings. With two diminishing loads, both at a significant distance on either side of the center of gravity, very careful management of fuel consumption will be essential.

Some tandems incorporate the pitch controls—the elevators—in the wings themselves while others carry them behind as a separate conventional tail. Some carry rudders within the span of the wings (usually the rear), while others carry them behind.

Overall, it can be said that the tandem design has been the least successful of the "conservative" unconventional aircraft configurations, but latter-day technology is giving it another chance.

Langley Aerodrome

The first—and beyond a doubt the most famous—of the tandem-wing aircraft is the Langley Aerodrome of 1903 (FIG. 2-1).

Professor Samuel Pierpont Langley was a scientist of note and also Secretary of the Smithsonian Institution, which sponsored his experiments in aeronautics in the 1890s. He was systematic in his approach to the problem, and built and successfully flew a quarter-size-steam-powered model of his proposed Aerodrome in 1896 and a gasoline-powered one in 1903. These were tandem-wing designs with a separate cruciform tail behind the rear wing. (A cruciform tail has the horizontal and vertical surfaces in the form of a cross. On the Langley and some others, the whole unit pivoted about a forward point to function either as a rudder or an elevator.) There was no provision for control about the roll axis; later stability was provided by the generous dihedral angle of the wings. Several straight-ahead flights with distances up to 4,200 feet were made from catapult launches.

With government funds at his disposal, Langley built his full-scale Aerodrome in 1903. The span was

Fig. 2-1. The famous tandem-wing Langley Aerodrome poised for a catapult launch over the Potomac River in October 1903.

48 feet 5 inches, length 52 feet 5 inches, and the gross weight of 750 pounds combined with the wing area of 1,040 square feet to produce the fractional wing loading of only .81 lbs./sq. ft.

When a suitable powerplant couldn't be found, his pilot, Charles Manly, designed and built a really remarkable five-cylinder water-cooled radial engine that produced 52 horsepower for a weight of only 124 pounds. This was mounted crossways in the fuselage. Shafts extending from each end turned 90-degree bevel gears at the ends of steel tube outriggers. These drove other shafts that turned two propellers in opposite directions to neutralize torque.

No provision was made for landing gear. The Aerodrome was to be catapulted from the top of a houseboat and then ditch in the river. The first flight was scheduled for October 7, 1903, and it looked like Langley's creation would become the first heavier-than-air man-carrying machine to achieve controlled powered flight. It was not to be.

What happened is still controversial; a wire on the machine apparently snagged on the catapult and caused the Aerodrome to dive into the river. The damage was relatively minor, and it was ready to try again on December 8.

Again failure, and again controversy—some claim that wires again snagged while others maintain that the rear wings collapsed under the air load because of their fragile construction and improper bracing. In any case, the Aerodrome was destroyed and Langley abandoned the project.

In 1914, aircraft manufacturer Glenn Curtiss was defending the famous patent infringement suit brought against him by the Wright Brothers. In his attempts to invalidate the Wright patent, he resurrected all sorts of pre-Wright flying machines that might have been capable of flight. This activity included rebuilding the wrecked Langley Aerodrome with the permission of the Smithsonian.

Curtiss made some essential modifications to the rigging and wing structure (which were hotly disputed by Orville Wright) and put the plane on pontoons. In the process, the wing area was reduced to 988 square feet and the weight increased to 1,170 pounds for a wing loading of 1.18 pounds per square foot. The Aerodrome was flown briefly with its original engine/propeller arrangement on May 28, 1914, but Curtiss installed a more powerful V-8 engine of his own and a single propeller in the nose for some research on tandem wings (FIGS. 2-2, 2-3).

The Smithsonian then had the Aerodrome restored to its 1903 configuration and put it on display over a sign that proclaimed it to be "the first man-carrying aeroplane in the history of the world capable of sustained free flight." This statement so angered Orville Wright that he sent the restored 1903 Flyer to England

Fig. 2-2. After its early failures, the Langley Aerodrome was rebuilt as a seaplane by Glenn Curtiss. Here it still has its original powerplant and propeller arrangement in 1914.

Fig. 2-3. The Aerodrome did fly with its original engine, but Curtiss installed an engine of his own with a single propeller on the nose for further flights, as shown here.

to display in 1928 rather than to the Smithsonian. It did not come back until after World War II, when the wording on the sign had been revised to Orville's satisfaction.

Kress Triple Tandem

Austrian inventor Wilhelm Kress also tackled the problems of flight in a remarkable parallel to Langley's methods without knowing of his work. He, too, flew models in 1898 and 1899, but powered them with rubber bands.

He then built a full-size seaplane with three monoplane wings in tandem and a cruciform tail behind. A gasoline engine was centrally located and drove two pusher propellers mounted above the airframe (FIG. 2-4.).

The first trial was in October 1901, but the craft turned over while maneuvering on the water prior to takeoff. In view of the extensive damage, Kress abandoned the project.

Even if it had become airborne, it is doubtful how well it would have performed. It had no provision for roll control, and no dihedral for lateral stability as Langley had. Further, the extremely flimsy wing structure would probably have deflected under load, if not failed completely, so it may have been just as well that this triple-tandem did not get into the air. The same can

be said for several other designs of that era, which had workable aerodynamics but inadequate structures.

Specifications: Powerplant, Daimler 24-hp; wing area 366 square feet.

27

Voisin-Bleriot Water Glider

Many inventors were working on the problems of flight simultaneously in several countries. The December 1903 success of the Wright Brothers was largely unnoticed at the time and the others continued their independent lines of development.

In France, Gabriel Voisin built flying machines to his own design and to the designs of others. In 1905 he built a tandem biplane glider with a canard for Louis Bleriot and fitted it with twin pontoons. This machine was later numbered Bleriot II in the Bleriot line.

The glider was a true tandem, with the rear wings having only a slightly shorter span than the forward set. There was also a small forward canard (FIG. 2-5). The glider was successfully flown from the River Seine when towed by a fast motorboat, but had no lateral stability. As a glider on tow, the directional stability provided by the vertical panels was enhanced by the strong straight-ahead pull of the tow rope.

While it did not achieve free flight, Bleriot II is recognized as the first man-carrying aircraft to fly off of water, even though it was towed.

Fig. 2-4. The Austrian Kress triple-tandem of 1901 preceded Langley's full-scale design but came after his quarter-scale flying models.

Fig. 2-5. The Voisin-Bleriot tandem glider on floats in 1905.

Fig. 2-6. The Jones tandem biplane of 1905.

Jones 1905 Tandem

One serious effort at manned flight that failed was the unorthodox—even by the 1905 standards—Jones tandem (FIG. 2-6). It was designed and built by Charles Oliver Jones of Dayton, Ohio, and powered by a 25-hp air-cooled engine provided by Glenn Curtiss. Curtiss was a bicycle and motorcycle manufacturer at the time and had not yet become involved in aviation beyond supplying some of his light engines to airship builders. The Jones machine was the first heavier-than-air aircraft that Curtiss had seen (he is holding a strut at the left of the photo).

The engine was located amidship and drove two outrigged propellers through shafts and gears a la Langley. Jones' machine did not fly; it was so heavy that 25 hp could only get it up to 10 mph on the ground. With no airfoil sections on the wings, which had only flat single surfaces, it could not possibly have flown except as a box kite at a high angle of attack.

The landing gear, however, was a significant milestone in aircraft development and influenced later Curtiss designs—three wheels to permit a rolling takeoff at a time when the Wrights were still using a dolly on a monorail.

Montgomery Glider

The most successful of the early tandem designs was the glider built in 1905 by Professor John J. Montgomery of the University of Santa Clara in California (FIG. 2-7). This was based on Langley technology, with a cruciform tail behind but with roll control achieved through wires worked by the pilot's body motion somewhat in the manner of the Wrights.

Montgomery was not a pilot; he left that to Daniel Maloney, a professional acrobat. The glider would be carried aloft under a hot-air balloon. Maloney would then cut loose and put on a spectacular (for the time) demonstration of maneuverability on the way down to a spot landing. He was killed when some bracing wires snagged during a balloon launch; after he cut loose, the wing collapsed. Montgomery then abandoned the tandem configuration and built other gliders to what had become the standard tractor design, but he was killed in one in 1911.

1907 Voisin

By 1907, aircraft development in France was booming, and the pioneering Voisin firm was one of the

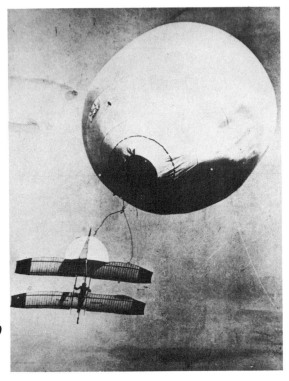

Fig. 2-7. The successful Montgomery Tandem Glider of 1905.

30

leaders. This 1907 tandem biplane was representative of the period. It qualified as a tandem because the "tail" was increased in span and provided with an airfoil to generate significant lift. It was also a canard because of the forward elevator (FIG. 2-8). Note the great amount of down elevator needed to keep the machine trimmed for level flight; apparently the forward wings were set at too great an angle of attack relative to the rear wings and therefore generated more lift and an unbalanced condition that had to be corrected by a down load on the nose.

This condition, known as *trim drag*, where one surface had to be displaced considerably to keep the machine trimmed, was a severe aerodynamic handicap to the marginally-powered early-day planes and is still a speed stealer on modern designs.

Specifications: Powerplant, 50-hp Antionette; span 33 feet 6 inches; gross weight 1,145 pounds.

Cesar Tandem Biplane

Little is known of the French Cesar biplane beyond the photo (FIG. 2-9). It is representative of many experiments of the 1907-11 era that failed and have been forgotten, their inventors going on to other activities and the firms that built them dissolved.

An earlier version of this machine had two outboard propellers chain driven by a central engine; this

Fig. 2-8. The French Voisin tandem biplane of 1907. Note nose-down position of canard surface.

Fig. 2-9. The French Cesar tandem with 50-hp engine, circa 1909.

one had a single direct-drive propeller with the slipstream blowing directly on the pilot. Both sets of wings were double-surfaced airfoils ahead of the rear spar, and single-surfaced behind it. The design capitalized on the presence of two sets of wings to reduce the span for a given area. Roll control was by interplane ailerons in the manner of the 1909 Curtiss and there was a forward canard for elevator control. Double rudders were installed behind the rear wings.

Koechlin Tandem

In contrast to the complexity of the Cesar, the little French Koechlin of 1908 represents an extremely simplified approach to the same basic design. The Koechlin had notable differences, however.

The space between the front and rear upper wings was filled in to provide additional lifting surface, leaving the lower wings the only true tandems (FIG. 2-10).

No further information is available, but it is doubtful that the machine ever flew, first because of the obvious inadequacy of the small pusher engine, and second because of the flat airfoil section.

Oertz Schooner

The most successful of the early tandem-wing airplanes was the German Oertz W.6 Schooner of 1916

(FIG. 2-11). This flew well enough for the single one built to be accepted by the German Navy and put in service as an unarmed observation plane.

It followed the Langley concept in having separate tail surfaces behind the short hull that consisted of conventional fixed stabilizer and vertical fins with elevators and rudders. Ailerons were in the forward upper wing.

Two 240-hp Maybach engines in the hull each drove a pusher propeller behind the forward wings through shafts and gears. The big W.6, with a span of 65 feet 7½ inches, was heavy (11,066 pounds), and its top speed was only 73 mph. It was sluggish in roll, so a second set of ailerons was added to the rear set of wings.

Fig. 2-10. The tiny French Koechlin tandem of 1908.

Fig. 2-11. The German Navy's Oertz W.6 Schooner of 1916.

32

Five-Wing Fokker

The Dutch aircraft builder Anthony Fokker established his plant in Germany in 1913 and was one of that country's major suppliers of fighter planes through 1918. One of his most famous designs was the nimble Dr-1 triplane fighter that was introduced in mid-1917 and made famous by such pilots as Manfred von Richthofen, the Red Baron.

Fokker was also a great innovator, and turned out over 50 different models from 1913 through 1918. Many of these were minor variations of an established production model, or even a mixing of major parts of two models to create a third.

The little triplane was subject to a number of modifications, the most extreme of which was this tandem, identified as V.8 in Fokker's experimental series. The fuselage was lengthened and the 110-hp rotary engine was replaced by a 160-hp water-cooled in-line model. A standard set of triplane wings was mounted far forward, a new biplane set consisting of the upper and lower wing of a regular triplane set was located amidships, and tail surfaces from a stock triplane were carried aft (FIG. 2-12).

Fig. 2-12. The German Fokker V.8 of late 1917 had tandem wings plus conventional tail surfaces.

Fokker tested all new models himself. It is reported that he made one flight in the five-wing model, landed it safely, and ordered it dismantled.

Caproni Flying Houseboat

The most ambitious tandem-wing airplane project ever was the Italian Caproni CA-60 of 1920. This firm was famous for the giant twin-fuselage bombers that it

Fig. 2-13. It is perhaps fortunate that the 100-passenger Caproni CA-60 of 1920 was damaged on its short first flight and was scrapped.

built during World War I. The magnitude of the CA-60 was best expressed in Italian as "Capronissimo!"

The CA-60 used three sets of triplane wings left over from wartime bomber production; these were set atop a 100-passenger hull that resembled a houseboat more than any conventional airplane component (FIG. 2-13). The combined area of the nine wings was 9,000 square feet, a total exceeded by only one airplane since—the giant Hughes H-4 flying boat of 1947.

Connecting the center wings of each triplane set were two parallel structures resembling fuselages. Each contained one 400-hp American Liberty engine at each end. A power pod containing one pusher and one tractor engine was located between the fuselages at the forward and aft wing sets for a total of eight engines. Ailerons were fitted to all nine wings, but the rear ones were rigged as elevators. Vertical fins and rudders were installed outboard of the fuselages between all the rear wings.

The CA-60 made one short straight-ahead flight. It is perhaps fortunate that it was damaged enough at the end of this flight to justify abandoning the project.

Specifications: Powerplants, eight 400-hp Liberty; wing span 100 feet; wing area 9,000 square feet; gross weight 55,000 pounds; top speed 90 mph (estimated).

Peyret Glider

The most successful tandem-wing aircraft, in terms of accomplishing what it was designed to do, was the French Peyret glider of 1923 (FIG. 2-14). It was designed during the period when the new sport of gliding was catching on in postwar Europe. The move-

Fig. 2-14. The French Peyret tandem glider of 1923 set a world's glider endurance record in England. Here it is being hauled up a hill in French Morocco for further slope soaring.

ment was sparked by the Germans, who were denied military flying and much civil activity by the Treaty of Versailles. The popularity of the sport spread to France and England, and soon international competitions were being held.

In the early meets, the gliders did just that—descended from a launch point on a hill and landed in the valley below. Contestants were judged on distance from the starting point or on duration. In either case, light wing loading was the key to success. Designers quickly found that increasing the wing area through the use of biplane surfaces was not the way to go; the interference drag between the wings pretty much overcame any advantages of the lighter wing loading that was supposed to reduce the sinking speed. The added drag increased the sinking speed.

The Peyret lightened the loading by going to a clean tandem monoplane arrangement, with both wings ahead of conventional fin and rudder. Airplane-type landing gear was installed forward.

The Peyret had an unorthodox control system. In addition to the standard rudder at the rear of the fuselage, it had a set of full-span "elevons" in each wing that combined the functions of elevator and aileron. For roll, both sets operated differentially as ailerons. For pitch, the forward set was raised to lower the nose while the rear set was lowered to perform the same function since it was on the opposite side of the center of gravity.

The new tandem glider made brief history by setting a world's glider endurance record of three hours, 23 minutes at an international meet held at Itford, England, in 1922. Unfortunately, this performance did not reflect any superiority of the tandem design, but of the technique of slope-soaring—flying back and forth across the side of a hill in a wind that is directed upward with a vertical component greater than the sinking speed of the glider. Orville Wright had first used this technique when he set a record of nine minutes, 45 seconds in 1911. It was forgotten until rediscovered in the early 1920s. It just so happened that the Peyret was at the right place at the right time to be among the first to cash in on it.

Needless to say, its record did not stand for long, nor did the idea of absolute minimum wing loading for reduced sink. Subsequent improvement in glider performance came from cleaning up the basic tractor monoplane design, not by decreasing the wing loading.

The Peyret had given the tandem its one brief moment of triumph.

S.F.C.A.-Peyret Taupin

Following the success of his tandem-wing glider, Louis Peyret carried his basic design on into powered aircraft, which culminated in the Peyret VI of 1929 (FIG. 2-15). Following Peyret's death, the design was acquired by the Societe Francaise de Constructions Aeronautique (S.F.C.A.) in 1935. The Peyret VI was refined, fitted with a two-cylinder 30-hp air-cooled Mengin engine, and named Taupin. Some 60 were built, making the "Taupin" the most numerous factory-built tandem-wing design of all time.

One Taupin is flying today in the French antique airplane movement, powered with a 60/70 hp Regnier inverted four-cylinder in-line engine intended for a two-seat development of the "Taupin."

Specifications: Powerplant, one 30 hp Mengin engine; wing span 25 feet 4 inches; gross weight 693 pounds; top speed 68.7 mph.

Fig. 2-15. The Peyret glider of 1923 was easily developed into a powered model. This model VI is the sole survivor of some 60 built in France in the late 1930s as the S.F.C.A. "Taupin."

34

Stout Amphibian

A most unusual tandem was the little all-metal twin-engine amphibian built by William B. Stout in 1927. Stout had designed several airplanes previously, and his company had been absorbed by the giant Ford Motor Company; one of his designs evolved into the famous Ford Trimotor transport, ("Tin Goose") after Stout's departure. He developed several subsequent innovative designs on his own, but none reached production status.

The tandem amphibian was of the flying boat type, with a hull wide enough, apparently, not to need wingtip floats for stability. The forward wing, with full-span ailerons, was mounted on very short struts just above the bow. The rear wing, with full-span elevators, was similarly mounted behind the raised tandem cockpit structure that also supported the center rudder. Other fins and rudders were under the rear wing. Power was provided by a pair of British Bristol Cherub 32-hp two-cylinder air-cooled engines mounted in separate nacelles (FIGS. 2-16, 2-17).

Some good thinking was shown in the wing arrangement that earlier designers had apparently not considered. By having the forward wing below the rear, the rear wing operated in clean air, not in the wake of the forward wing.

Only these photos, dated May 12, 1927, are available today to record this unique amphibian. It is not known whether it flew or what happened to it.

Mignet Flying Flea

The record for the first tandem design built in quantity must go to the infinite variations of the *Pou du Ciel*, or Sky Louse, developed in 1934 by a Frenchman, Henri Mignet. In England this was usually called the Pou, but in the U.S. it became the Flying Flea.

When it appeared, it promised to fulfill everyman's dream of a low-cost easy-to-fly airplane that he could build himself. The reality turned out to be something different.

In its initial successful version, the Pou was a tan-

35

Fig. 2-16. The unique Stout all-metal, twin-engine tandem.

Fig. 2-17. The Stout amphibian was of the flying boat type.

Fig. 2-18. The original production form of the French Mignet H.M.14 Pou du Ciel, widely known as the Flying Flea.

dem monoplane with the forward wing slightly above the rear and overlapping it by a few inches (FIG. 2-18). The control system was unique; fore-and-aft movement of the stick moved the upper-wing, which doubled as the elevator. There were no ailerons; lateral stability came from the curved dihedral built into the early models. The rudder forced the Pou into a skidded turn and was activated by sideways motion of the stick—left stick for left rudder, etc. Mignet maintained that the conventional rudder control was not instinctive and that a non-technical person like himself could not master it. The limited controllability made crosswind landings difficult.

The original powerplant was a 17-hp motorcycle conversion. The refined HM-14 version of the Pou worked for Mignet, and worked well. It was limited in performance, which was acceptable since its only purpose was to get the pilot into the air for the joy of flying, not to serve as transportation. Mignet's meager finances were the saving grace of the design. Since he could only afford the smallest engines, the subsequent low speed of the plane kept it out of trouble. Its takeoff, cruise, and landing speeds were about the same. Serious trouble developed when the design became popular and other people began making "improvements."

The first of these, of course, was to install more powerful engines—as much as 65-hp—to develop more speed. This brought on a series of unexplained crashes that led to a ban on the design in England and France.

Investigation in full-scale wind tunnels revealed that the tilting of the forward wing upward, serving as an elevator to raise the nose to climb or recover from a dive, narrowed the gap between the trailing edge of the upper wing and the leading edge of the lower. This meant that the mass of the air flowing under the upper wing and over the lower had to move through the gap, or slot, at a greater velocity. This increased the lift of the rear wing from accelerated airflow more than the lift of the forward wing was increasing from its increased angle of attack, so the plane went into a dive; the pilot doing the natural thing and pulling back on the stick only made the situation worse.

By the time the facts were determined and fixes worked out to lift the ban, the appeal of the Pou had passed. It was revived on a small scale after World War II, and versions with notably increased separation of the wings in height and horizontal distance are still being built. Some of these latter-day Pous retain the movable wing feature; others delete it and have elevators built into the trailing edge of the rear wing—or move the rear wing (FIG. 2-19).

The Pou is now a minor novelty in the homebuilt airplane movement rather than the mainstay that it started out to be.

Delanne Duo-Mono

A new approach to tandem-wing design was taken by the French designer Maurice Delanne. His concept was for an otherwise conventional tractor monoplane with the rear of the fuselage shortened and the normal horizontal tail surfaces lengthened to become a second wing. Since this would be a load-carrying surface, the center of gravity would be moved aft, so he placed the cockpit well aft of the normal position (FIG. 2-20).

The original Delanne model 20 was a light two-

Fig. 2-19. After the early deficiencies of the Flying Flea were corrected, the design continued to develop. This Croses Criquet, a 90-hp two-seater with pivoting forward wing but with elevators in the rear wing, is one of several different Mignet-based, tandem-wing designs now being built in France.

seater built in 1937. The designer followed Flying Flea concepts in placement of the wings, claiming that the vertical gap between these formed a slot that directed air over the rear wing and made the plane virtually stall-proof. The first prototype soon crashed, but a second logged 600 flying hours. Others, including glider versions, were built.

The military potential of the design as a two-seat fighter with an excellent field of fire for a rear gunner was recognized and the French government funded the construction of the Delanne 10C-2 prototype (the C in the designation mean *Chasseur*, or pursuit plane, while the -2 indicated a two-man crew). Delanne didn't have

Fig. 2-20. The close-coupled French Delanne 10C-2, with a gunner at the extreme rear, was taken over by the Germans in World War II.

a suitable shop, so the 10C-2 was built by the Arsenal firm. Power was a 1,010-hp Hispano-Suiza. Span was 33 feet 1¼ inches, wing area 242 square feet, and gross weight 6,287 pounds. Top speed was reported to be 340 mph, unusually high for a plane of that size, weight, and power.

Germany occupied France just as the 10C-2 was completed, so the testing was done under German control.

Westland Tandem

The British Westland firm picked up the Delanne tandem concept in 1941 and took a shortcut in developing it. Instead of designing a new model from scratch, it took an existing Westland Lysander Army cooperation model (actually the prototype), cut the original fuselage off aft of the wing, and spliced in a new aft section that contained a four-gun turret as used in the tail of heavy bombers (FIGS. 2-21, 2-22). The fitting of the turret indicates that the tandem-winger, unofficially named the Wendover (and sometimes Lysander Mk. V), was intended to be a low-cost trainer for turret gunners—certainly its performance didn't suit it for combat. On the other hand, the design may have been intended for aerodynamic research with the dummy turret added to show a practical application.

Fig. 2-21. The Westland Lysander, a standard British liaison plane of World War II.

Dornier 212

The German Dornier Model 212 flying boat of 1942 (FIG. 2-23) had several novel features that qualify it for other chapters of this book, but since it became a tandem-wing of necessity, it is presented in this chapter.

The 212 was an experimental amphibian flying boat that showed some of the compromises, or "trade-offs," that have to be made in order to achieve certain design goals. To achieve a very aerodynamically clean design by avoiding the traditional engine/propeller combination above the hull, the 450 hp Hirth Hm512

38

Fig. 2-22. Tandem-wing conversion of the Westland Lysander, with shortened fuselage and dummy machine gun turret.

Fig. 2-23. The German-designed, Swiss-built Dornier Do.212 had conventional tail surfaces expanded to a tandem wing. Note upward-tilted propeller shaft to keep propeller clear of the water.

engine was installed inside the hull to drive a behind-the-tail propeller through a long extension shaft. To keep the propeller out of the spray during takeoff and landing, it was necessary to raise it for these operations. This was achieved by pivoting the drive shaft at the engine end so that it angled 12 degrees upward to elevate the propeller.

The tandem wing appeared when the behind-the-wing location of the engine, dictated by the need for cabin space, brought the center of gravity to a point well aft of the normal rear limit. This was offset by giving the horizontal tail a significant lifting function through a span approximately two-thirds that of the main wing and an area 56 percent of the main wing. Because all of Dornier's German plants at the time were committed to war work, the non-military Model 212 was built in Dornier's Altenrheim plant in Switzerland, hence the Swiss registration.

Specifications: Wing span 33 feet 10 inches; gross weight 5,280 pounds; wing area 159 square feet.

Quickie

The tandem-wing concept went into eclipse again after the World War II experiments, but reappeared in a highly successful form in 1977. The new design was

the Quickie, a low-powered homebuilt designed by Tom Jewett, Gene Sheehan, and Burt Rutan, as Rutan Model 54, using an 18-hp Onan two-cylinder industrial engine. The secret of its performance is in the glass fiber/foam construction that allows a slick finish and highly accurate laminar airfoils.

The configuration is a bit hard to define. With wings of very nearly equal size and area, the Quickie is a tandem, but the builders call it a canard because the elevators are on the forward wing while the ailerons are on the rear. It can also be regarded as a tailless biplane with extreme negative wing stagger. A novel detail is the location of the mainwheels in the tips of the lower wing (FIG. 2-24).

Fig. 2-24. The most popular tandem-wing design to date is the homebuilt Quickie.

Because the plans appeared on the homebuilt market in 1980, more Quickies have been built than all other tandems back to Langley put together. Its success had the usual result—the development of a slightly larger two-seat version, the Q-2, and an imitator, the two-seat Dragonfly.

Quickie Model A specifications: Span 16 feet 8 inches; total wing area 53.6 square feet; empty weight 240 pounds; gross weight 480 pounds; top speed 126 mph.

Lockspeiser LDA

The British Lockspeiser LDA (for Land Development Aircraft, FIG. 2-25), is in a shadow area between a true tandem-wing and a canard with a heavily-loaded foreplane. While there are flaps on the foreplane of the LDA, the flight controls, consisting of ailerons that double as elevators (elevons), are located aft, so we can safely consider the LDA to be a tandem-wing.

The all-metal LDA was built in 1981 as a 70 percent-size proof-of-concept prototype for a proposed aerial equivalent of the famous British Land Rover all-terrain utility truck. The one-piece forward wing has half the span of the rear wing, and can be substituted for either the right or left rear wing panel. So far, only the reduced-scale prototype has been built and flown.

Specifications: Powerplant, one 85 hp Continental C-85 engine; main wing span 20 feet; length 22 feet 6 inches; gross weight 1,300 pounds; test speed 83 mph.

Amsoil Racer

In 1981 Burt Rutan introduced a larger development of the Quickie as his Model 68 (FIG. 2-26). To meet the requirements of the custom biplane racing class, it was larger, with a wing area of 75 square feet, a 160-hp Lycoming IO-320 engine, and interplane struts. Although the wings were cantilever as on "Quickie," the struts were required by the biplane racer rules.

A notable change from Quickie is the use of a one-piece horizontal tail. This does not make the racer a tandem-with-tail like the Langley or the Oertz in that the forward wing is fitted with a full-span elevator. The elevator on the tail is not the primary pitch control, but

40

Fig. 2-25. The British Lockspeiser LDA has the smallest forward wing of any tandem-wing design but is a true tandem and not a canard.

Fig. 2-26. The Amsoil Racer, designed by Burt Rutan, before installation of the totally unnecessary wing struts that were required by the biplane racing rules.

Fig. 2-27. The Rutan Model 72 Grizzly is a tandem-wing design with conventional tail surfaces on a long moment arm.

is actually a trimmer connected to the forward elevator to keep it in optimum position for the flight condition of the airplane.

Specifications: Forward wing span 20 feet 5 inches; rear wing span 22 feet; empty weight 854 pounds; gross weight 1,167 pounds; top speed 232 mph.

Rutan Grizzly

The Rutan Model 72 Grizzly of 1982 marks a return to the Langley and Oertz concepts of tandem wing designs in that a conventional tail group is located behind the two wings, which unlike the Quickie and Amsoil Racer, are on the same level (FIG. 2-27). There are overtones of triple-surface canard in that the forward wing is notably smaller than the rear. Both wings are fitted with Fowler flaps to increase lift and the forward wing does not provide pitch control.

Grizzly is a one-only experimental design powered by a 180-hp Lycoming IO-360B engine and was built to test the suitability of tandem wings for STOL operations and to develop various new structural and control concepts.

3
CHAPTER

Tailless Aircraft

FOR NEARLY AS LONG AS MAN HAS BEEN BUILDING FLY-
ing machines, the so-called "tailless" type has received
serious consideration. In fact, one of the first inanimate
flying objects that man became familiar with was a tailless glider—the inherently stable seed of the tropical
Zanonia bush. The seed drops from the bush and glides
for a distance before reaching the ground to take root.

ADVANTAGES

At first glance, tailless aircraft appear to have
many advantages over the conventional types—great
savings in weight, drag, and cost through elimination of
the aft fuselage and tail surfaces, plus enhanced maneuverability through the corresponding lower inertia. In
really big types, cargo and passengers can be carried
inside a roomy wing structure. For most tailless aircraft
built, however, the engine, crew, etc., have been carried in a shortened version of a conventional fuselage,
often called a *pod*.

DISADVANTAGES

The tailless types have two basic factors working
against them that pretty well nullify the advantages.
One is pitch instability, the tendency of the wing to
rotate (or tumble) about its own lateral axis if the center
of lift (center of pressure, or CP) is not closely aligned
with the center of gravity (CG). Stability is easy to
achieve for a single speed, but any speed or attitude
change that causes the CP to move results in instability.

The second disadvantage is the short control force
moment in pitch. Since the conventional trim controls,
the elevators, are very close to the center of gravity on a
straight-wing tailless, their effectiveness is greatly
diminished by the decreased distance, or moment arm.

This means they must have a greater displacement in
order to exert the greater force needed to make up for
the shorter moment. For minor trim corrections in level
flight, this means that the elevators are displaced,
thereby adding what is known as *trim drag*.

Another problem with tailless designs is where to
put the rudder and vertical fin. A very few have managed with none at all, but most have needed them—and
of greater area due to the reduced effectiveness through
the shortened moment arm. Some lengthened the short
fuselage a bit to put a single rudder at its end for
increased moment; others put rudders on each wingtip
for maximum moment, or closer inboard on each side
of the fuselage or pod.

CORRECTING TAILLESS PROBLEMS

Corrections for the stability and control problems
were found in the Zanonia seed. The trailing edges of
its wingtips project well aft of the central portion, cre-
ating in effect a swept-back wing. Also, the tendency to
pitch forward is overcome by the tip trailing edges
being reflexed upward, exactly like up elevator, so that
the airstream exerts a downward force that balances the
pitch-forward tendency.

For man-made wings, it was easy to sweep the
wing back and put the elevators at the tips so they now
were a greater distance aft of the CG and were therefore more effective. Since the ailerons were also to be
at the wingtips for maximum moment relative to the
longitudinal (roll) axis, it was logical to combine aileron and elevator into a single surface known as a
elevon. The surfaces on opposite wingtips operate in
the same direction as elevators and in opposite directions as ailerons, with necessary variations between.

For steady flight, the pitch-over tendency of the tailless is countered by reflexing the wingtips to a decreased angle of attack—in effect, using the wingtips as permanent up elevators instead of displacing the elevators or elevons themselves.

This practice had a disadvantage that the early designers might not have fully understood. By decreasing the angle of attack toward the wing tips, the lift of the "twisted" portion of the wing was decreased significantly and the drag was increased—two of the very things that the elimination of the conventional tail and rear fuselage was supposed to reduce.

A very few tailless designs have flown with straight rather than swept wings, but the most successful of these have been light gliders with a low speed range.

Staunch advocates keep pushing the tailless design, but until the advent of the hang glider and ultralight sport flying movements of the 1970s and 80s, the only tailless design to be produced in any quantity was the German Messerschmitt 163 rocket-powered interceptor of 1944/45.

The weight/cost/drag advantages of the tailless design pay off handsomely in the glider and ultralight fields, and the relatively narrow speed range of the aircraft greatly minimizes the trim and control problems. Further, the location of the pilot (who usually weighs more than the entire airframe) is located several feet below the CG of the structure and adds a very significant stabilizing moment that helps overcome pitch instability and allows the use of a straight, rather than swept-back, wing.

Etrich Gliders

The Austrian Igo Etrich was one of several independent experimenters working with gliders in the late 1890s. Having discovered the stability secret of the Zanonia seed, he was a jump ahead of the others. Instead of running down a hillside with a small hang glider controlled by the shifting of the pilot's weight, he built a larger machine mounted on a three-wheel undercarriage and rolled it down an inclined wooden ramp (FIG. 3-1).

44

Fig. 3-1. The Austrian Etrich tailless glider of 1900 and its inclined launching ramp.

By 1904, Etrich was building and successfully flying even larger gliders that looked still more like the Zanonia seed, complete with the rear-projecting upturned wingtips that imparted pitch stability to a tailless aircraft (FIG. 3-2). He had the stability problems licked, but this stability made control difficult. To overcome this problem, he added a long narrow horizontal tail in 1908, and then moved on to experiments with powered aircraft.

These retained the Zanonia wing which, combined with the long tail, gave his 1911 machine the planview appearance of a dove. The word for dove in German is *Taube*.

The design became very popular, and quite a few German firms built Taube variations from 1912 into early World War I.

Dunne

An Englishman, John W. Dunne, introduced a successful tailless glider in 1907; he developed it over the next four years into a powered biplane that pretty well established the standard for most tailless designs that followed, right up to the present.

The longitudinal stability of the 50-hp modified Dunne D.5 was imparted by the high degree of sweepback combined with a greatly decreased angle of attack of the wingtips—in effect, a turning-up of the trailing edges relative to the rest of the wing in the manner of the Zanonia seed, which Dunne knew about. In airplane rigging procedures, this decrease of positive angle of attack (actually, *angle of incidence* when there is no airflow to "attack") toward the wingtips is called *wash-out*. (The opposite is *wash-in*.)

Dunne was also the inventor of the elevon, which combined the function of elevator and aileron in a single surface. He was not very successful in selling his unique design, however; the imminence of World War I depressed the civil market. While the Royal Flying Corps tested one, it did not meet military requirements. Dunne sold a manufacturing license to the Burgess firm in the United States and a few were built as Burgess-Dunnes from 1914 to 1916.

45

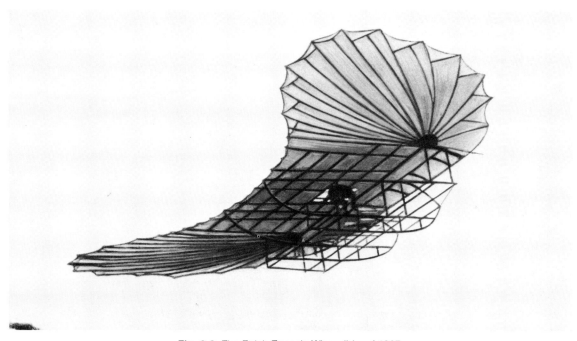

Fig. 3-2. The Etrich Zanonia-Wing glider of 1907.

Fig. 3-3. A U.S. Army Burgess-Dunne of 1914. Note the pronounced washout of the wings between the fuselage and the wingtips.

FIGURE 3-3 shows a 1914 U.S. Army Burgess-Dunne, with enclosed pod for the crew and protective skids under the wingtips.

Specifications: Powerplant, salmson 120-hp; wing span 46 feet; wing area 527 square feet; gross weight 2,140 pounds.

Lippisch Hang Glider

The sport gliding movement that started in Germany right after World War I produced a great number of designs that sought to increase performance through the use of unconventional configurations. One of the earliest tailless types seen in this program was designed and built by Alexander Lippisch, a young German engineer, in 1921.

This was a major step ahead of the hang gliders of the time and featured a relatively long span, slightly swept wing with heavily reflexed elevons, an open-frame "fuselage" for a seated pilot, a centerline wheel

for rolling starts and landings, and two sticks projecting downward from the wing for control actuation. The fins and rudders were underneath the wingtips, where the fins doubled as skids to keep the wingtips off the ground when the machine was at rest or rolling at less than flying speed (FIG. 3-4).

As a competitive glider, this early Lippisch design was no world-beater, but it gave the designer experience and encouragement that were to make him the world's foremost authority on tailless designs in an association that was to last for over 40 years.

Lippisch's Powered Deltas

Alexander Lippisch carried on his tailless work with further gliders and light, powered airplanes. Performance, stability, control, and accommodation comparable to contemporary light civil models were achieved with the refined Delta I of 1930.

The notable design detail of the Delta I was that

Fig. 3-4. German designer Alexander Lippisch and his tailless glider in 1921. Note the upward deflection of both elevons.

while the leading edge of the wing was still swept back at a comparatively shallow angle, the sweep of the trailing edge was eliminated by having it run in a straight line from tip to tip (FIG. 3-5). This is historically significant in that it started the development of the *delta* wing, which was not to become successful until after World War II—and then proved to be pioneered by Lippisch.

Because his new wing was more like a broad-based triangle than an inverted letter V, Lippisch named it Delta after the Greek capital letter, even though the proportions were way off. Delta I was not put into production, but led to later Deltas (FIG. 3-6).

The many Lippisch designs of the 1920s and 1930s are hard to track in the standard references under his name. Lippisch was a researcher and had no regular production facility of his own, so most of his designs were built by others, generally under their own names. An example is the Fieseler W-3 *Wespe* (Wasp), a unique twin-engine tailless that Lippisch called Delta IV. In addition to the novelty of two 75-hp British Pobjoy engines, one pushing and one pulling, the Wespe

had folding wings (FIG. 3-7). It was also one of the first aircraft—if not *the* first—to use a fixed canard surface to redirect airflow over the wing root. This feature has become very popular on the high-performance deltas of the 1980s.

Westland-Hill Pterodactyls

Too many firms have worked with tailless aircraft to provide coverage of them all in this chapter, but the case of one major British firm—not a small experimental shop—deserves comment.

The Westland Aircraft Company was founded during World War I and is still a major independent manufacturer today. In 1925 it became interested in the ideas of Geoffrey Hill and built several different tailless airplanes of his design. The first was a little single-seat development model powered with a 32-hp Bristol Cherub engine and called Pterodactyl I because the angularity of its wing vaguely resembled that of the prehistoric flying reptile (FIG. 3-8).

Fig. 3-5. The Lippisch Delta I of 1930, with swept-back wing leading edge and straight trailing edge.

The wing followed the now-traditional swept-back pattern, but instead of using elevons, it had elevators in the trailing edge and separate pivoted wingtips that served as ailerons. This type of wingtip had appeared on various experimental models since before World War I, but its disadvantages—particularly, greater drag and lack of "feel"—outweighed the alleged advantage of greater effectivity.

The landing gear featured two wheels in tandem under the podlike fuselage and stabilizing outriggers under the wings at the inboard ends of the elevators.

Hill's developments were finalized in a powerful

Fig. 3-6. Another Lippisch tailless, this with elliptical wing leading edge and thin canard surfaces installed close enough to the wing to form a slot.

two-seat fighter that was named the Pterodactyl V. It was unique among the tailless designs in being a tractor (with a 600-hp Rolls-Royce Goshawk engine) and being a *sesquiplane,* (a biplane with a lower wing having less than half the area of the upper), the upper wing had the same planform as the Pterodactyl I, the narrow lower wing, which also supported the small stabilizing wheels, was straight (FIG. 3-9).

The reason for the tractor engine installation was to give a gunner in the rear cockpit a wide, unrestricted field of fire for his machine guns, which were mounted on the standard gun ring used since 1916. This two-seat fighter concept didn't work out and the Pterodactyl V remained a one-only. Its principal function in the Royal Air Force, which bought it, seemed to be appearances at air shows.

Specifications: Powerplant, Rolls-Royce Goshawk 600-hp; wing span 46 feet 8 inches; gross weight 5,100 pounds; top speed 190 mph.

Horten Flying Wings

Inspired by Lippisch's work, the German Horten brothers, Reimar and Walter, built some very interesting gliders that truly deserved the names of "flying wing." In the interest of increasing performance through aerodynamic refinement, they did away with the now-traditional short fuselage or pod. To achieve this, the pilot lay prone in the center of the highly-tapered cantilever wing. For forward visibility, the leading edge of the wing was made transparent (FIG. 3-10).

Even the surface and intersection drag of vertical

Fig. 3-7. The Lippisch-designed Fieseler Wasp, a two-engine tailless with folding wings. Note the canard surface behind the forward engine for airflow control.

50

fins and rudders was eliminated. To initiate a turn, a high degree of differential was built into the aileron movement—the up aileron moved upward much farther than the opposite one moved down. This, aided by a spoiler on the upper surface, put more aerodynamic drag on the inside of the turn, in effect pulling that wing back. Further reductions in drag were achieved in the Horten VI model of 1944 by the use of wings having a higher-than-average aspect ratio (AR, or the total wing span divided by the average wing chord, expressed as a ratio: 32.4:1 for the Horten IV). High AR is a very important parameter in high-performance sailplane design.

Altogether, five different Horten wings were built from 1934 through 1944 (the Horten V of 1941 was a twin-engine powered version of the Horten III glider). They achieved very good lift-to-drag ratios (L-over-Ds, or the distance that the glider will move forward for each foot of altitude that it loses, expressed as ratio such as 28:1 for the III compared to contemporary sail-

planes. The Horten III of 1938 is shown in FIG. 3-10. Both IIIs built were lost at the same time. They flew into a severe thunderstorm during a prewar German glider contest and broke up in the extreme turbulence. Both pilots parachuted; one was dead when found later but the other was kept aloft by rising air currents in the storm for nearly two hours! (This was not the first time that parachutists were kept aloft by strong updrafts.)

Limitations on pilot mobility and comfort, limited maneuverability, and aeroelasticity problems in the Horten VI resulting from extremely long (24 meters, or 60.8 feet), thin wings kept the innovative Hortens from becoming more than limited research vehicles. After World War II, when aircraft production was prohibited in Germany, the Hortens moved to Argentina and continued their development of both gliders and powered airplanes.

Horten III specifications: Wing span 65.6 feet; area 403 square feet; aspect ratio 10.66:1; gross weight 770 pounds, climbing speed 2.13 fps.

Fig. 3-8. The British Westland-Hill Pterodactyl I, a 32-hp single-seater. Note the full-chord ailerons, or pivoting wingtips, and the absence of rudders.

Fig. 3-9. The Westland-Hill Pterodactyl V two-seat fighter.

Fig. 3-10. The German Horten III tailless glider of 1938.

Northrop N-1/N-9 Series

The American designer John K. Northrop had been a leading advocate of "clean" airplane design even before he developed the famous Lockheed Vega in 1927. He carried on his concepts in three succeeding companies of his own. In 1940 he accomplished the ultimate cleanup by eliminating the fuselage and tail and retaining only the wing. Like the Hortens that preceded him by a few years, he also eliminated the traditional tip-mounted vertical fins and rudders to create another line of pure "flying wings" (FIG. 3-11).

As a major manufacturer, he was able to interest the U.S. Army in the possibilities of tailless aircraft (the Army had purchased one Burgess-Dunne in 1915) after demonstrating a small company-funded test model N-1M.

The N-1M was powered by two 65-hp Franklin engines buried in the wing and driving pusher propel-lers through extension shafts. Since the N-1M was an airplane and not a sailplane like the Hortens, the drag of a bubble canopy enclosing a properly-seated pilot was acceptable. His downward vision was severely handicapped by his position, well back from the leading edge, but this was a minor handicap for an aerodynamic research tool. The structure was simple wood and metal, and was adaptable to extensive changes.

An unorthodox original feature of the N-1M was the use of turned-down outer sections of the wings. Elevons were used, but in place of rudders the N-1M had split trailing edge flaps outboard of the elevons that opened both upward and downward on one wingtip or the other to increase drag and pull the wing into a turn. The turned-down wingtips were soon straightened.

The first flight of the single N-1M was on July 3, 1940, and over 200 subsequent flights were made. After a change to 120-hp Franklin engines, the top speed was 200 mph. Wingspan was 38 feet, area 300 square feet for an AR of 4.81, and the gross weight was 3,900 pounds.

After the Army awarded Northrop a contract to develop a four-engine tailless heavy bomber, Northrop built four N-9Ms (FIG. 3-12), basically the N-1M with wing span increased to 60 feet, as flying scale models of the XB-35. The first three had 275-hp Menasco engines; the fourth had two 300-hp Franklins. All had straight-across wings from the start. The first flew on December 27, 1942, but crashed after 50 flights. The other three flew intensive test programs for the next three years. One is now preserved by the National Air and Space Museum and another is being restored. The gross weight of the N-9M was 7,100 pounds, wing area

Fig. 3-11. The American Northrop N-1M of 1940 with its original turned-down wingtips.

Fig. 3-12. The Northrop N-9M, used as a flying scale test model for the later XB-35 bomber.

490 square feet for an AR of 7.34, and the top speed was 257 mph for No. 4.

Northrop XP-56

A unique byproduct of the Northrop N-1/N-9 research was the XP-56 tailless fighter for the U.S. Army. Like the Curtiss XP-55, this was one of several new experimental fighters that were to use the new Pratt & Whitney X-1800 engine. Like the XP-55 and others, however, the XP-56 had to be redesigned for another engine, the 2,000-hp P & W R-2800-29 radial, and suffered because of it.

Two XP-56s were built. Aerodynamically, they were like the original N-1M, with the turned-down wingtips, but with a fat pod-like fuselage and twin vertical fins ahead of coaxial propellers. The co-axial arrangement was chosen over a single unit to reduce

propeller diameter and minimize the length of landing gear required for ground clearance (FIG. 3-13).

The directional control system was unique. It consisted of the split trailing edge flaps of the N-1/N-9, but they were not actuated directly by the pilot. Ram air passed continuously through a duct on each wingtip. When the pilot wanted to turn, he actuated a shutoff valve on that side that blocked air flow and directed it into a bellows that expanded to exert the force necessary to open the flaps.

Other than its aerodynamics, the XP-56 is notable for being the first all-welded and first all-magnesium airplane. As a fighter, the armament was a formidable battery of four .50-caliber machine guns and two 20mm cannon.

The No. 2 XP-56 is preserved by the National Air and Space Museum.

Fig. 3-13. The Northrop XP-56 fighter, with coaxial pusher propellers and turned-down wingtips.

Specifications: Wing span 42 feet 6 inches; area 307 square feet; gross weight 11,350 pounds; top speed 467 mph.

54

Messerschmitt Me. 163 Komet

The rocket-powered German Messerschmitt 163B interceptor that entered combat in May 1944 was one of the world's most unusual as well as advanced military airplanes. In the subsequent four decades of aeronautical history, no directly comparable production model has come along to match it.

The prototype was the DFS 194, which was built by the Deutsches Forschungsinstitute fur Segelflug (DFS) the German Research Institute for Soaring (glider) Flight, and first flew in August 1940. Since the DFS was essentially a research organization, production was turned over to Messerschmitt, then the leading German producer of fighter planes, and the designation Me. 163 was assigned. It is fortunate for the Allies that enormous technical development problems (associated mainly with the liquid-fuel rocket engine), further complicated by politics, delayed the combat debut of the Komet as long as they did.

In configuration, the Me. 163 was a conservative swept-wing tailless designed by the experienced Alexander Lippisch. It featured simple elevons on a wooden wing and a large vertical fin and rudder at the rear of a stubby aluminum fuselage (FIG. 3-14). To avoid the weight and stowage problems of a retractable landing gear, the Komet had none. Takeoff was made on a droppable two-wheel dolly and landing was on a single sprung skid, glider-fashion. However, there were no wingtip skids or rollers; nearly every landing ended in a whole or partial ground-loop if not a complete turn-over.

All the available space in the fuselage was needed for storage of the liquid rocket fuel. This consisted of two separate liquids which, when brought together, burned spontaneously with intense heat that was converted to propulsive energy. One, a mixture of methyl alcohol, hydrazine hydrate, and water, was called *C-*

Fig. 3-14. The phenomenal German Messerschmitt Me. 163 Komet rocket-powered interceptor of World War II on its takeoff dolly. The skid extended for landing.

Stoff. The other, *T-Stoff,* was hydrogen peroxide. There were many instances of Me. 163s blowing up when these two got together in other than the combustion chamber of the 4,410-pound-thrust Walter HWK 509C-1 rocket engine. Sometimes even the impact of a hard landing would set it off.

In spite of the great quantity of fuel carried (4,409 pounds*), the consumption was enormous and the engine could only run for about twelve minutes on that supply. This meant that the interceptors had to be based pretty much on the flight route of the Allied bombers to be able to engage them before flaming out. By the time they reached an altitude of 32,000 feet, they had only six and a half minutes of fuel left. In some cases, fully-fueled Komets were towed to altitude behind airplanes to intercept the bomber streams. After their engines were air-started at altitude, they had a few more minutes available for combat.

Glide tests of the first Me. 163V-1 prototype began in the spring of 1941; the first powered flight was made in July. The Me. 163V-4, closer to the production version, flew on October 2, 1941, and exceeded the long-sought goal of 1,000 kilometers per hour (622 mph) on its first flight. It was also the first aircraft to encounter the compressibility problems associated with high speeds in level flight, so some aerodynamic fixes had to be worked out. Due to the Komet's swept wing and tailless design, the compressibility problems were not as bad as they could have been—swept wings have since been the principal means of minimizing compressibility problems.

Armament was two 20mm cannon in the wings. With a wing span of only 32 feet 2 inches, the Komet was one of the smallest fighters of World War II. Wing area was 219 square feet and gross weight was 11,684 pounds to give the then-phenomenal wing loading of 53.5 pounds per square foot. Top speed of the production Me. 163C model was 596 mph and it could climb to 39,690 feet (12,100 meters) in three minutes and 20 seconds. Initial rate of climb was 11,810 fpm.

Altogether, 364 Komets were built. Other liquid-rocket airplanes have been built since for research, but none have been put in production as first-line combat aircraft.

Northrop Bombers

In September 1941, Northrop proposed a tailless heavy bomber design to the U.S. Army Air Force and was given a contract in November for the development of ten, to be designated XB-35 for two prototypes and YB-35 for eight service test models. In July 1942, the four N-9M research models were authorized. It was recognized at the time that the bombers would require a long development time and could not be expected to contribute to the war effort. As it was, the first XB-35 did not fly until June 25, 1946.

This was the largest and heaviest tailless built to that time (or since), with a wing span of 172 feet, area of 4,000 square feet, and loaded weight of 209,000 pounds. It followed the planform and aerodynamic details of the 60-foot N-9Ms. The powerplant installation was complex, with four huge 3,000-hp Pratt & Whitney R-4360-17 air-cooled radials buried in the wing and driving coaxial propellers behind the trailing edge through extension shafts (FIGS. 3-15, 3-16). There

55

Fig. 3-15. Underside view of the Northrop XB-35 showing the leading edge air intakes for the buried engines, the wing planform, and the wingtip slots.

*The output of rocket and jet engines is measured in pounds of thrust rather than horsepower, and fuel is measured in pounds rather than gallons. One pound of thrust equals one horsepower at about 375 mph, less below that figure and more above it.

Fig. 3-16. The fairings for the extended propeller shafts of the Northrop XB-35 provided enough vertical fin area to assure directional stabilily. Propellers were later changed to single-rotation type.

was a 15-man crew; defensive armament was to be 20 .50-caliber machine guns in seven remotely controlled turrets above and below the wing. The bomb load for a 7,500-mile range was to be 10,000 pounds, and the maximum speed was 391 mph.

Only three of the eventual 15 flying wing bombers started were delivered as piston-engined B-35s. In May 1946, the order stood at two XB-35s, eleven YB-35s, and two jet-propelled YB-49s. With the introduction of jet propulsion at the end of the war, the U.S. Army got Northrop to rework two of the YB-35s as YB-49s powered with eight 4,000-pound thrust Allison J-35A-15 jet engines (FIG. 3-17). The first flight of a YB-49 was on

October 21, 1947. The jets provided a great improvement in powerplant operation and maintenance, besides reducing the weight by over 12,000 pounds. Top speed was increased by 102 mph to 433. It was necessary to add four small vertical fins to the YB-49s to improve directional stability; this function had been performed by the drag of the propellers and propeller shaft housings on the Ns and the B-35s.

The Northrop bomber program had a troubled history that was both technical and political. The coaxial propellers of the XB-35s were major technological headaches, and their late delivery delayed the initial flights. For a while, undesirable single-rotation propel-

Fig. 3-17. The Northrop YB-49 substituted jet engines for the propeller types of the XB-35 and found that it was necessary to add vertical fins for directional stability.

lers had to be fitted. Before the war ended, the Army decided that the Martin Company should build 200 production B-35s, but this program was soon cancelled.

Even before two of the three B-49s flown were lost to crashes, the Army had decided to have Northrop convert the nine uncompleted B-35 airframes to B-49s. Before this work could be completed, however, the entire flying wing bomber program—and the unfinished B-35/B-49 conversions—was scrapped.

Following the demise of the B-49 program, the tailless configuration for heavy airplanes was a dead issue until the Northrop B-2 appeared in early 1988 (the last airplane in the original U.S. Army/Air Force B-for-bomber series was the North American B-70 of 1964; the series started over with the Rockwell B-1 of 1974). B-numbers from 71 through 87 were assigned to unmanned tactical and strategic missiles given airplane designations.

Vought F7U Cutlass

The only true tailless design (not including delta wings, see Chapter 4) other than the Me. 163 to achieve production and first-line military service was the American Vought F7U Cutlass ordered in 1946. The U.S. Navy bought 197 and operated them from aircraft carriers starting in 1950 (see Chapter 13). The F7U sat on tricycle landing gear at a very high ground angle in order to be able to make carrier takeoffs and landings at high angle of attack for maximum lift (FIG. 3-18).

Although it had a short service life, the F7U was

Fig. 3-18. The American Vought F7U Cutlass was the only tailless fighter other than the Me.163 to be produced for first-line service. Note that the elevons are raised slightly to trim the fighter to the relatively low speed of the camera airplane.

57

pioneer in that it was the first fighter that was designed from scratch to use after burners on its two jet engines.

Specifications: Powerplants, two 4,600-pound thrust Westinghouse J46 WE-8A; wing span 38 feet 8 inches; area 496 square feet; gross weight 31,642 pounds; maximum speed 680 mph.

Recreational Tailless Designs

As previously mentioned, glider builders have been experimenting with tailless designs since the early 1920s in attempts to improve performance through reduced weight and drag. While many of these were successful in varying degrees, none got into production. With the German Horten designs providing inspiration, serious studies were undertaken in the early 1950s, and some interesting new designs began to appear in the recreational field.

Fauvel AV-36 This French single-seater appeared in 1951 and was built in significant quantities throughout the world by amateur constructors using purchased plans. The AV-36 had a more practical seating arrangement than the Hortens; the pilot sat upright in a short pod. A major break with traditional tailless design was the use of a tapered wing without sweep (FIG. 3-19). While it was a satisfactory sporting glider, its relatively low performance rendered it non-competitive and it soon faded from the soaring scene. However, the designer went on to develop powered versions.

Specifications: Wing span 41 feet 10$\frac{1}{2}$ inches; area 157 square feet; gross weight 569 pounds; L/D 26.5:1 at 51 mph; sinking speed 4.26 feet per second at 62 mph.

Fig. 3-19. The French Fauvel AV-36 broke with tailless glider tradition in not using a swept-back wing. Pitch and roll control are by elevons; that is a trim tab between the rudders.

Fig. 3-20. The powered Mitchell Wing B10 ultralight was easily adapted from the earlier Mitchell rigid-wing hang glider.

Mitchell Wings When the modern hang glider movement began in the late 1960s, most of the designs utilized traditional rigid aircraft structures, both in monoplane and biplane form. It was logical for some designers to try the old reduction of weight and drag through tailless design, but now something new was added. The pilot was now suspended well below the wing in most cases, thereby imparting a very high degree of *pendulum stability* since he outweighed the structure by nearly 2:1. This cut down greatly on the amount of sweep needed for longitudinal stability, and tailless designs became quite significant in the early stages of movement.

Outstanding examples are the American Mitchell Wings, developed by old-time traditional glider designer Don Mitchell. The first featured a rigid cantilever wing, with control by pilot weight shift. When power began to enter the picture, the Mitchell Wing was one of the earliest to be adapted to the new movement. A "fuselage" with three wheels, a proper seat for the pilot, manual controls, and a two-stroke-cycle pusher engine were added (FIG. 3-20). As long as the machine could be launched by the pilot standing on his feet, it could be flown without either a pilot's or aircraft license, just as the hang gliders were allowed to do by the FAA.

In 1979, a new Mitchell design, the U-2, was designed from scratch to use power (FIG. 3-21). This had much higher performance, and since it did not have foot-launch capability, had to be licensed as an amateur-built airplane; the pilot had to have a license.

In 1982, the FAA announced new rules for the low-powered designs that were derived mainly from hang gliders and were called *ultralights*. If they

Fig. 3-21. The Mitchell U-2, with engine on a tubular tail boom, was designed from the start as a powered aircraft and is not a converted hang glider.

weighed less than 260 pounds empty, carried no more than five gallons of fuel, did not exceed a maximum speed of 63 mph (55 knots), they could operate unlicensed. Anything above these figures requires licenses. The U-2, designed long before the rules were set, does not qualify as an ultralight.

Mitchell B-10 wing specifications: Powerplant Honda 20-hp; wing span 34 feet; area 136 square feet; gross weight 430 pounds; top speed 55 mph.

Mitchell U-2 specifications: Powerplant Honda 20-hp; wing span 34 feet; area 136 square feet; gross weight 480 pounds; top speed 95 mph.

Modified Rogallo Wings The original delta form of the unique Rogallo wing did not last long in the hang glider movement. The sweep angle of the leading edge was soon decreased to the point where the planform resembled a traditional tailless planform with generous taper and very little sweep. Chordwise battens similar to ribs were added, and the wing now operated as a true airfoil rather than as a kite. Performance was greatly improved.

New designs using the basic Rogallo structure and single-surface cloth covering proliferated in the 1970s and were hard to tell apart. The Phoenix shown in FIG. 3-22 is representative of these elongated Rogallo wing hang gliders, with the pilot suspended in a near-prone position well below the wing to provide pendulum stability. Control is by the pilot shifting his weight, supplemented on some by wing-warping.

When the ultralight movement began, it was easy to adapt many of the tailless hang gliders to ultralights by adding a framework for a seated pilot, engine, wheels, and manual controls. Some added canard surfaces to improve their maneuverability (FIG. 1-29).

Representative "expanded Rogallo" hang glider specifications: wing span 31 feet; wing area 190 square feet; gross weight 275 pounds; L/D 8 or 10:1; stall speed 17 to 20 mph.

59

Fig. 3-22. The Phoenix hang glider is representative of many now in use with the basic Rogallo wing expanded to high aspect ratio with battens installed to give a chordwise airfoil shape and increase efficiency.

4
CHAPTER

Delta Wings

THE *DELTA* WING, SO-CALLED BECAUSE ITS GENERALLY triangular shape resembles the Greek letter of that name, is now a relatively common feature on two widely separated types of aircraft—very high performance military and civil types, and some hang gliders and ultralights at the very bottom of the performance scale.

In both cases, the use of delta wings is relatively recent practice—from the early 1950s for the high-performance types and from the 1970s for the recreational. Technology advances in other areas were necessary to make them workable.

In concept, the delta-wing aircraft can be regarded as a tailless design with a high degree of leading edge sweepback—45 degrees or more—in which the area forward of a straight line connecting the trailing edges of the wingtips has been filled in. This greatly increases the area of the wing relative to its span, producing very low or even fractional aspect ratios. Aspect ratio (AR) is the ratio of the span of a wing to its average, or mean, chord (MAC), expressed as a ratio such as 2:1 for a typical delta wing. For odd shapes on which it is hard to determine the MAC, the AR is found by the formula $AR = \frac{span^2}{area}$. With a delta wing, a given area can be provided with a wing of much shorter span.

A minor oddity of modern high-performance delta airplanes is that none are driven by propellers. Props were on their way out when the delta made its appearance after World War II, so were never used except on a few experimental models—and then with a special feature.

ADVANTAGES

Reduced span and light wing loadings are the primary benefits of the delta wing. Further, since it has such a long chord, its physical thickness for a given aerodynamic thickness is great, allowing much of the payload, fuel, and equipment normally carried in a conventional fuselage to be carried inside the wing, thereby reducing drag through elimination of the fuselage. This arrangement has been used mainly on larger types such as bombers. On the other hand, some single-seat fighters have fuselages that are very large relative to the wing; these capitalize primarily on the advantages of very short span for a given area.

DISADVANTAGES

The shorter the wingspan gets, the less effective it is in resisting the tendency of the airplane to roll in a direction opposite to the direction of propeller rotation. An extreme example of this is seen in the ConVair XFY-1, a propeller design with enough power in its turboprop engine to permit vertical takeoff. With this much power and a single-rotation propeller, this single-seat delta would virtually spin about its longitudinal axis under full power. To avoid this, coaxial propellers were used, the single engine driving two propellers in opposite directions to neutralize the roll effect. This is a prime example of some of the tradeoffs that must be made when trying to capitalize on the advantages of a certain configuration.

Another inherent disadvantage of the delta wing in most applications is that conventional trailing edge flaps cannot be used to reduce landing speed. Their maximum distance from the center of gravity causes them to act more like elevators than flaps. This disadvantage is offset somewhat by the fact that the delta wing can fly at a considerably higher angle of attack than conventional wings, and so can generate more lift and therefore land more slowly. Further, stopping after a still relatively "hot" landing is aided by deployment of a braking parachute (this is also used on many high-performance types besides deltas, such a procedure being acceptable for military aircraft). Except for the few supersonic transports built in the 1970s, high-performance delta-wing airplanes are entirely military.

ROGALLO WING

At the opposite end of the scale, the hang glider movement boomed when it adopted the Rogallo wing. This was developed by Francis M. Rogallo of the National Aeronautics and Space Administration (NASA) as sort of a gliding parachute for aerial cargo delivery. It was soon adapted to powered airplane-like vehicles in the late 1950s. Nothing came of these, but the concept caught on strongly in the hang glider movement. The low cost and structural simplicity offered major advantages over more traditional rigid structures of comparable performance. Further, the Rogallo wing could be "rolled up" and transported on a car-top carrier, allowing storage at home and avoidance of airport hangar costs.

The initial appeal of the Rogallo was its simplicity. It consists essentially of a sail-like cloth stretched between three aluminum tubes that form the two leading edges and a centerline spine. As long as the wing has forward speed or airflow past it, and maintains a positive angle of attack, it stays "inflated" much like a parachute and can generate lift (FIG.4-1).

Oddly, the true delta form worked its way right out of the hang glider movement through the desire for improved performance. The span of the basic Rogallo wing was gradually increased and the chord decreased until the planform became essentially a tailless with a very shallow angle of leading edge sweep.

Prior to the hang glider boom, some propeller-driven homebuilt deltas appeared—there were no small jets available to the amateur designers. Because of the relatively low power of these recreational types, the roll tendency was minimal and could be handled by the short-span wing.

Lippisch DM-1

The DM-1, designed by Alexander Lippisch, was the first true delta-wing aircraft—one with a leading-edge sweep angle more than 45 degrees from a line

Fig. 4-1. A representative example of an early Rogallo-wing hang glider.

normal to the airplane centerline. The DM-1 had a sweep of 60 degrees at the leading edge and 15 degrees forward sweep at the trailing edge. It was developed late in World War II as a full-scale glider mockup of an innovative delta-wing fighter to be powered by ramjet engines. The purpose of the DM-1 was to verify that the configuration had acceptable handling characteristics at the low end of the performance scale. In the absence of a high-powered prototype, the high-speed data had to be obtained in a wind tunnel. Intermediate-range data were to be obtained by towing the DM-1 to high altitude—25,000 or more feet—or carrying it piggyback on a larger airplane, and releasing it. It would then accelerate to the desired test speed in a long dive. Of course, the relatively light weight and construction of the DM-1 put a limit on the diving speed—approximately 347 mph.

Lippisch was aided in his design work by two *Akademisch Flieger grupes,* sort of engineering-oriented flying organizations, at the Universities of Darmstadt and Munich—hence the DM-designation.

Except for the absence of an engine, the DM-1 was a complete airplane, with retractable tricycle landing gear. For light weight and ease of construction, it was all wood with a thin plywood covering. Other than its innovative wing shape, the unique feature of the design was the integration of the cockpit with the lower lead-

Fig. 4-2. The wooden Lippisch DM-1 glider developed late in World War II.

ing edge of the thick-section vertical fin (FIGS. 4-2, 4-3). Wing span was 19 feet 8 inches; length 20 feet 9 inches, and wing area 214 square feet. Maximum speed at a gross weight of 1,012 pounds was 446 mph at a wing loading of 4.7 pounds per square foot. The sinking speed was high by ordinary glider standards, 16.4 feet per second, and the glide, or L/D, was steep—only 7:1.

The DM-1 was liberated by American occupation forces and brought to the U.S. for testing late in 1945. The data obtained were encouraging and a contract was awarded to Consolidated-Vultee Aircraft (ConVair) to develop a jet-propelled derivative. The DM-1 survives today in the U.S. Air Force Museum near Dayton, Ohio.

Fig. 4-3. The Lippisch DM-1 was the first delta-wing aircraft.

Fig. 4-4. The American ConVair 7002/XF-92A was the first successful powered delta-wing aircraft.

ConVair F-102 Delta Dagger

The enormous potential of the DM-1 encouraged the U.S. Army Air Force (changed to U.S. Air Force in 1947) to develop the design further and produce the high-performance fighter that it was intended to be.

A contract was awarded to the Consolidated-Vultee Aircraft Corporation (ConVair) for one jet-powered research aircraft, Model 7002. Although not a combat model, this was soon redesignated XF-92A (FIGS. 4-4, 4-5). It drew heavily on the DM-1, and in fact Alexander Lippisch was on hand as a consultant. The sweepback angle was 60 degrees but the airfoil was much thinner than that of the DM-1, and the thick fin/cockpit combination was eliminated. Power was a 4,500-pound thrust Allison J-33A. Its first flight was on September 18, 1948.

The success of the 7002/XF-92A program resulted in the production of an all-weather interceptor fighter, the F-102A Delta Dagger (FIG. 4-6). This was the first delta wing design to go into service, and 1,088 in all were built starting in 1953. With extensive changes of fuselage geometry, the F-102 used the XF-92A wing scaled up 1.22:1.

The service test YF-102 model flew on October 24, 1953, but in spite of the power of its 17,000-pound thrust Pratt & Whitney J-57P-23 engine, it could not achieve supersonic flight. Compressibility was holding it back. A redesign of the fuselage, which narrowed it in the area of the wing root (area rule) according to the theories of Richard Whitcomb of the National Advisory Committee for Aeronautics (NACA), overcame the problem.

Production F-102As entered service in 1956. The F-102 was the first fighter to dispense with the tradi-

tional machine gun or cannon armament. Instead, it was armed with unguided rockets and guided missiles.

One hundred and eleven F-102As were completed as two-seat TF-102 trainers with side-by-side seating in a widened fuselage. With a span of 38 feet 1½ inches, the F-102A weighed 28,000 pounds and had a top speed of 825 mph at 36,000 feet.

A further development was the F-106A Delta Dart (originally to have been the F-102B), which had changes to tail and air intakes and used a P & W J-75 series engine (FIG. 4-7). With a 50 percent increase in power, the F-106A could reach 1,525 mph at 40,000 feet. A total of 340 F-106As and Bs, plus TF-106As were built from 1956 to 1961.

Fig. 4-5. ConVair XF-92A. Note tufts on right wing for aerodynamic testing.

Fig. 4-6. The ConVair F-102A Delta Dagger was the production result of the 7002/XF-92A program.

Fig. 4-7. The ConVair F-106A is a further improvement over the F-102.

ConVair B-58 Hustler

Since it was logical to adapt the delta wing configuration to supersonic bombers as well as fighters, this was quickly done, and the now-experienced ConVair firm was given a U.S. Air Force contract in October 1954 for a four-jet bomber, designated XB-58. This was basically a scaling-up of the F-102A wing to slightly more than double the area (1,542 square feet) and a wing span of only 56 feet 10 inches. Since the wing was far too thin to accommodate four 15,600-

pound thrust General Electric J79 engines internally, they were mounted in individual pods beneath it (FIG. 4-8).

A unique feature of the design was that the nuclear weapon was not carried in the traditional bomb bay in the fuselage but in a large pod under the belly that could also accommodate other stores and extra fuel.

The first of 13 test models, XB-58 and YB-58, flew on November 11, 1956. An additional 17 test articles were ordered. These were followed by 86 B-58As, with the first delivered in September 1959.

Fig. 4-8. The wing of the ConVair B-58 Hustler bomber was a direct scale-up of the F-102 wing.

Fig. 4-9. The wing of the British Avro Vulcan bomber was thick enough to allow the four jet engines to be installed inside of it.

The high speed of the B-58A—1,385 mph at 40,000 feet—made traditional swivelling machine gun turrets useless. Instead, a radar-aimed tail turret with a 20mm multi-barrel cannon was fitted. Gross weight of the B-58A was 163,000 pounds for a wing loading of 105 pounds per square foot.

Avro Vulcan

While the XB-58 was a supersonic bomber that was scaled up from a fighter, the British Avro 698 Vulcan started as a bomber for the top of the subsonic range—actually transonic (650 mph plus). It capitalized on the thick wing root of a large delta wing to house four jet engines to reduce the drag of external installations. The early models (prototypes and Mark I production models) had a span of 99 feet and an area of 3,554 square feet. First flight of the prototype was September 3, 1953.

The leading edge sweep was relatively shallow—50 degrees—but this was greatly increased at the outer quarter of each wing (FIG. 4-9). Early models through the Mark I had separate ailerons and elevators; the Mark II used elevons. Since the selected 10,000-pound thrust British Olympus jet engines were not ready on schedule, the first prototype was flown with 6,500-pound thrust Rolls-Royce Avons. The final Mark IIs, which had their wing span increased by 12 feet, had 20,000-pound thrust Rolls-Royce engines.

The speed of the Vulcan made defensive armament unnecessary. It could carry a nuclear weapon or up to 21,000 pounds of conventional bombs.

Specifications: Span 111 feet; gross weight 180,000 pounds; cruising speed 625 mph.

Payen 49B Katy

The little French Payen 49B of 1954 is hard to exactly classify. It is not a true delta-wing because the trailing edge also has significant sweepback (FIG. 4-10). The low aspect ratio, however, pretty well keeps it from being called a true tailless type. (M. Payenne is noted for hard-to-classify designs; see the PA-22 in Chapter 16.)

Fig. 4-10. The design of the little French Payenne 49B was strongly influenced by the Lippisch DM-1.

Built of wood and powered with a small Turbomeca Palas jet engine of 730-pound thrust, the Katy owed much to the Lippisch DM-1. Its span was 16 feet 11 inches; the area was 121 square feet with an aspect ratio of 2.38:1. Gross weight was 1,430 pounds; top speed was 310 mph. Since the Katy was built for research, maximum performance for the power was not a goal, so the landing gear was fixed.

A unique feature was the split rudder. Both sides could be opened outward to full normal travel to act as an air brake, a vertical application of the wingtip rudders of the Northrop tailless models.

The Douglas Deltas

Delta wings do not have to be perfect triangles with acute base angles, as shown by the Avro Vulcan. Further, delta wings are not limited to use on tailless aircraft. The Douglas Aircraft Company of Long Beach, California, developed two major production models that illustrate both points well.

The first was the F4D Skyray, a carrier-based fighter for the U.S. Navy. It flew in its XF4D-1 prototype form on January 23, 1951, with a single 5,000-pound thrust Allison J35 jet engine substituting for the intended Westinghouse J40. The F4D featured a combined fuselage/wing root structure that enclosed the large engine and tapered sharply downward to the wing

Fig. 4-12. Front view of the Douglas F4D-1 shows the blending of the wing into the fuselage. Note folded-up wingtips to save space on aircraft carriers.

67

surface proper, which had the leading edge rounding gently into the wingtip, and a rounded trailing edge at the tip (FIGS. 4-11, 4-12). The leading edge of the wing root was squared off to provide dual air intakes for the engine. To reduce the already short wingspan of 33 feet 6 inches for stowage on aircraft carriers, the tips of the wing could be folded upward.

Altogether, 420 F4D-1s were delivered between June 1954 and December 1958. The production F4D-1 had a top speed of 695 mph from a later 9,700-pound thrust Pratt & Whitney J57 engine (10,500 pounds with afterburner). Armament was four 20mm cannon and up to 4,000 pounds of bombs, rockets, or other stores.

To combat the trend of single-seat combat designs toward greater size and weight, Douglas designer Edward H. Heinemann was charged in 1950 with the task of reversing the trend without decreasing combat capability. The result was the A4D-1 Skyhawk, also called "Heinemann's Hot Rod" because of its perfor-

Fig. 4-11. The delta-wing Douglas F4D-1 Skyray was produced as a carrier-based fighter for the U.S. Navy.

mance. It was (and is) primarily a bomber and ground attack type, not a fighter. The XA4D-1 prototype flew on June 22, 1954, with a Wright J65 (American-built British Armstrong-Siddeley Sapphire) engine. While it featured a classic delta wing with straight leading edges and sharp wingtips, it also had a horizontal tail (that in planform was a smaller version of the wing), a big jet engine in the small fuselage, and little room for fuel in the thin 27 foot 6 inch wing (FIG. 4-13). The bare Skyhawk was a short-range plane. Extra fuel could be carried in external drop tanks, and the new technique of aerial refueling by the hose-and-probe method (see Chapter 15) could extend the range indefinitely, leaving the under-wing racks available for military stores. Armament was two 20mm cannon and up to 500 pounds of bombs. Maximum speed at a gross weight of 24,500 pounds was 570 mph at sea level.

The A4D series (A-4 since 1962) established a most remarkable production record—some 2,960 were delivered between August 1954 and February 1979, a quarter-century of production for a first-line combat airplane. A switch to the 11,200-pound thrust Pratt & Whitney J52 in 1957 resulted in the A4D-3 (later A-4D). Skyhawk designations ultimately reached A-4M.

A-4E specifications: Wing span 27 feet 6 inches; area 260 square feet; gross weight 24,500 pounds; top speed 675 mph.

68

Fig. 4-13. Douglas also used a delta-wing on the long-produced A4D Navy attack plane that was later redesignated A-4. This differed from traditional Deltas in having standard horizontal tail surfaces, with ailerons and trailing edge flaps in the delta wing.

Homebuilt Deltas

The fact that the delta wing was used almost exclusively in the high-performance military field and associated with jet propulsion did not keep amateur builders from trying it for recreational designs. It got off to a bad start when a widely-publicized design (because it was the first) crashed on its first flight, killing the pilot. This was not blamed on the propeller-driven design; it was a high-performance aircraft by homebuilt standards and the pilot, who insisted on making the first flight through pride of authorship, was not qualified to handle an untried "hot" airplane that might hand an inexperienced pilot some surprises.

Baker Delta Kitten The first notably successful amateur design was the Delta Kitten built by Marion Baker of Akron, Ohio, in 1960. Powered by an 85-hp Continental piston engine in the nose, it was all-metal (a rarity in homebuilts at the time) and owed much to the DM-1 in the fin/cockpit arrangement (FIG. 4-14). Baker did not leap right into a full-scale design immediately; he tested it carefully as a gasoline-powered flying scale model first. The Kitten's span was 18 feet, area of the 45-degree delta wing was 98 square feet, and gross weight was 843 pounds. Its maximum speed was 135 mph.

Dyke Delta A somewhat different amateur designer's approach to the delta was made in 1964 by John Dyke of Fairborn, Ohio. He built a four-seater (also a rarity among homebuilts) and used a 180-hp piston engine in the nose. The structure used a steel tube fuselage. The 22-foot span wing also used a steel-tube frame, another rarity.

The wing was not a true delta, but was more like a diamond due to the extensive forward sweep of the

Fig. 4-14. The propeller-driven recreational Baker Delta Kitten shows strong influence of both the Lippisch DM-1 and the Payenne Katy.

Fig. 4-15. The Dyke Delta is misnamed because its wing has a trapezoid or diamond planform, not a true delta.

Fig. 4-16. The delta-wing of the Concorde supersonic transport has a fractional aspect ratio because the root chord is slightly greater than the span.

trailing edge (FIG. 4-15). This permitted a long root chord with great depth that faired into a relatively broad and shallow fuselage tapering outward from the nose. The top of the cockpit canopy was of airfoil shape from the front of the windshield aft to contribute to the overall lift.

The Dyke Delta performed so well—190 mph at a gross weight of 1,800 pounds—that the designer put the plans for the JD-2 version on the market. Several have now been built by others.

Concorde

One of the hottest political potatoes of the international civil aircraft industry has been the supersonic transport, or SST. The cost of developing such a plane of sufficient size to carry a suitable payload was beyond the financial ability of any single manufacturer.

In Western Europe, a French-British consortium formed in 1962 and backed by the respective governments produced the Concorde. The two firms were Aerospatiale in France and British Aircraft Corporation Ltd. in England. The four 38,050-pound thrust engines were also a joint effort between Rolls-Royce in England and SNECMA in France.

The first prototype (FIG. 4-16) flew on March 2, 1969, but this triumph was dimmed by the fact that the very similar-looking Russian Tupulev 144 SST had flown on December 26, 1968. The Russian model entered service within Russia on December 26, 1975, which is highly indicative of the extensive "de-bugging" time required for such a complex aircraft. Com-

mercial transatlantic service with the production Concorde was inaugurated on May 24, 1976. An operational handicap is the fact that the SST can only fly supersonically over the oceans; the noisy shock wave of supersonic flight is unacceptable over inhabited land, so the full potential of SST operation cannot be realized.

The Concorde can carry up to 128 economy-class passengers at a cruising speed of Mach 2.04 at 51,300 feet. Sixteen Concordes were built, but with the novelty wearing off and the cost of petroleum fuel increasing greatly in the 1974-1980 time frame, SST service has been serously curtailed.

Specifications: Wing span 83 feet 10 inches; area 3,856 square feet; gross weight 408,000 pounds.

Lockheed SR-71 Blackbird

The ultimate delta-wing airplane is also the fastest at 2,193 mph (Mach 3+) and the highest-flying at 85,069 feet (FIG. 4-17). It entered service in 1966 as the SR-71, the figure 71 being a continuing number in the B-for-Bomber series. However, the letters SR stand for Strategic-Reconnaissance. Some were also built as F-12A fighters (the F-for-Fighter series started over again after reaching F-111; the B-series started again after reaching B-87).

Over 90 percent of the airframe is titanium, and because of the friction of the air at high speed, the outer skin temperature can reach 1,200 degrees Fahrenheit. Since some of the cooling is by radiation, the entire air-

69

Fig. 4-17. The American Lockheed SR-71 and its immediate predecessors, the A-11 and F-12, are consistently the world's fastest and highest-flying airplanes. Note the irregular shape of the trailing edge and the inward slant of the vertical tail surfaces on this third of three YF-12A airplanes.

70

plane is painted black, hence the unofficial name "Blackbird." The SR-71s are still in service and, in spite of their age, much of the data concerning these remarkable twin-engine single-seaters is still classified.

Available specifications: Powerplants two 32,500 pounds of thrust Pratt & Whitney J-58 turbojets, wing span 55 feet 7 inches; length 107 feet 5 inches, service ceiling over 80,000 ft.

5
CHAPTER

Rotary Wings

HONORS FOR THE SINGLE DESIGN FEATURE THAT DID the most to create unconventional aircraft configurations must go to the rotary wing. The idea for the device, initially conceived as a screw boring its way upward through the air, was actually put down on paper by Leonardo da Vinci around the year 1500 (FIG. 5-1). Like other concepts for mechanical flight, however, it took a few centuries for advancing technology to make the rotary wing workable.

The first serious and potentially workable helicopter configurations date from 1907, and experimentation has been continuous thereafter. A few did hop off the ground and support their weight for short periods of time before and after World War I, but none managed to get out of ground effect or to move about under really effective control until 1937. Development was rapid after the appearance of Igor Sikorsky's breakthrough

VS-300 design in 1940 (he had started his helicopter experiments in 1907), and helicopters of various configurations are a common sight today.

ADVANTAGES

The principal advantage of the rotary wing (for helicopters) is that it generates lift by rotating in place and is not dependent on forward speed of the aircraft itself for lift. This makes vertical takeoff and landing possible without the need for thrust equal to the weight of the aircraft. Power-to-weight ratios remain essentially the same as for conventional airplanes. The wing loading of rotary-wing aircraft is not determined by the area of the individual wings themselves—called *blades*—but by *disc loading*. This is the area of the disc swept by the rotor blades divided into the weight of the aircraft.

Another great advantage is that the helicopter can hover over one spot, a feature of value for observation, loading or unloading cargo at points where an aircraft cannot land, lowering medical or rescue personnel on cables, etc. Entire books can and have been written on the subject.

With no forward speed during part of its flight regime, the helicopter does not need conventional wings or control surfaces. Primary control is through the rotor or rotors, which are tilted slightly in the desired direction of movement by the pilot.

DISADVANTAGES

As with any special feature, there is a major price tag associated with the advantages of the rotary wing. The primary drawback is mechanical complexity, with attendant high initial and maintenance costs. In helicopters, the rotors are not connected directly to the

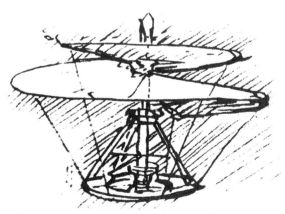

Fig. 5-1. Leonardo da Vinci's concept of a helicopter, circa 1500.

powerplant as is a propeller; they are driven through complex systems of gears and shafts and the rotor blades themselves attach to the shaft through an elaborate hinge that allows movement relative to the shaft vertically, laterally, and axially for pitch change.

The wearout period for major moving parts is much shorter than for comparable components of conventional aircraft. Operating costs per flight hour are so high, in fact, that small commercial helicopters are usually moved from their base to a job site relatively few miles away by truck rather than being flown.

Another inherent disadvantage, discovered by the earliest helicopter experimenters, is the tendency of the fuselage, or body of the aircraft, to rotate in a direction opposite to the rotation of a single rotor. The pioneers overcame this by using multiple rotors turning in opposite directions to cancel out the torque effect.

Two approaches were (and still are) used here. One is to have two (or more) opposite-turning rotors spaced some distance apart (and sometimes overlapping or even intermeshing) and the other is to mount two rotors, one above the other on coaxial shafts but rotating in opposite directions. The primary disadvantage of both of these systems is the mechanical complexity and additional structure, weight, and cost involved in multiple rotors.

The problem was solved for the desirable single-rotor helicopter when Sikorsky developed a variable-pitch tail rotor with a transverse horizontal axis that could be pitched both ways from zero. This acted like a rudder to apply a reversible sideward force that not only countered the turning tendency but provided directional control for the helicopter. A minor disadvantage of the helicopter tail rotor is that it absorbs a significant percentage of the available power; on multi-rotor helicopters, all of the power is available for lift.

DETOUR: THE AUTOGYRO

None of the helicopters developed into the 1920s were notably successful. The essential improvements that were needed to make the rotary wing practical resulted from a different line of development—the autogyro.

In 1922 Spanish inventor Juan de la Cierva combined a helicopter-like rotary wing with a conventional airplane fuselage, using the rotary wing as a substitute for the standard wing. The rotor was not connected to the powerplant; rotation had to be started manually or by taxiing the craft about so that the airstream got the blades rotating. Airflow then kept them rotating. Later, a power drive from the engine was developed to simplify spinning-up the rotor prior to takeoff but not to drive it in flight. This power drive was later used to overspeed the rotor. Then, after the power was disconnected, the pitch of the blades could be increased collectively and the surplus energy use to let the autogyro "jump" into the air. However, it could not hover over the takeoff spot like a helicopter; it had to pick up forward speed immediately through the thrust of its conventional propeller.

The early autogyros had rudimentary wings that supported ailerons for roll control; later designs were able to delete both of these details.

The autogyro cannot take off vertically, but can still climb at a steeper angle than an equivalent airplane with the same power-to-weight ratio. It can descend nearly vertically, however, the rotor acting essentially as a rotary-wing parachute. This phenomenon is *autorotation,* another trick borrowed from nature. The maple seed is a single-blade rotary wing that rotates rapidly about its center of gravity while falling and generates enough lift to significantly reduce its rate of descent. Since it comes down more slowly, the wind can carry it farther from the parent tree in nature's plan. Airflow striking the man-made rotor from below, even at a very shallow angle, keeps it rotating and generating lift.

The autogyro has been completely displaced in military and civil aviation by the more versatile helicopter, and survives today only as a recreational vehicle for the amateur aircraft builder. It is of enormous historical significance, however, in that it introduced the blade-hinging and cyclic-pitch-change features and the blade structure, proportions, and aerodynamics that made the successful helicopter possible. In effect, it showed other inventors how to put it out of business.

Cornu Helicopter

While not the first attempt at a helicopter since da Vinci, the tandem-rotor design of Frenchman Paul Cornu is the first known to have actually lifted itself off the ground (FIG. 5-2). This was on November 13, 1907, and achieved an altitude of one foot for a duration of 20 seconds. A later flight lifted two people and reached an

Fig. 5-2. The first helicopter to lift a man off the ground was the French Cornu tandem-rotor design of 1907.

altitude of 6¹/₂ feet, but all that was really accomplished was to prove that a rotary-wing aircraft could be made to fly.

With his tandem rotors, Cornu anticipated the Piasecki/Vertol/Boeing line that was to come 37 years later (and is still in production) and also proved his understanding of one of the major problems of rotary-wing aircraft, the tendency of the fuselage or body to rotate in a direction opposite to that of a rotor. Cornu overcame this by using two rotors rotating in opposite directions. His drive system was simple; a vertical shaft from the engine drove a pair of belts from a wheel on the end of the drive shaft to larger wheels that formed the hubs of the rotors. Opposite rotation of one rotor was attained by crossing its drive belt. Deflector vanes at each end of the four-wheel body were supposed to impart a degree of directional control, but were ineffective.

Although his design worked, Cornu received no encouragement from others for continued development. Out of funds, he abandoned his experiments.

Ellehammer Helicopter

The first consistently successful helicopter was built in Denmark by Jacob Christian Ellehammer, who had been experimenting with aircraft since 1905 and with helicopters since 1910. His first full-scale machine (FIG. 5-3) was flown late in 1912.

Ellehammer also understood the rotor-torque reaction problem and used two rotors installed coaxially one above the other and rotating in opposite directions. This system was to be used by many others right up to the present.

The Ellehammer rotors were unique by modern and even contemporary standards. Two 19-foot diameter steel tube rings anchored the roots of six vanes nearly five feet long that projected beyond the rings. The vanes were adjustable in pitch, a forerunner of the

73

Fig. 5-3. The first notably successful helicopter was the Danish Ellehamer coaxial rotor design of 1912. The propeller was to cool the engine, not provide propulsion.

modern collective pitch that is so essential to successful helicopters today. Further, Ellehammer's helicopter was what is today called a compound helicopter in that it was fitted with a propeller.

Ellehammer himself did not make the first flight. Indoor tethered flights without a pilot proved that the machine would fly, but it could not lift its builder's weight. The first pilot was Ellehammer's lightest employee, the young apprentice Erik Hildesheim, who was to be honored in later years as World Helicopter Pilot No. 1.

The 1912 helicopter underwent improvement and flew continuously until September 1916 when it rolled over on takeoff and was damaged beyond repair.

Karman-Petroczy Captive Helicopter

The first helicopter to achieve more than momentary liftoff and an altitude of more than a few feet was a unique substitute for a captive Army observation balloon designed by Lt. Stefan von Petroczy of the Austrian Army Balloon Corps; and built in Austria in 1916. The hyphenated name came from association with Professor Theodore von Karman.

This had three 120-hp rotary airplane engines in a three-arm steel tube framework driving 20-foot coaxial rotors that were similar to standard wooden airplane propellers working in a vertical direction (FIG. 5-4). As such, it was not a true rotary-wing aircraft, but still utilized direct lift and was capable of hovering, which it was built to do.

It had no means of directional control nor was it stable. While it was able to reach an altitude of several hundred feet, it did so while pulling against three cables that held it level.

The observer rode in a cylindrical basket installed on the end of the vertical propeller shaft—a most precarious location and one impossible to leave via parachute as could be done from a balloon basket. Instead, a parachute was provided to let the whole machine down, crew and all.

For descent, the helicopter maintained lift against the three cables, and was winched down like a balloon. This procedure, using a single cable, was readopted many years later to bring naval helicopters down on small landing platforms aboard ships in rough water. This is a prime example of technique being developed

Fig. 5-4. The Austrian Karman-Petroczy rigid-rotor coaxial helicopter of 1916.

some 35 years before helicopters could make regular use of it.

Needless to say, the Karman-Petroczy helicopter never got beyond the prototype stage, and crashed on its 15th flight.

Pescara Biplane-Rotor Helicopter

From 1919 into 1924 the Spanish Marquis Raul Pescara (FIG. 5-5) developed a series of three helicopters with very unique rotors. The two rotors were co-axial, which was nothing new, but each of the six blades per rotor on Models One and Two were biplane structures, complete with interplane struts and bracing wires, to give a total of 24 lifting surfaces. The Model Three reduced the biplane sets to four per rotor.

With only 45 hp, Model One was too underpowered to fly. Number two, with 170 hp, was able to struggle off the ground in May 1921. After Pescara moved to France in 1922, he improved Model Two and was able to hover it at an altitude of five feet.

Model Three, built in 1923, was a major milestone in helicopter development in that its biplane rotors incorporated an early form of pitch control, had tilting rotor heads as a means of providing thrust, and was capable of autorotation landings in case of power failure. On April 18. 1924, the improved 180-hp Model Three set a World's helicopter distance record of 735 meters (2,414 feet).

Berliner Helicopter

For the first serious American effort toward developing a helicopter, Henry A. Berliner took a notable shortcut. Instead of designing his machine in total, he adapted an existing airplane, a World War I surplus Nieuport 21 (an 80-hp version of the famous Nieuport 17 combat model that was used for advanced training).

From 1920 into 1924, Berliner tried various arrangements of twin rigid rotors driven by shafts and gears from the nose-mounted engine. In the version shown in FIG. 5-6, longitudinal vanes installed below

75

Fig. 5-5. The Spanish Pescara Model Two helicopter of 1922 with unique biplane rotor blades.

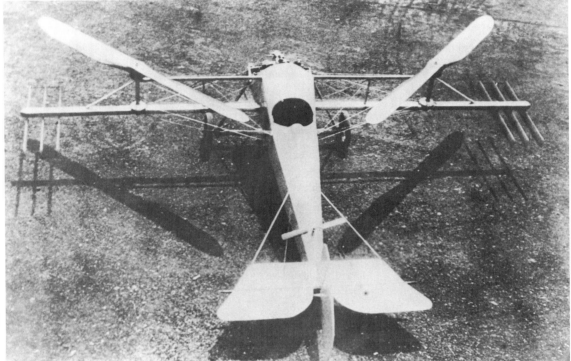

Fig. 5-6. The American Berliner helicopter of 1922, adapted from a conventional Nieuport 21 airplane.

each rotor were intended to provide a degree of directional control by deflecting the downwash of the rotors. This was an advanced concept that would not be utilized significantly until the advent of convertaplanes capable of taking off vertically in the 1960s.

Another advanced feature was the use of a small vertical-thrust propeller just ahead of the tail for pitch control.

The Berliner helicopter made a number of short hops, but made no performance breakthroughs. Berliner himself went on to more conventional lines of aircraft development. His helicopter is preserved in the National Air and Space Museum.

de Bothezat Helicopter

One of the most serious of American helicopter design efforts as far as official support and funding went was the four-rotor machine developed by expatriate Romanian designer Prof. Georges de Bothezat. His theories were convincing enough to get the U.S. Army Air Service to put $20,000 into his helicopter and build it in the Air Service shops at McCook Field, Dayton, Ohio.

The de Bothezat was built in the form of a steel-tube cross, with a single six-blade rotor 25 feet in diameter at the end of each trusswork arm and a 190-hp engine at the center (FIG. 5-7). The Professor acted pretty much like his machine looked and became a well-known character around the field while it was being built.

The helicopter was expected to be stable in pitch and roll because of its four rotors, which did have one advanced and very significant feature—they had variable-pitch blades, so each rotor could be controlled to increase or decrease the lift on that corner. Considerably underpowered for its gross weight of 3,600 pounds, the de Bothezat did manage to lift off the ground a few times, once for a record two minutes and 45 seconds on February 21, 1923, but never achieved

Fig. 5-7. Rumanian engineer Georges de Bothezat built this four-rotor helicopter for the U.S. Army Air Service in 1922.

horizontal movement, either forward or sideways. The Army refused to appropriate additional funds and dropped the project.

Curtiss-Bleeker Helicopter

One of the more extreme efforts to overcome the tendency of the fuselage to rotate beneath a single rotor was taken by Maitland B. Bleeker. In 1929 he persuaded the giant Curtiss-Wright Corporation to finance and build his unique design.

While it was actually a single-rotor helicopter with one 420-hp Pratt & Whitney Wasp engine in the podlike fuselage, it was in effect a fleet of four separate airplanes pivoting about a central point on their right-hand wingtips. Each blade of the rotor had a winglike lifting surface, with trailing horizontal "stabolator" surfaces to control angle of attack, and a four blade propeller to pull it (FIG. 5-8). This machine certainly had the highest ratio of rotor mass to overall weight of any helicopter ever built.

The Curtiss-Bleeker never flew. After a few ground runups and tethered liftoffs at Curtiss Airport, New York, the drive gear broke. With the worldwide economic depression then under way, and already disenchanted with the helicopter, Curtiss-Wright could not justify the cost of the special and very expensive part in depressed times and terminated the project.

Focke-Achgelis FW 61

The Focke-Achgelis FW 61 of 1936, developed by the German designer Dr. Heinrich Focke, was influenced by the American Berliner in two major respects. First, it used the fuselage and powerplant of an established airplane, (the Focke-Wulf FW 44 *Stieglitz* training biplane) which was then fitted with two outrigged rotors. As on the Berliner, the 160-hp Siemens SH-14A engine remained in the nose (FIG. 5-9). A short stump of a propeller was retained simply to cool the engine, but its presence led some people to insist that the craft was an autogyro rather than a helicopter. (The Berliner used a rotary engine, which cooled itself simply by running.)

The major advantage that the FW 61 had over the Berliner was the later rotor technology developed by Cierva on his Autogyros. Dr. Focke was well familiar with these, having built Cierva C-19 and C-30 Autogyros under license. The rotors were independently adjustable to permit roll control and lateral movement of the machine. The FW 61 was also the first helicopter to be able to disengage the rotors from the engine and land in autorotation.

The FW 61 was a success from the start and almost immediately began to establish world helicopter records for duration, altitude, and distance. One of the more spectacular demonstrations of its controllability was in April 1938, when aviatrix Hanna Reitsch flew it

77

Fig. 5-8. The Curtiss-Bleeker helicopter of 1930 had each blade of the rotor driven by its own propeller to eliminate rotor torque reaction on the fuselage.

78

Fig. 5-9. The German Focke-Achgelis FW 61 of 1936 was the most successful helicopter up to that time.

Fig. 5-10. The first convincing demonstration of helicopter versatility was made by famed German woman pilot Hanna Reitsch, who flew the Focke-Achgelis FW 61 inside the Berlin Deutschlandhalle in February 1938.

inside the *Deutschlandhall,* an indoor sports stadium (FIG. 5-10).

Sikorsky VS-300

The most significant single helicopter ever built was the Sikorsky VS-300 of 1939. It has been well said that there was no helicopter industry until after the VS-300 appeared.

The awkward-looking VS-300 (FIG. 5-11) was the brainchild of Igor Sikorsky, a Russian who had started experimenting with helicopters in 1907, emigrated to the United States after World War I, and established the Sikorsky Aircraft Corporation, noted for its amphibians and transoceanic flying boats. The designation VS-300 was far out of sequence with Sikorsky's own design numbers, which were up to 43 in 1939. The VS stood for Vought-Sikorsky, the result of a merger between the Chance Vought Aircraft Company and the Sikorsky firms, both of which were subsidiaries of the giant

United Aircraft Corporation conglomerate. The -300 carried on Vought's numbers, not Sikorsky's.

The key to the success of the VS-300 was the use of controllable pitch tail rotors to counteract rotor torque and provide directional control. This system was not simple at first; there were also two additional rotors with vertical axes to help control the VS-300 in pitch. Through extensive test and refinement over a three-year period, the design was cleaned up and perfected to the point where only the single "rudder" rotor on the tail was necessary. This arrangement—a single main rotor over the center of gravity, a single tail rotor, and the powerplant also on the CG—became the standard for most subsequent helicopter designs.

The 51-year old Sikorsky did all of the test flying on the 75-hp (later 90 and then 150-hp) VS-300 himself; he personally broke the world's helicopter endurance record and demonstrated the previously unmatched maneuverability of the craft. The VS-300 was retired in 1943 and Sikorsky himself flew it from

80

Fig. 5-11. An early form of the American Sikorsky VS-300, the design that revolutionized the helicopter business in 1939-40.

his factory in Bridgeport, Connecticut, to the Ford Museum in Dearborn, Michigan, for permanent display.

The U.S. Army quickly ordered an improved model, the 165-hp YR-4 (R for Rotorcraft in Army designations) for test. This was followed by a total of 30 service test YR-4As and Bs. These were followed by 100 200-hp R-4Bs. The Navy ordered 25 as HNS-1s (H for helicopter, N for Training, and S for Sikorsky), most of them transfers from the Army R-4B contract (FIG. 5-12). No further production was undertaken, however, since improved models were being developed so quickly that the R-4s (changed to H-for-Helicopter in 1948) were obsolete as soon as they were delivered.

Bell Model 47

Shortly after World War II the Bell Aircraft Company, then of Buffalo, N.Y., went into production with its Model 47, a small and very versatile two-seat heli-

copter (FIG. 5-13). It used the single tail rotor of the final Sikorsky VS-300 configuration and the R-4. In this it was representative of the majority of subsequent production single-rotor helicopter designs regardless of size and the number and type of powerplant.

It was distinctive, however, in using a two-blade rotor, with the Bell-developed stabilizer bar, when other designs were using three and four-blade main rotors. The versatility of the Model 47, plus its convenient size and relatively low cost, made it very popular. Over 2,000 were sold to the U.S. Army or Air Force as H-13s while the Navy bought 178 as HTLs (H for Helicopter, T for Training, L for Bell) and 31 HULs (U for Utility).

The Model 47 was in production for 28 years and evolved from a steel-tube two-seater with 175 hp to a sleek aluminum four-seater with 250 hp. Over 5,000 were built by Bell and by British, Italian, and Japanese licensees.

Fig. 5-12. The U.S. Army ordered the improved R-4 development of the VS-300. This is an HNS-1, the Navy's version of the R-4, approaching a makeshift landing platform.

Fig. 5-13. A Bell YH-13H, a U.S. Army and Air Force version of the civil model 47, changing crew members in the course of a 57-hour endurance record flight in 1956. Note wheels retracted above landing skids.

Fig. 5-14. The Piasecki HRP-1 transport helicopter for the U.S. Navy featured tandem rotors, which had first been used with moderate success in 1907.

Piasecki/Vertol Tandem Helicopters

The idea of using two rotors in tandem originated on the French Cornu helicopter, which made a 20-second hop in November 1907. The idea of tandem rotors then lapsed until revived by American designer Frank N. Piasecki. He flew his first single-rotor helicopter, the PV-1, in April 1943, and quickly decided that tandem rotors were the way to go. In 1944, he received a U.S. Navy contract for his Model PV-3. This flew in March 1945, and led to an order for two further prototypes designed to specific Naval requirements as XHRP-1 (X for experimental, HR for Helicopter Transport, P for Piasecki, and -1 for initial configuration in the U.S. Navy designating system of the time). The first of 10 production HRP 1s flew in August, 1947 (FIG. 5-14).

Power was provided by one 600-hp Pratt & Whitney Wasp air-cooled radial engine amidship, with both 41-foot diameter rotors being driven through shafts and

gears. Gross weight was 8,000 pounds, making the HRP-1 the heaviest helicopter to that date as well as the first production tandem-rotor model.

The success of the 20 HRP-1s led to follow-on orders for improved HRP-2s with semi-monocoque aluminum fuselages and the similar H-21 workhorse for the U.S. Army and Air Force (H for Helicopter in the Army/Air Force system).

Vertol 107 The Piasecki firm reorganized under the name of Vertol, an acronym for Vertical Take Off and Landing, in 1956. In addition to continued military production, Vertol developed a commercial model, the 44, powered with an 1,150-hp Wright Cyclone engine. To avoid excessive length, Piasecki installed the rear rotor on a pylon that raised it above the forward rotor and permitted a significant overlap. Production was short-lived because an improved model, the 107 (FIG. 5-15), was being developed to take advantage of the high power-to-weight advantages of gas turbine engines (in

Fig. 5-15. The Royal Canadian Air Force version of the Vertol Model 107 demonstrates the flotation and tailgate-loading capability of the design. Note the high pylon for rear rotor to permit rotor overlap.

effect, jet engines turning shafts instead of expelling a jet of high-velocity air). This was powered by two 860-hp Lycoming T-53 turbine engines. First flight of the 25-passenger, three-crew 107 was on April 22, 1958. Later versions of this one are still in production by Vertol (a division of the Boeing Company since 1960) and by licensees outside the U.S.

Several hundred military variants of the 107 are in service with the U.S. Army, Navy, and Air Force and Foreign governments as the CH-46 Sea Knight. A larger development is the CH-1B Chinook of 1961 (redesignated CH-47A in 1962) (FIG. 5-16). This was originally powered by two 2,200-hp Lycoming T-55 turbines, but later versions have 3,750-hp T-55s. Gross weight of the current (1983) CH-47D is 50,000 pounds.

Kaman Intermeshing-Rotor Helicopters

A different approach to the design of twin-rotor helicopters was taken by the Kaman Aircraft Corporation of Windsor Rocks, Connecticut. To avoid the excessive span of side-by-side rotors, the length of the tandem type, and the complexity of the coaxial type, Kaman put the two rotors close together by meshing them on canted shafts oriented side-by-side (FIG. 5-17). If the shafts were not canted to put each rotor on a different plane and eliminate blade interference, the shafts would have had to be positioned slightly more than one-half-rotor-diameter apart. This practice was not new (it had been introduced by Flettner in Germany during World War II) but Kaman perfected it and brought it to production status.

Fig. 5-16. The U.S. Army Vertol CH-47A Chinook helicopter has the rear rotor mounted on a pylon that allows it to overlap the forward rotor. Compare with Fig. 5-14.

Fig. 5-17. A U.S. Air Force Kaman H-43A with ski/wheel landing gear displays the unique Kaman meshing-rotor system.

After testing and producing piston-powered models for the Navy and Air Force, Kaman received large U.S. Navy and Air Force orders starting in 1950 for later utility models powered by 850-hp Lycoming turbine engines. The 211 Air Force models were designated H-43 and the 107 Navy models were HOK (83) and HUK (24).

Hiller Ramjet Helicopters

Another scheme to drive a single rotor while avoiding the torque reaction that tends to turn the fuselage in the opposite direction was tried by Hiller Helicopters Inc. of Palo Alto, California, with its series of tiny two-seat Hornets introduced in 1952.

The two-blade rotor was driven by a 38-pound thrust Hiller ramjet engine mounted on the tip of each blade (FIG. 5-18). Fuel was pumped to the ramjets through the rotor hub. Since ramjets require high-velocity air to flow through them before they will start, it was necessary to pre-rotate the rotor from another energy source before lighting the ramjet.

In addition to the civil test model, Hiller built 17 service test models for the military, 14 YH-32s for the Army and three HOE-1s for the Navy. These flew quite well and their simplicity was commendable. However, they were too short-ranged to be practical; their 50-gallon fuel supply would keep them airborne for only 20 minutes.

Specifications: Rotor span 23 feet; gross weight 1,080 pounds; cruising speed 69 mph.

Flying Scooters

The successful adaptation of small two-stroke-cycle engines and even four-cycle outboard motorboat engines to recreational aircraft use made possible the development of quite a few ultralight one-person helicopters for short-range use, such as getting a foot soldier to the other side of an unbridged river.

These ranged from the simplest example (quickly abandoned) of an outboard motor strapped to the pilot's back and driving an overhead rotor through more substantial structures with the pilot sitting on the aeronautical equivalent of a campstool. Still others were flying platforms, with the pilot standing, either above or below a set of coaxial rotors, and steering by leaning in the desired direction, as in a hang glider.

In spite of the talent and treasure expended in developing these, none ever progressed to the production stage. A few representative American examples, none of which achieved production, are illustrated here.

85

Fig. 5-18. The author demonstrates the small size of the two-seat Army Hiller YH-32 ramjet-powered helicopter in 1956.

Fig. 5-19. Improved form of the Pentecost Hoppicopter of 1946 with conventional seat and landing gear.

Pentecost Hoppicopter One of the earliest midget helicopters was the Pentecost Hoppicopter of 1946. This started as a 20-hp outboard motor strapped to the pilot's back and driving two coaxial rotors. This concept was soon replaced by the model 102 shown in FIG. 5-19, still with coaxial rotors but with a conventional

seat and landing gear. Powerplant was a 35-hp two-stroke-cycle engine, rotor diameter 16 feet, gross weight 363 pounds.

Rotorcraft RH-1 The RH-1 of 1954, designed to carry one fully-armed soldier short distances, featured a single main rotor and a belt-driven tail rotor. The main rotor was driven by a 20-pound thrust liquid rocket motor at the tip of each blade (FIG. 5-20). Fuel was 90 percent hydrogen peroxide; rotor diameter 16 feet; gross weight 400 pounds; cruising speed 70 mph.

De Lackner Aerocycle With coaxial rotors, the 1956 De Lackner Aerocycle was one of the most unconventional of the one-man helicopters. The pilot was on top of it and leaned in the direction that he wanted to go while bicycle-like handle bars controlled the heading (FIG. 5-21). The powerplant was a 43-hp two-stroke Kikhafer outboard motor, empty weight 218 pounds, range 15 miles at 75 mph on one gallon of fuel.

Gyrodyne Rotorcycle The Rotorcycle was the most successful of the "flying motorcycles" in that it was produced in small service test quantities for the U.S. Navy and Marine Corps in 1960-61 (FIG. 5-22). The two Marine XRON-1s had 40-hp Nelson two-stroke engines driving coaxial rotors. The three YRON-1s had 62-hp (and later 72-hp) converted

86

Fig. 5-20. The Rotorcraft RH-1 featured liquid-fuel rocket motors on the tips of the main rotor blades, but still incorporated a tail rotor for directional control.

Fig. 5-21. The De Lackner Aerocycle placed the one-man crew above the coaxial rotors in the style of the 1916 Karman-Petroczy.

Porsche automobile engines. Later conversions of both X and Y models were fitted with 62-shaft hp Solar T62 turbine engines. The YRON-1 (with Porsche engine) had a rotor diameter of 17 feet, gross weight of 700 pounds, and top speed of 68 mph.

Fig. 5-22. The Gyrodyne XRON-1 with a Porsche automobile engine driving the coaxial rotors.

Cierva Autogiros

The autogyro (to use the common term) appeared after many years of unproductive helicopter experimentation. The new design was derived from the helicopter only in the use of a rotary wing. However, the improvements to the rotary wing made by Spanish inventor Juan de la Cierva were used by subsequent helicopter designers to finally achieve success.

Cierva believed strongly that the way to make flying safe was to develop a stallproof airplane. The conventional fixed wing could not meet this requirement, so he searched for another form. The rotary wing had possibilities but as driven by engine power on helicopters to the time (1920) it was not working. He discovered that a rotor could be kept spinning freely by air flowing into it from below—not necessarily at 90 degrees as on a windmill or the autorotating maple seed, but at a relatively shallow angle corresponding to the angle of attack of a regular airplane wing.

He then installed a four-blade rotor on a conventional airframe. This did not require wings for lift but

Fig. 5-23. The first successful Cierva Autogiro, the C-4, which flew in Spain on January 9, 1923.

did need ailerons for roll control, so had rudimentary wings to hold the ailerons. Cierva named his new flying machine the C-1 Autogiro, with a capital A. (This word is used in reference to Cierva products only; all others are *autogyros* with a small "a" and "y" instead of an "i.")

With no power from the engine to spin the rotor prior to takeoff, other means—either by hand or by a rope spindled on the rotor shaft and pulled by a ground crew or a car—had to be used. Once started in rotation, the rotor was brought up to proper speed by taxiing the machine fast enough to get the necessary airflow past the blades. The C-1 had a rigid rotor like the preceding helicopters, and because of that fact it did not work.

With no forward speed on the aircraft, all blades of the rotor move at the same speed relative to the air mass and therefore generate equal lift all the way around the circle. As the machine acquired forward speed, however, this speed was added to the advancing blade and subtracted from the retreating blade. This resulted in unbalanced lift on opposite sides of the circle that tipped the Autogiro over before it had a chance to leave the ground. This also happened on the C-2 and the C-3, and it looked for a while as if the Autogiro would join the long list of unsuccessful rotary-wing aircraft.

Cierva's breakthrough came with his development of a rotor blade hinge that allowed three axes of motion. The most important of these was a twist that allowed the advancing blade to take on a lower angle of attack (pitch) relative to the airstream, thereby generating less

lift, while the retreating blade took on a greater pitch to generate more lift proportional to its decreased airspeed. These simultaneous changes of lift through cyclic pitch change kept the lift on both sides of the disc equal regardless of changes in airspeed. Cierva had his successful Autogiro. The first flight of the C-4, which used the fuselage of a prewar French Deperdussin monoplane powered with a 110-hp Le Rhone rotary engine, was on January 9, 1923 (FIG. 5-23).

The rotary wing then did what was expected of it, allowing shorter takeoffs and steeper climbs than equivalent conventional designs. However, it was difficult to demonstrate slow-flight characteristics in an Autogiro powered with a rotary engine. This type of engine had two speeds—wide open or off—and could be throttled down (and then only briefly) by cutting off the ignition to several cylinders. Real progress in Autogiro development came after Cierva was able to build new aircraft from scratch instead of adapting cheap surplus, and power them with conventional engines.

Development was rapid, especially following an association with Harold F. Pitcairn in the United States and formation of the Pitcairn-Cierva Autogiro Company in 1928. Pitcairn overcame the rotor-starting problem by developing a driveshaft from the engine that got the rotor up to speed and then disengaged to let it rotate freely (FIG. 5-24). Some taxiing was still necessary. The principal product of the American firm was the three-place PCA-2, with a 300-hp Wright Whirlwind engine. Two other American firms, Buhl and Kel-

88

Fig. 5-24. The American Pitcairn PCA-2 Autogiro used by the Marine Corps as the XOP-1. Note drive shaft from back of engine to prespin the rotor prior to takeoff.

lett, built autogyros under Cierva licenses. Kellett went into production on several models, but Buhl built only a prototype before being shut down by the world economic depression in 1932.

The PCA-2 still needed ailerons to bank it into a turn just as a regular airplane so that there would be a horizontal component of the lift vector to pull it around the turn. It, as all other Autogiros of the time, was fitted with undersize wings of conventional construction to hold the ailerons and provide a little extra lift during forward flight.

The next major advance came from Cierva's English firm, the Cierva Autogiro Company. An articulating hub was developed for the rotor that allowed it to be tilted in the desired direction of turn, thereby eliminating the need for ailerons and their supporting wing panels. The prototype of the new wingless Cierva C-30, a modified C-19, first flew late in 1932 (FIG. 5-25).

The final step in the perfection of the Autogiro was the development of the "jump takeoff" procedure that allowed vertical takeoffs. These had to be followed immediately by forward motion, however, since the rotor, which was driven to an overspeed condition in flat pitch and then disengaged and given a collective pitch change to maximum lift, was now freewheeling and needed the airflow of forward motion to keep it spinning.

In a major act of irony, Juan Cierva was killed in a civil airline crash in December 1936, in just the kind of accident his Autogiro was designed to eliminate.

Autogyro production continued on a small scale by several manufacturers throughout the world until World War II, in which its unique but limited capabilities could not be used. By war's end the greater versatility of the helicopter, thanks to Cierva's key rotor developments, was able to surpass the autogyro and establish a major role in civil and military aviation far beyond Cierva's dreams.

Fig. 5-25. Cierva's English firm developed the wingless direct-control C-30 Autogiro in 1932.

Bensen Gyros

The only significant area of autogyro operations subsequent to World War II has been in the recreational field of homebuilts. The pioneer and still leading figure in this endeavor is Igor Bensen of the Bensen Aircraft Corporation, Raleigh, North Carolina.

The idea came from late wartime attempts to develop a rotary-wing parachute for the precision airdrop of supplies. Bensen saw the recreational possibilities of this and fitted a two-blade rotor autogyro-fashion to a simple three-wheel framework supporting a pilot's seat. Pitch and roll control stick attached to a tilting rotor hub (FIG. 5-26). Called the B-8 Gyro-Glider, this was to be towed straight ahead by a car on a long airport runway or equivalent clear space. Its first flight was in 1954.

While all this did was get the pilot off the ground briefly, it was appealing in that the Federal Aviation Agency (FAA) regarded the B-8 as a kite as long as it

was attached to the towline and therefore did not require licensing of either the aircraft or the pilot. If released in the air, however, it instantly became a glider and subject to all the technical and legal requirements. Because of the unlicensed status, Bensen was able to sell prefabricated kits and even complete machines, something not allowed under the "51 percent rule" that requires the builder to actually fabricate 51 percent or more of a licensed homebuilt. The Bensen Gyro-Glider that went on the market was the B-8.

Bensen soon found a suitable powerplant to convert his glider to a true autogyro, the B-8M Gyro-Copter (M for Motorized). This was the 72-hp McCullough 0-100, a four-cylinder two-stroke engine used to power military target drones. It was installed behind the pilot as a pusher. Since it was built for a short operational life, the 0-100 needed extensive reworking to deliver the reliability needed for continuous man-carrying use. A shortage of 0-100's developed, so, many later B-8M

Fig. 5-26. The earliest recreational autogyro was the American Benson B-8 Gyro-Glider of 1954, shown here being towed by a car along an airport runway.

Fig. 5-27. Two Benson B-8M gyrocopters; gyrocopter in foreground, pilotd by designer Igor Benson, has the standard overhead control stick; background gyrocopter has a convential airplane-type upright control stick.

variants now use different two-stroke engines developed for the ultralight airplane movement while some use aircraft conversions of Volkswagen automobile engines.

Most Gyro-Copters retain the overhead control stick of the glider, but some pilots prefer a conventional airplane-type stick control (FIG. 5-27). Individual variations are many, mostly consisting of pilot enclosures

and windshields. Some go so far as to add a model airplane engine to start the rotor. Normal procedure is to reach up from the seat, give the rotor a few turns by hand, and then taxi some to bring it up to speed.

Thanks to the enormous popularity enjoyed by these unique rotorcraft, their numbers today far exceed the total of all other civil and military autogyros built from the 1920s on to World War II.

6
CHAPTER

Other Wing Shapes

THE SIZE AND PROPORTIONS OF THE "CONVENTIONAL" wings that are seen today are pretty much the same relative to the rest of the machine as those established by the inventors of the last century. The Wrights proved them to be practical, and we are still using wings with average aspect ratios on the order of 6:1 and horizontal tail surfaces that are approximately 12 to 25 percent of the planform wing area and located approximately three times the chord behind the CG.

Some inventors, however, took entirely different approaches while others merely made major alterations to the established standards. Some of these departures worked well enough to warrant further development and have become accepted to the point of being recognized as special categories of "standard" aircraft. These include the tailless, delta, and rotary-wing designs discussed in preceding chapters.

The unconventional wings have taken on many forms and some have even tried to operate on different principles. Most, however, still depend on lift generated by the airstream passing over (or sometimes through) the surface. Some are merely "different" wings on a relatively conventional fuselage, while others incorporate other major features of the aircraft within themselves.

MULTIPLANES

The fact that some conventional wings are used in more than conventional numbers, or are positioned in other than the traditional places on the aircraft, does not qualify them as being different, nor does the fact that some fold. Some of the multiple-wing arrangements qualify the aircraft as tandems (see Chapter 2).

The most common form of multiplane seen today is the biplane, which now totals less than five percent of the world's aircraft. Before World War I the ratio was closer to 50-50, but the maneuverability and strength advantages of the multiplane virtually obliterated the monoplane until the late 1920s. Even triplanes were common during WWI. The biplane made up about 95 percent of the fleet until 1930.

The major advantage of more than one wing on an otherwise conventional airplane was distribution of the required wing area over a shorter span. This enhanced maneuverability, manufacture, ground handling, and storage. As the wartime military influence began to wane, the streamlining, range, and cost advantages of the monoplane made economic sense. The military fought the trend for a few years, but eventually joined the revolution. About the only biplanes being built today are for crop dusting, competition aerobatics, or sport flying. Biplanes are very popular in the antique airplane movement simply because they *are* biplanes, individualistic anachronisms in this day of sleek metal monoplanes that all look like they were designed by the same computer.

d'Ecquevilly Multiplane

If one wing is good and two are better, why not go for *seven?* A *septuplane* is certainly the rarest of all forms of multiplane.

This 1909 creation is not a true round-wing, but the unique enclosure of the flat panels with an oval frame gives it that appearance (FIG. 6-1).

Note the rather common practice of driving a relatively large diameter propeller from a faster-turning engine by means of chain-and-sprocket or belt-and-pulley arrangement that permitted both remote location of the propeller axis from the engine and a reduction in propeller speed relative to the engine. Also notice that

92

Fig. 6-1. The French d'Ecquevilly of 1909.

some people did not yet fully understand propeller theory—they figured that all the work was done by the backside, as with an oar. However, some aircraft did fly successfully with "paddle" propellers like this.

FLYING PANCAKES

The name "flying pancake" was applied to various aircraft long before the term "flying saucer" was coined after World War II to describe real or imagined spaceships. The term was a natural one for aircraft that had wings of circular shape or nearly so. Ever since the days of the Wright Brothers, inventors have been popping up with circle-wing aircraft. Some worked to some extent, others never got off the ground. One early example, whose name and details have been lost to history, was among the various pre-Wright flying machines that Glenn Curtiss resurrected in his vigorous defense of the Wright Brothers' patent infringement suit. By proving that some earlier designs incorporated details of the Wright control system, Curtiss hoped to invalidate their patent. The "circle wing" biplane shown in FIG. 6-2 had surfaces for roll control that resembled ailerons, but this and other machines with three axes of control were of no help in fighting the patent suit.

In order for airplane construction to proceed during World War I, a patent pool was established that included the Wright patent as well as the more numerous Curtiss patents, plus others. The original suit was never resolved, and the Wright patent was allowed to expire in 1923.

Half-Round Farman 1020

Some "flying pancakes" do not have perfectly circular wings, they are more like a pancake cut in half. The French Farman Model 1020 of 1934 is such a

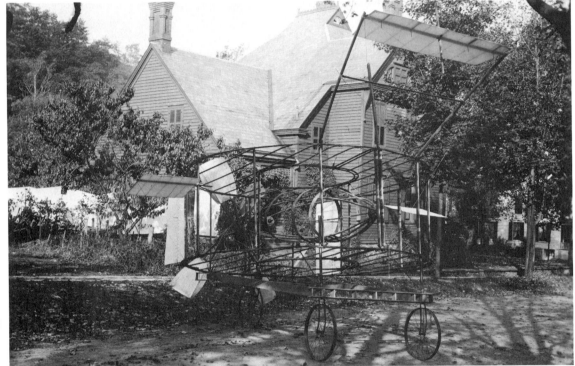

Fig. 6-2. An early 1900s round-wing design with three axes of control.

design (FIG. 6-3). Even though it was not a perfect circle, the wing shape posed interesting problems in control surface installation.

Conventional ailerons were installed on projecting wingtips while the trailing edge contained long-chord

Fig. 6-3. The French Farman 1020 of 1934 with conventional tail surfaces behind a semicircular wing fitted with trailing edge flaps and projecting ailerons.

flaps. Conventional tail surfaces were carried at the end of the fuselage.

Nemuth Parasol

The first airplane to fly consistently with a perfectly circular wing was the American Nemuth Parasol of 1934 (FIG. 6-4). This was a conventional parasol monoplane (wing above the fuselage on struts like the upper wing of a conventional biplane) except for the shape of the wing, which had short ailerons at the very tips.

The claimed advantages for this two-seater, powered with a 110-hp Warner Scarab radial engine, was that the low aspect ratio of the wing permitted flight at higher-than-usual angles of attack and made slow and safe full-stall descents possible, almost as though the machine were being lowered with a parachute.

Needless to say, the Nemuth, which was built by students at Miami University, never got beyond the prototype stage.

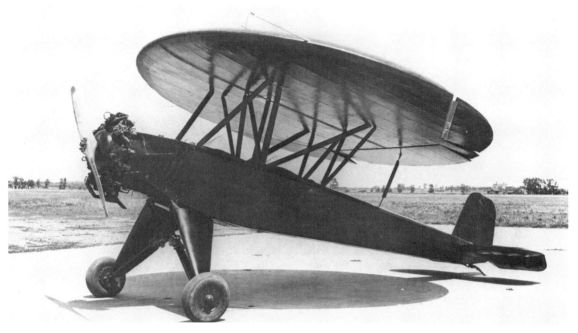

Fig. 6-4. The American Nemuth parasol had a perfectly circular wing fitted with ailerons and a flap.

Arup Flying Wings

One of the "half pancake" designs successful enough to pass through four airframes was the creation of a medical doctor, Cloyd Snyder of South Bend, Indiana. In 1928 he was impressed by the apparent stability of a felt heel-lift that he had tossed through the air. This got him to thinking that the shape was suitable for an aircraft wing, so built a series of flying models.

These were successful; Snyder applied for an received a patent and then designed a man-carrying glider that was built by shop students at the local high school. This had the "heel" shape, with an elevator full-span across the rounded rear of the wing. Two thin board-like fences along the top of the wing near the tips held rudders at the rear and ailerons at the front (FIG. 6-5). After a series of successful flights that started in 1932, a 26-hp aircraft conversion of a four-cylinder motorcycle engine was installed at the leading edge, but performance was disappointing.

With the help of a professional engineer, Raoul Hoffman, Snyder then designed a second ship along more conventional airplane lines. This was named Arup No. 2, the word being a contraction of "air-up." Powered with a 37-hp Continental A-40 airplane engine, it flew very well for several years. Its wing span was only 16 feet, one of the benefits of the low aspect ratio, but pivoted ailerons beyond the wingtips raised the span to 19 feet (FIG. 6-6). A conventional fin and rudder were used while the trailing edge had two elevators at the edges and a large flap in the center. For the power, the Arup-2's performance range was sensational, with a top speed of 97 mph and a landing speed of only 23 mph.

The Arup-2 was followed by an 80-hp Arup-3 that moved the horizontal tail surfaces to a conventional stabilizer-elevator combination at the top of the vertical fin in what is today called a T-tail. The Arup-3 had inset ailerons. It did not fly well, and was destroyed by a saboteur before it could be de-bugged.

The Arup-4 was essentially an improved -3, and flew for several years before Dr. Snyder went broke and his two surviving "flying heels" were scrapped.

Fig. 6-5. The Arup Flying Heel glider of 1932.

Fig. 6-6. The powered Arup No. 2 with projecting ailerons.

Vought V-173/XF5U-1

By far the most successful "flying pancake" was the American Vought V-173 of 1942 (FIG. 6-7). This was a lightweight, low-powered flying mockup of a proposed high-performance fighter of unconventional design, much in the manner of the C-W 24B. It was built by the Chance Vought Aircraft Company of Stratford, Connecticut.

This unique design was the brainchild of Charles H. Zimmerman, who had built successful flying models of it in the mid-1930s. He then got Vought interested in the military possibilities, and the V-173 mockup was completed early in 1942. In a reversal of customary procedure, the single prototype was tested in the full-scale NACA wind tunnel at Langley Field, Virginia, to verify its capability for flight—not to clean up and improve a design that had already flown.

The secret of the V-173's success was the use of two very large and slow-turning propellers, each driven through shafts and gears by a separate 80-hp Continental A-80 engine buried in the wing. The airflow from

the propellers passing over the wing added lift equivalent to a sizeable increase in wingspan, thereby reducing the induced drag associated with low-aspect-ratio wings at low speed. The V-173 had "ailavators" attached to horizontal stabilizers. These were adjustable in flight and projected from the edge of the wing just ahead of the conventional fins and rudders.

The V-173 first flew on November 23, 1942, and accumulated 131 hours of flight time. It had a top speed of 150 mph and could land at 35 mph at the amazing angle of attack of 36 degrees.

The success of the V-173 led to a 1943 U.S. Navy contract for a twin-engine fighter, the XF5U-1 (X for Experimental, F for Fighter, 5 for the fifth Navy fighter design from Vought, and U for the letter that identified Vought in the Navy designating system). This was powered with two 1,350-hp Pratt & Whitney R-2000-7 engines (FIG. 6-8). Mechanical problems and low priorities delayed completion until 1948. By then the Navy had moved into the jet age and ordered the XF5U-1, which it had paid for, scrapped. Entreaties by Vought to

97

Fig. 6-7. The famous Vought V-173 Flying Pancake built for the U.S. Navy in 1942 as a proof-of-concept prototype.

Fig. 6-8. The concept of the V-173 was incorporated in the design of the U.S. Navy's XF5U-1 fighter.

98

permit at least one test flight were refused—in fact, the Navy specifically prohibited it.

XF5U specifications: Powerplants, two P&W R-2000, 1,350 hp, wing span 32 feet 6 inches; length 28 feet 7^1/$_2$ inches; gross weight 18,635 pounds; top speed 388 mph at 15,000 feet (estimated).

Bonnet-LaBranche

A different approach to the low-aspect ratio aerondynamics of the "flying pancake" was taken by the French Bonnet-LaBranche of 1908. This was basically a Voisin or Farman-type tailboom pusher with the area between a full-span upper wing and conventional (for the time) biplane horizontal tail filled in to provide additional lift area. The fact that it was fitted with a canard surface was incidental to the wing design (FIG. 6-9).

Note that the lower of the two horizontal stabilizers has camber to provide a degree of lift while the top one is flat to serve as the trailing edge of the wing.

1909 Givaudan Tandem

Because of its equal-size wings fore and aft, the Givaudan qualifies as a true tandem, but the unique wing form earns it a more prominent place with the round wings (FIG. 6-10).

It is hard to fathom the thinking behind a wing of this form—there is very little horizontal component to provide effective lifting area and the near-vertical portions provide no lift at all. Since the surface of the "wings" were flat, they obviously did not generate lift in the manner of a regular wing. With equal size units at each end, the Givaudan looked like an oversized box kite with its cells rounded off. The forward cell was movable for control.

SWEPT WINGS

Swept wings have been in use since before World War I, but should be regarded basically as standard wings with a relatively slight modification for special purposes. In general, the proportions, structure, and attachments (such as ailerons and flaps) remain the same regardless of the angle of sweep.

For straight wing (with constant chord from root to tip), the angle of sweep is measured at the leading edge. For tapered wings, the sweep is measured at the quarter-chord line. The sweep for delta wings is again measured at the leading edge.

Fig. 6-9. The French Bonnet-LaBranche of 1908, with the space between the upper wing and the horizontal tail filled in.

Fig. 6-10. The round-wing French Givaudan of 1909.

Sweep-back (or sometimes sweep-forward) is utilized for three primary reasons: to solve a balance problem, to put pitch controls a suitable distance from the center of gravity on tailless aircraft, and, since the end of World War II, to delay the onset of compressibility on high-speed (600-mph plus) aircraft.

High speed has resulted in a new feature—variable sweep. The wing is set to a nearly-straight position to give maximum lift for takeoff and landing and is mechanically swept back in flight to obtain the benefits of sweep at the high end of the performance range.

The design problems of a "swing wing" are enormous, and add greatly to the structural complexity and the cost. Some of these are the aerodynamic and balance problems of relocated wing area, the need to have a hinge or pivot strong enough to carry the entire load of the wing panel, and the need to have the pylons for underwing stores remain parallel to the line of flight through the full range of wing sweep.

A bit more should be said here about the effect of variable sweep on aircraft performance. Physically, two things change when the wing moves to the swept position: The wing span is decreased and the thickness of the airfoil section is also decreased, thereby altering its characteristics. Since the wing panel is a rigid structure, it is obvious that its physical thickness does not change. It is the relationship of wing thickness to the chord that is acted on by the airflow—the aerodynamic thickness—that changes as a function of the sweep angle. See FIG. 6-11.

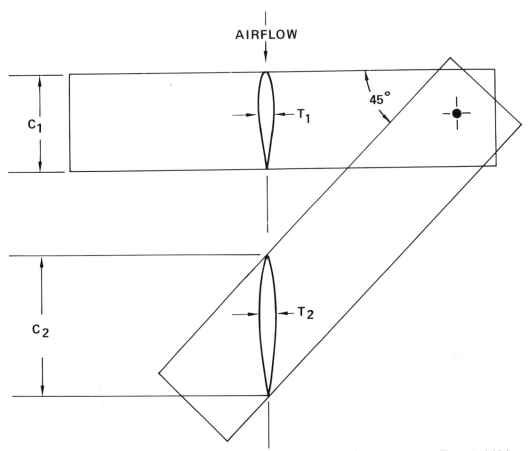

Fig. 6-11. The aerodynamic thickness of a wing decreases as the sweep-back angle increases. The actual thickness remains the same ($T^1 = T^2$), but the chord parallel to the airflow increases (C^1 to C^2).

Junkers Ju.287

The first large airplane to capitalize on the aerodynamic advantages of swept wings turned up by German World War II research was the Junkers Ju.287, a truly revolutionary airplane. Not only did it have swept wings—which were swept *forward* rather than back—but it was a four-jet bomber with the jets in pods attached to the fuselage as well as the wing, and it used jettisonable solid-fuel rockets for extra thrust on takeoff (FIG. 6-12).

It was also a "quickie" design that used the fuselage of the established Heinkel 177A bomber and the tail of the Junkers 388. For a 500-mph airplane, it had the surprising anachronism of fixed landing gear. Of course, this was another shortcut on a proof-of-concept prototype. The four 2,095-pound thrust Junkers Jumo 004B jets drove the first Ju.287V-1, which flew in February 1945 to a top speed of 506 mph, faster than any piston-engined fighter. Gross weight was 49,723 pounds.

The second Ju.287 flew soon after. Both were captured by the advancing Russians.

North American F-86 Sabre

Following the successful demonstration of turbojet engines in both Germany and England early in World War II, all major aircraft-producing countries began a race to develop jet-powered combat airplanes. The first to see service was the German Messerschmitt 262, which had a very slight sweep to its wing. All of the other jet fighter designs started before the end of the war had straight wings, and several of these went into produciton.

When Allied aeronautical engineers found the war-time German research on swept wings, they saw the improvements in maximum speed that such wings could deliver, so a second generation of jet fighters was designed.

In the U.S., North American Aviation, Inc. developed a straight-wing jet for the Navy as the FJ-1 (F-for Fighter and J for North American, which was successor to Berliner-Joyce, also identified by J). This was the basis for a new design for the Army (U.S. Air Force after September 1947), the XP-86, with a 35-degree swept wing and tail. The XP-86, which flew on October 1, 1947, pretty well established the world standard for jet fighters (FIG. 6-13).

Power was supplied for the fastest (F-86D) model by a 7,650-pound thrust General Electric J-47. Gross weight was 17,100 pounds and the armament was six .50-caliber machine guns. The high fuel consumption of the jet was compensated for somewhat by external auxiliary fuel tanks (and later, by the use of in-flight

101

Fig. 6-12. The German Junkers Ju.287 jet bomber of 1945 with swept-forward wing.

Fig. 6-13. The North American F-86 Sabre was the first production fighter with a 35-degree swept-back wing. This is an F-86-E-10.

refueling). Adverse stall characteristics of this early swept wing were countered by automatic leading edge slats that popped open at low speed to create slots that improved the airflow over the wing and delayed the stall. While the P/F-86 was fast, with a top speed of 707 mph at sea level and capable of exceeding Mach 1 in a shallow dive, the age of the supersonic fighter had not yet arrived.

A version for the Navy became the FJ-2 even though it differed greatly from the FJ-1. Altogether, 9,623 P-86s (F-for-Fighter 86s after June, 1948) were built and were the mainstay of USAF fighter operations in Korea. The last one was delivered in December 1956. A few are still used for test work in 1989, 42 years after the XP-86 first flew.

F-86H specifications: Powerplant, General Electric J-73, 8,920 pound thrust; wing span 39 feet 1 inch; area 313 square feet; gross weight 21,852 pounds; top speed 692 mph at sea level, 603 mph at 43,900 feet.

Grumman F9F Panther and Cougar

Some jet airplane builders were able to switch a basic model from a straight-wing type to swept wings in the middle of production. Such was the case of the Grumman Aircraft Company, leading builder of fighters for the U.S. Navy.

Grumman built a single-jet carrier-based fighter as the F9F (F for Fighter, 9 for ninth Grumman Navy fighter, and the second F to identify Grumman) Panther and reached the -5 variant with straight wings (FIG. 6-14). The prototype XF9F-2 flew on November 24, 1947. An entirely new 35-degree swept wing was fitted to the same fuselage and tail in the variant that was produced as the F9F-6 and -8 Cougar (FIG. 6-15). First flight of the XF9F-6 was September 20, 1951.

The combination of the swept wing and the change from a 6,250-pound thrust Pratt & Whitney J-48-6 to a 7,250-pound thrust J-48-8 increased the top speed from 579 mph at 5,000 feet for the F9F .5 to 690 mph at sea level for the F9F-6. Altogether, 3,077 Panthers and Cougars were delivered.

Boeing B-47 Stratojet

The first swept-wing jet bomber after the Ju.287 was the far more advanced Boeing XB-47, which first flew on December 17, 1947. This had been started as a straight-wing jet bomber on an Army contract, but was redesigned completely for swept wings after Boeing engineers got a look at the wartime German research data. Telegrams home from engineers touring Germany halted work on the straight-wing model. The resulting

Fig. 6-14. The Grumman F9F-5 Panther U.S. Navy fighter with straight wing.

Fig. 6-15. A 35-degree swept-back wing on a Panther fuselage resulted in the F9F-6 and -8 Cougar. This is the unarmed photo reconnaissance F9F-8P (P for Photo). Note camera ports in extended nose.

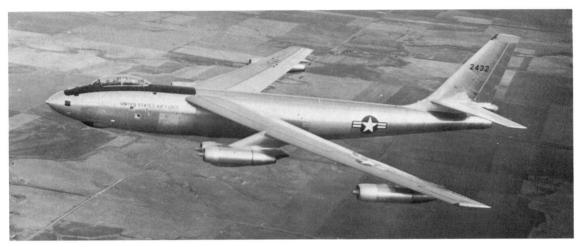

Fig. 6-16. The famous six-jet Boeing B-47 with 35-degree swept wing appeared in 1947. Shown above is a 1953 model B-47E-85.

production models became the first swept-wing bombers to equip any air force. The sweep angle was 35 degrees.

The XB-47 had six 3,750-pound thrust General Electric J-35-2 engines in four pods below the wing, which had the unusually high aspect ratio of 9.42:1. Instead of being bunched near the center of the wing, two jets on each side were paired on a single strut while the third was located near the wingtip to distribute the weight (FIG. 6-16.). Thanks to the swept wing, the new bomber was so fast that it was not expected to come under standard fighter attack patterns, so only a remotely controlled tail turret firing to the rear was provided for defensive armament.

Deliveries of B-47As with 5,200-pound thrust General Electric J-47 jets began in December, 1950. The last of 2,060 built by Boeing and licensees Lockheed and Douglas was delivered in February 1957. The last was not retired from the Air Force until 1969. Performance of the 206,000-pound B-47E-II with 6,000-pound thrust J-47-25s was 606 mph at 16,300 feet. Range without in-flight refueling was 4,000 miles.

Grumman X-29A

After its brief appearance on the Junkers Ju.287, the swept-forward wing vanished from the high-speed scene for nearly 40 years until the single-seat Grumman X-29A research plane made its first flight on December 14, 1984. Although the X-29A (FIG. 6-17) is a canard and would logically be presented in Chapter 1, it was developed for research into forward-swept wing design and Grumman emphasizes this point by designating it as the FSW (Forward Swept Wing) Technology Demonstrator.

The claimed advantages of the FSW are improved maneuverability, nearly spin-proof characteristics, better low-speed handling, and reduced stalling speeds. Wind tunnel testing revealed a pronounced tendency, when using conventional metal structures, for the FSW to deflect unfavorably, twisting the outer portions of the wing to higher angles of attack at high speeds, thereby increasing lift and adding further flight loads that could lead to structural failure. Grumman avoided this by using latter-day composite materials that produced a torsion-resistant wing that permitted full utilization of FSW benefits.

As a design shortcut to reduce cost and airframe development time, Grumman used much of the fuselage and other components of an existing Northrop F-5A fighter for the X-29A.

Specifications: Powerplant General Electric F404 16,000 pounds thrust; wing span 27 feet 2^{1}/$_{2}$ inches; length 53 feet 11^{1}/$_{4}$ inches; wing area 188.8 square feet; gross weight 17,700 pounds; max speed approximately Mach 1.6.

104

Fig. 6-17. Although fitted with a prominent canard, the Grumman X-29A was built specifically for research into swept-forward wings and is designated the FSW (Forward Swept Wing) Technology Demonstrator.

VARIABLE SWEEP WINGS

Following the adoption of swept wings as a standard feature of high-speed aircraft, various designers sought to combine the high-speed advantages of sweep with the slow-speed benefits of the straight wing by pivoting each wing panel at the fuselage so that the wing could be swung from a straight position to one of significant sweep (FIGS. 6-18 through 6-20).

General Dynamics F-111

After a series of experimental prototypes by various builders, the U.S. government held a design contest for a "swing-wing" fighter that was called at the time the TFX, for Tactical Fighter Experimental. This was won by the ConVair Division of General Dynamics and ordered into production as the F-111A, the first swing-wing fighter in any air force. The feature is now commonplace in most major air forces.

The TFX/F-111 was also the first modern fighter designed to meet the requirements of two different services, the U.S. Air Force and the U.S. Navy. The basic missions were not compatible and resulted in two models being built, the Air Force F-111A built by ConVair and the longer-winged F-111B built for the Navy by Grumman.

A two-seater with side-by-side seating, the first F-111A flew on December 21, 1964. Power was provided by two 20,000-pound-thrust Pratt & Whitney TF-30 jets. Wing sweep was from 16 degrees to a maximum of 72.5 degrees, reducing the span from 63 feet to 31 feet 11 inches. The F-111B has a maximum span of 70 feet. On both, the trailing edge of the wing is closely aligned with the leading edge of the horizontal tail to make the design a delta-wing when folded.

Fig. 6-18. ConVair F-111A variable-sweep-wing fighter, photographed at roll-out in October 1964; wings extended.

Fig. 6-19. F-111A with wings fully swept.

At a gross weight of 70,000 pounds, the F-111A has a maximum speed of 1,650 mph at 40,000 feet (Mach 2.5). Armament consists of various air-to-air and air-to-ground missiles, and the FB-111 version is equipped as a bomber.

NASA AD-1 Oblique Wing

A greatly simplified variation of the variable-sweep wing was made with the NASA AD-1. The concept of a rigid wing pivoting about a center point to change its angle relative to the fuselage with one side

Fig. 6-20. Flight views of the F-111A showing the full cycle of wing sweep.

swept forward and the other aft—was developed by the Dryden Flight Research Center of the National Aeronautics and Space Administration (NASA). Design and construction of the airplane was contracted to the Rutan Aircraft Factory.

The AD-1 is a relatively conventional high-wing monoplane with tricycle landing gear and small jet engine in a pod on each side of the fuselage behind the wing. Wing sweep is variable to 60 degrees relative to the fuselage. The idea is to have a high-lift wing for takeoff and landing and a high-speed wing for cruising flight.

Flights with a straight wing began December 21, 1979. The first flights in which the wing was skewed in flight began in February 1980. The first flight with the wing at the full 60 degrees was made on April 24, 1981 (FIG. 6-21).

Upon completion of the NASA test program, the AD-1 was turned over to Mr. Rutan. No information has been released as to details of the testing, or how the known different characteristics of swept-forward and swept-back wings were reconciled.

Specifications: Powerplant, two 220-pound thrust Ames Industrial TRS 180046 turbojets; wing span 32

Fig. 6-21. The NASA AD-1 in 1981 with its oblique wing in the 45-degree position.

feet; area 93 square feet; gross weight 2,000 pounds; top speed 200 mph.

ODD SHAPES

Many inventors have tried completely different wing forms other than those previously described on relatively standard fuselage tail powerplant landing gear combinations. Some of these attachments have worked to varying degrees, but none to the point of entering production or becoming an accepted part of the aviation scene. Others have developed radical flying machines on which the wing forms the main part of the vehicle, with engine, controls, and landing gear being incorporated in sometimes non-standard positions. A number of these are illustrated and described on the following pages and others will be found in Chapter 16. (The sail-like Rogallo wing has been covered in Chapter 4 and rotary wings have been covered in Chapter 5.)

A.E.A. Cygnets

As one of its first experiments, Alexander Graham Bell's Aerial Experiment Association flew a man-carrying kite named Cygnet that had been designed by Dr. Bell. This departed from established boxkite construction by having a wing that was built up of a framework containing hundreds of small tetrahedrons, small flat surfaces arranged in Vs to provide the lift for the Tetrahedral Kite.

Cygnet, which had no means of control for the pilot, made one successful flight when towed into the wind by a boat. It was destroyed after coming down in the water while still being towed. Because of the lack of control, the A.E.A. pursued other lines of development for its flying machines.

Dr. Bell persisted, however, and built a larger, powered version named Cygnet II (FIG. 6-22). This had a wing span of over 40 feet, was fitted with a biplane canard elevator, and a Curtiss V-8 engine was installed behind the wing as a pusher. The pilot sat ahead of the wing.

Cygnet II was tested on the ice at Baddek, Nova Scotia, Canada, on February 22 and 24, 1909, and again on March 15, but was too heavy to fly with the available power. In March, 1912, a cut-down version named Cygnet III, powered with a 70 hp Gnome rotary engine, a monoplane canard elevator, and with a rudder and fixed stabilizer behind the wing, made a series of successful straight-ahead flight on the ice, not so much to advance aviation, but as a sentimental gesture to prove that the venerable Dr. Bell's unique wing would work.

Curtiss-Goupil Duck

As a further effort in his defense of the Wright Brothers' patent suit, Glenn Curtiss resurrected still

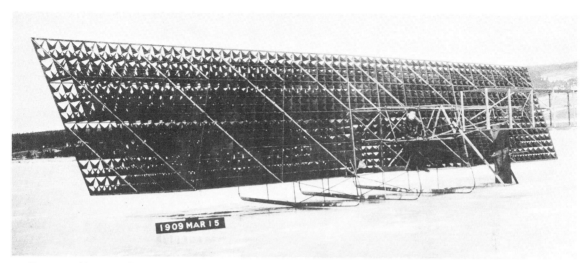

Fig. 6-22. Alexander Graham Bell's Cygnet II was a canard pusher with a very unconventional wing consisting of hundreds of tetrahedron cells to provide lift.

another pre-Wright design to show prior application. This was an 1883 invention by a Frenchman, Alexander Goupil, who applied for and received a patent for his odd-looking design but did not build it for lack of a suitable powerplant. The importance of the design to Curtiss was that it incorporated three axes of control, and applied lateral, or roll, control by means of auxiliary surfaces that functioned exactly like latter-day ailerons.

Working from Goupil's patent drawings, Curtiss was able to build a flyable example that incorporated a few state-of-the-art improvements that did not enhance the original control system. Major changes were to add a 100 hp Curtiss OXX engine and install a latter-day landing gear in place of Goupil's skids.

The gull-winged monoplane, with a low-aspect-ratio wing blended into the horizontal tail (FIG. 6-23), was called the Duck by Curtiss. It was first tried late in 1916 as a seaplane on the old Langley Aerodrome floats, but was barely able to hop off the water because of its weight. Refitted with wheels, it flew successfully on January 19, 1917, but was not a successful defense of the suit.

Flettner Rotor Wing

A round wing of an entirely different kind was tried by this oddity of the early 1930s, which featured a

wing built in the form of a Flettner Rotor. This cylindrical arrangement had worked previously on small experimental sailing ships which mounted them vertically as substitutes for sails. On the boats, the cylinders were spun by motors. When this rotation was acted upon by the wind, the air pressure differential known as the Magnus effect, was built up on opposite sides of the cylinder to exert a directional force at right angles to the air flow—much the way a baseball pitcher throws a curve ball by spinning it.

The boat worked, but had no commercial advantages over sail in the age of steam—and powered cylindrical sails certainly had no place in the sport of sailing.

In spite of its odd wings and spidery fuselage landing gear wing truss frame, the components were arranged conventionally, with a 300-hp Wright J-6 engine and propeller in front, pilot seated at the center of gravity, and conventional tail surfaces behind (FIG. 6-24). A second airplane engine, an 85-hp American Cirrus, was used to spin the rotors.

Lanier Vacuplane

The Lanier Vacuplane of 1935 took an entirely different approach to wing design. Instead of having the low-aspect ratio wing use the conventional double-surfaced configuration, Professor Edward M. Lanier of

109

Fig. 6-23. Glenn Curtiss built the Duck from an 1883 design in a further attempt to invalidate the Wright Brothers' patent on three-axis airplane control.

the University of Miami tried an "open top" airfoil that supposedly created a partial vacuum in the open area that created lift by virtually sucking the airplane upward. The flat bottom prevented free air beneath the plane from flowing in to fill the vacuum (FIGS. 6-25, 6-26).

The Vacuplane, built by the Professor's students at Miami U., was powered with a 36-hp Aeronca two-cylinder-engine and used parts of some existing airplanes. The stub wings outboard of the vacuum section were there to support the ailerons, but doubtless contributed significantly to the lift. The plane flew, slowly but stably, and demonstrated a steep parachute-like descent at low speed.

Fig. 6-24. An early American 1930s experiment involving the use of Flettner Rotors as airplane wings.

Fig. 6-25. The American Lanier Vacuplane of 1935.

Fig. 6-26. Lanier Vacuplane.

Specifications: Wing span 14 feet 4 inches; wing area 73 square feet; gross weight 574 pounds; top speed 96 mph; cruising speed 80 mph; landing speed 30 mph.

Custer Channel Wing

Some inventors come up with "different" features that have certain demonstrable virtues that blind them to the obvious disadvantages. Instead of the first prototype being a convincing failure, it works and further encourages the inventors, who fight to promote their dreams for years.

Such was the unique Channel Wing developed by the American inventor Willard R. Custer. His inspiration came from seeing the roof of a barn blown off by a strong wind. This, he reasoned, was done by the speed of air moving past the object, not an object flying as the

result of being moved through the air. His approach, then, was to move the air through the flying machine, not the machine through the air.

After testing some models, the first full-scale Channel Wing, the CCW-1 (Custer Channel Wing No. 1) was completed in 1942. The key to its performance was the half-circular section of each wing close to the fuselage. The inner surface of each had an airfoil shape. A pusher propeller driven by a 75-hp Lycoming airplane engine in each channel sucked high-velocity air through the channel and generated static lift. The CCW-1 did fly—not well by contemporary airplane standards, but well enough to prove Custer's theories. There were conventional wing panels with ailerons outboard of the channels, and these were large enough to fly the plane on their own. However, the extra lift from the channels, which existed even at zero airspeed, allowed the overall wing to have a notably reduced stall speed. The low speed introduced other problems such as lack of lateral control effectiveness because the surfaces were outside the high-velocity air of the channels. This was corrected on the CCW-1 by putting small ailerons across the tops of the channels.

The military investigated the Channel wing briefly during the war, but nothing came of it. Afterward, Custer built the CCW-2 on the fuselage and tail of a prewar Taylor J-2 Cub lightplane (FIG. 6-27). Faced into a slight

111

Fig. 6-27. The second version of the Custer Channel Wing, the CCW-2, flew soon after World War II.

Fig. 6-28. The 1953 Custer CCW-5 used the fuselage and tail of a production Baumann Brigadier light twin-engine airplane.

Fig. 6-29. Custer CCW-5.

breeze, this actually lifted off the ground, restrained only by tiedown ropes. This flew unquestionably on the lift of its channels alone, although stub wings were added at FAA insistence.

The final Channel wing model was the CCW-5, which flew on July 13, 1953. It used the fuselage and tail of a Baumann Brigadier light twin-engine transport powered by 275-hp Continental engines (FIGS. 6-28, 6-29). The effectiveness of the channel concept was considerably diluted by the presence of conventional wing panels outboard that were obviously large enough to support the CCW-5 on their own. The CCW-5 with its combination wing put on spectacular demonstrations of slow-speed flight and maneuverability. One "production" model was produced in 1964, but no backers could be found to finance plant and tooling for additional airframes.

Larsen Speed Bird

One way to take a time-saving shortcut in the development of a new aircraft feature is to simply install it on an existing conventional airframe. While the airframe might not permit optimum use of the new feature, it at least provides a test vehicle on which to see if it works.

A standard side-by-side two-seat sport trainer, the Taylorcraft BC-12, was used as the test bed for a relatively tiny wing developed by Merle Larsen of Concord, California (FIG. 6-30). This all-metal structure resembled a regular wing fitted with a full-span trailing edge flap divided at the centerline to allow differential movement for use as ailerons. Most of the wing area was within the high-speed slipstream of the propeller and so was able to generate more than normal lift. The engine used for the 1953 test was an 85-hp Continental removed from a Goodyear-class racer that Larsen had built.

The plane was doing well on its first flight when the engine overheated and froze; the air inlets for the engine were too small for adequate cooling. With no propeller blast on the wing, the Speed Bird began such a high rate of descent that the pilot took to his parachute.

Ryan Flexwing (Rogallo Wing)

An early and short-lived application of the Rogallo wing to a powered aircraft was made by the Ryan Aeronautical Company of San Diego under a U.S. Army research contract. The lift coefficient of the pure Rogallo wing is low compared to conventional airfoils that have two surfaces with a significant distance between them. The Rogallo wing flies at a high angle of attack—like a kite—with all the lift being derived from air deflected by the underside of the wing rather than by the airfoil splitting the air.

There are two major and significant features of the Rogallo wing. First, the wing is single-surfaced, using only a single thickness of air-tight cloth like the 1923 Platz glider. Secondly, the structure is extremely simple, as discussed in Chapter 4.

113

Fig. 6-30. The Larsen Speed Bird, with an experimental wing fitted to a standard Taylorcraft lightplane fuselage.

Fig. 6-31. The structurally and aerodynamically simple Rogallo wing was fitted to a powered test vehicle, the Ryan Flexwing, in 1962. Note the high angle of attack in level flight.

As demonstrated by the experimental Ryan Flexwing of 1962 (FIG. 6-31), lift entirely from below (like a kite) is not very practical for powered aircraft but it is fine for hang gliders, which operate in strong upslope winds. The combination of the single-surface cloth wing and the simple aluminum tube framework and wire bracing gave a great boost to the hang glider movement of the late 1960s. Control was still by the old procedure of the pilot shifting his weight.

In the search for better performance, the basic delta shape of the original Rogallo wing was gradually broadened into a conventional tailless wing shape and rib-like battens were added to give an airfoil shape to the cloth surface; now the structure operates like a conventional wing instead of like a kite.

With hang gliders perfected as recreational flying machines, the addition of small motors to increase their utility was inevitable, and so a new and booming industry was born. The early ultralights were converted directly from hang gliders, but later models, of which the Flight Design's Flight Star is representative, have

been designed from scratch to use their powerplants more efficiently, incorporate conventional landing gear, seat the pilot in a frame "fuselage" or pod, and replace weight-shift with varying degrees of mechanical control up to full three axis type (FIG. 6-32).

Fig. 6-32. An expanded Rogallo wing fitted to a 1982 ultralight, the Flight Design Flight Star.

Fig. 6-33. The Sawyer Skyjacker is a square-wing design that evolved from a conventional twin-tailboom pusher model.

Regardless of wing planform and fuselage/pod configuration, the majority of tailless single-surface wing designs owe much to the basic Rogallo design concept and follow the pattern of the Ryan Flexwing, with the pilot and "fuselage" suspended well below the wing to impart a high degree of pendulum stability.

Ryan Flexwing specifications: Powerplant Continental O-200, 100-hp; wing span 23 feet 5 inches; area 450 square feet; gross weight 1100 pounds; top speed 60 mph.

Flight Design Flight Star specifications: Powerplant, Kawasaki 30-hp; wing span 33 feet 6 inches; area 175 square feet; gross weight 460 pounds; top speed 55 mph.

Skyjacker

A nearly square wing was successfully flown on an all-metal 200-hp design developed by Ralph V. Sawyer of Lancaster, California (FIG. 6-33). Skyjacker, which appears to be a straight-wing tailless design with the unusually low aspect ratio of one, was not designed as such. It grew out of his earlier experiments with radio-controlled model airplanes, some of which were built in the configuration of traditional twin-tailboom pushers.

One of these developed unacceptable vibration in the booms that led to elevator flutter. Experimentation then resulted in expanded stabilizer span and wider boom spacing matched to reduced wing span, with the space between the wing and stabilizer being filled in to create an almost square wing with a slot in it for the pusher propeller.

After test of a glider model, the full-scale Skyjacker was built and made its first flight in March 1975. The three-segment trailing edge has an elevator in the middle and ailerons at the sides. Full-chord endplates, used to control span-flow and tip vortices on conventional wings, provide directional stability. Skyjacker development is continuing.

Specifications: Wing span 18 feet; length 17 feet 4 inches; gross weight 2,150 pounds.

7
CHAPTER

Where to Put the Engine?

THE WRIGHT BROTHERS HAD A PROBLEM WHEN THEY developed their ground-hugging 1902 glider into their 1903 powered airplane. They had to use propellers (two of them driven through chains by one engine) but had to keep them clear of the ground. This meant mounting their shafts high—up between the wings—while the engine was mounted solidly on the lower wing structure and right on the center of gravity (FIG. 7-1).

A few years later, others developed airplanes with wheeled undercarriages beneath them that kept the front of the fuselage a significant distance above the ground. This led to a more efficient engine-propeller hookup, with the engine in the nose and driving the propeller directly. This basic configuration is now the world standard and has come to be called the *tractor* because the propeller is out in front, pulling (FIG. 7-2).

For various reasons, there have been advantages in having the propeller behind the wings on some designs, where it is pushing, hence the term *pusher*. On most single-engine designs, the location of the pusher propeller prohibits the use of a conventional fuselage structure, so the tail surfaces are supported by booms that give the plane a distinctive appearance without actually being a freak (FIG. 7-3). In such cases, the occupants and engine are in a shortened structure that resembles a pod, so some pusher designs are called *pod and boom* types.

There are aerodynamic advantages to having the propeller clear back behind the tail, but it is not practical to locate the engine there because of its weight—it must be fairly close to the center of gravity. Most prop-behind-the-tail pushers have the engine forward and drive the propeller through a long shaft. This introduces many mechanical problems, some of which have not been solved until recent years.

When larger and heavier airplanes required more power, additional engines were installed. These introduced location problems. With two engines, one was usually located on each side of the fuselage, either as a tractor or a pusher, to equalize the thrust so the plane would fly straight. When planes got big enough to require four engines, it seemed logical to put the additions outboard of the pair already close to the fuselage for maximum propeller efficiency.

However there was a serious drawback to this—the outboard propellers acting at such a relatively great distance from the fuselage exerted quite a turning moment on the airplane. This was neutralized when both outermost engines were operating at approximately the same power, but if one engine quit—as was common in the old days—the opposite engine exerted more of a turning moment on the airplane than the rudder could overcome.

From 1915 on, when airplanes really began to get big, four-engine types and up had their engines clustered close to the fuselage to minimize asymmetric power conditions. Sometimes two engines were paired on a nacelle on each side of the fuselage, one a tractor and the other a pusher. In others, one pair of engines was mounted fairly low between the wings or actually on the bottom wing of a biplane while the other pair was mounted on or above the upper wing.

The basic fault of this scheme was that airplanes are much lighter about the pitch axis than about the yaw and the roll axes. Differential power settings between the high and low engines had a serious effect on trim. One brand-new six-engine bomber design crashed on its first takeoff when the power of the two top engines was cut in during the roll. They were approximately 28 feet above the ground and working against the drag of the wheels, exerted an irresistible nose-cover couple.

Fig. 7-1. The 1910 Wright Model B retained the chain-drive propeller arrangement and offset engine of the 1903 model. In 1903, the engine was offset because the pilot laid prone beside it and the weight of the two had to be equally distributed on each side of the centerline. When upright seating for two was adopted, the engine was still offset with the weight of the pilot balancing it. The passenger usually sat on the centerline, where his presence or absence did not affect the lateral balance. Here, the passenger is in the left seat, from which he will throw a dummy bomb in one of the first demonstrations of the airplane's possible use as a bomber, October 6, 1911.

Fig. 7-2. The 1909 French Bleriot XI pretty well standardized the tractor configuration that is still the most popular today.

Fig. 7-3. A British Vickers Gun Bus pod-and-boom pusher of 1915. Note the wide field of fire for the gunner.

Clustering four or more engines close to the fuselage prevailed to the end of the 1920s, when improved control design made stringing all engines out in a line practical. Another big step forward came in the late 1920s and early 1930s when the use of thick-section cantilever wings made it possible to build the engine nacelles into the leading edge of the wing and greatly clean up the design.

The development of flying boats, with the fuselage now a hull that floated on the water, brought back the problem of mounting the propeller or propellers high enough to clear the water and the spray. It became common practice to put single engines in nacelles between the wings or entirely above the wings or hull; this added drag, weight, and other complexities. Propeller placement is still a major problem in small flying boat development today.

Many other arrangements of engines and propellers for single and multiengine airplanes have been tried, each seeking a special advantage. Some of these have worked well and have become standard installations. Others have turned out to have disadvantages that more than offset their alledged advantages.

One particularly popular arrangement has been to put the engine (or engines) inside the fuselage and right on the airplane's center of gravity. The propeller (or propellers) is then driven by an extension shaft to either the nose of the tail for a single-propeller type, or by gears and shafts to side-mounted propellers. In most cases, such arrangements have been far more troublesome than they were worth.

Jet engines, with no need for propellers and therefore free of their clearance requirements, opened up many new installation possibilities for designers. Some jets were put in nacelles where they functioned virtually as direct replacements for piston engines. Others were integrated into designs that were developed specifically to capitalize on the many advantages of the jet engine, notably internal installation in the fuselage (FIG. 7-4) or even the wing.

Paulhan-Tatin Aerial Torpedo

Once the standard configuration was established with the wing in front of the fin, stabilizer, and rudder in back, the tractor locations of the engine became the

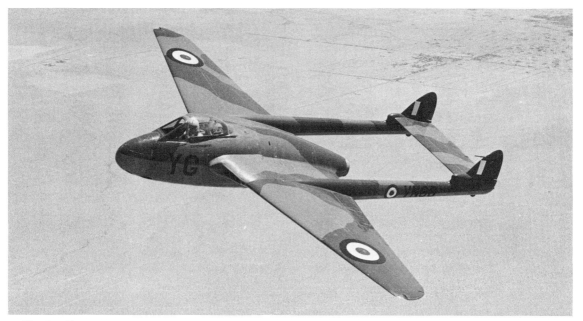

Fig. 7-4. The pod-and-boom pusher concept carried into the jet age with the postwar II British De Havilland Vampire.

most logical. However, there were advantages to having the propeller in back. One was to reduce the slipstream blast on the pilot in his open cockpit. The other, not really appreciated in the early days of slow airplanes, was the decreased drag of the fuselage passing through smooth air instead of air twisted into a spiral by the propellers. (A corresponding disadvantage was the lessened effectiveness of the tail surfaces without the slipstream acting on them.)

There were and are two major disadvantages of prop-behind-the-tail designs. One is the need to keep the propeller off the ground. Unless the main landing gear is built extra-high—adding to the drag—the ground angle is greatly decreased, increasing takeoff run and landing speed.

The other and major disadvantage is the need to keep the engine on or near the center of gravity and drive the propeller by means of a long extension shaft. The myriad mechanical problems associated with this have been resolved only since the 1950s by Molton B. Taylor and his Aerocars through the use of a dry fluid clutch at the engine end of the shaft.

The airplane in FIG. 7-5 is the French Paulhan-Tatin Aerial Torpedo, so named because of the (then) very streamlined shape of its fuselage. Note the high tailskid assembly and the level attitude of the plane relative to regular tractor types.

Tubavion

A really odd powerplant setup was used by the French Tubavion monoplane of 1911, built by the firm of Pouche & Primaud of Longchamps (FIG. 7-6). It was a tailboom pusher with a major difference—the propeller encircled the main tail boom, which was a metal tube. The water-cooled 70-hp Labor engine was installed backward and low inside the tubular frame of the "pod" beneath the wing. An extension shaft projected aft and turned a sprocket that drove a chain connected to a matching sprocket on the propeller hub.

Little is known of the Tubavion's history, but it is known that some notable designers, including Bleriot and Curtiss, tried the Tubavion propeller arrangement but did not put it into production.

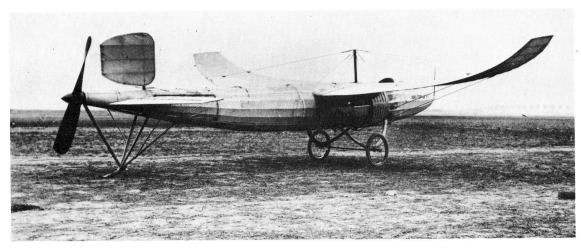

Fig. 7-5. The French Paulham-Tatin Aerial Torpedo prop-behind-tail pusher of 1911.

Fig. 7-6. The French Taubavion of 1911 had a complex drive system for a pusher propeller driven by a forward-mounted engine. An extension shaft from the engine drove a sprocket that powered a chain to a sprocket on the propeller.

Specifications: Wing area 160 sq. ft., length 27 feet 8 inches, top speed 73 mph.

Curtiss 1912 Flying Boat

When airplanes were developed that could fly from water, they were of two types—*seaplanes* that were simply standard landplanes with pontoons substituted for wheels, and *flying boats*, in which the fuselage became a boat-like hull. Both are actually seaplanes, but that word generally refers to pontoon-equipped aircraft (or "floatplanes") as distinct from flying boats.

Most floatplanes do not have propeller/water clearance problems, so an engine in the nose is accept-

Fig. 7-7. The American Curtiss flying boat of 1912 established the basic configuration used by most single-engine flying boats ever since.

able. The flying boat cannot have a propeller there for obvious reasons—it must be well above the water.

Glenn Curtiss had little trouble with this when he developed the flying boat in 1912. What he did was effectively substitute a hull for the undercarriage of one of his standard tail boom pusher biplanes, eliminate the boom, and put the tail surfaces on the rear of the hull. The engine was already mounted between the wings, and remained there (FIG. 7-7).

This arrangement remained standard for most large flying boats, particularly biplanes and even some monoplanes, right up to WW-II. For small single-engine types it is still the standard. Early production versions of the 1913 Curtiss model F flying boat were two-seaters with 75-hp Curtiss O engines and had a top speed of 54.8 mph. Hundreds were built, with many used by the U.S. Navy as trainers to the end of World War I.

Volmer VJ-22

The heritage of the 1912 Curtiss flying boat continues right up to the present with current single-engine flying boats—which are mostly monoplanes and amphibians—still having the engine in a nacelle above the hull and close to the center of gravity. Most are still pushers, but a few are tractors. The example in FIG. 7-8 is the Volmer Jensen VJ-22 Chubasco, also called the

Sportsman. It was built in 1958 for the homebuilt market, and features a wooden hull fitted with the wings and tail surfaces of a stock 65—100-hp production light-plane. There is enough work in the hull and engine setup to make up more than 51 percent of the total construction, so factory-built wings and tail can be used without violating the rule that says the builder of a homebuilt must do over 51 percent of the fabrication himself.

Other designers have followed the VJ-22 concept and also offer plans to the amateur builder.

Specifications: Powerplant, 100-hp Continental; span 36 feet 6 inches; gross weight 1,500 pounds, cruise speed 85 mph.

Gallaudet D-2

An early attempt at locating the engine of a single-propeller design internally on the center of gravity without the complexity of an extension shaft to the nose or tail was the American Gallaudet D-2 of 1916. This had two 150-hp engines mounted side-by-side in the fuselage of a single-float seaplane and driving a single propeller mounted on a ring encircling the fuselage. The D-2 flew successfully, but the later D-4 of 1918 (FIG. 7-9) used a single 400-hp Liberty engine.

No production was undertaken, but the D-4 was fast enough for the U.S. Navy to enter it in some early

121

Fig. 7-8. The homebuilt Volmer VJ-22 Sportsman of 1958 differs little from the 1912 Curtiss except for being a monoplane and an amphibian.

122

Fig. 7-9. The 1916 American Gallaudet D-2 with two side-by-side Dusenberg engines mounted amidship and driving a single propeller that encircled the rear fuselage.

post-WWI seaplane races. Other designers of the time tried the encircling-propeller concept but also abandoned it. For landplanes, there was the ground clearance problem. For seaplanes like the Gallaudet, there was the problem of spray impinging on the propeller.

Specifications: Wing span 46 feet 5 inches; weight 5,440 pounds; top speed 119 mph.

Bell P-39 Airacobra

The only single-engine piston-powered airplane with the engine buried in the fuselage and driving the propeller through an extension shaft to achieve mass production was the Bell P-39 Airacobra* of 1938-1944 (FIG. 7-10). Over 9,000 were built for the U.S. Army and the Allies for World War II.

---

*And its follow-on design, the Bell P-63 King Cobra.

Fig. 7-10. The Bell P-39 Airacobra fighter of 1938-44 mounted the engine directly over the wing and drove the propeller through a 10-foot extension shaft.

The main reason for the remote engine location was to allow a 37mm cannon to be installed in the front of the fuselage where it could fire through the hollow hub of the propeller. Other cannon had fired through hollow hubs since World War I, but they were nested between the cylinder banks of V-type engines in traditional nose positions with the propeller thrust line above the crankshaft, the propeller being driven by spur gears. Bell could have done this, but also cited the reduced inertia of an engine mounted right on the center of gravity as contributing to increased maneuverability. The 10-foot shaft passed under the pilot and drove the raised propeller through spur gears.

The P-39 was notably deficient as a fighter because its lack of a two-stage supercharger limited its altitude capability. However, its 37mm cannon and .50-caliber machine guns made it a very efficient low-level tank-destroyer, particularly in the hands of the Russians.

Specifications: P-39Q: Powerplant 1,200-hp Allison V-1710-85; span 34-feet; wing area 213 square feet; gross weight 8,300 pounds; top speed 385 mph at 11,000 feet.

Sikorsky Ilya Mourometz

The first-ever four-engine airplanes in the world, and the first giant bombers to go into action, were the Russian Sikorskys, starting with the "Grand" in 1913 and developing through the Ilya Mourometz models to 1917 (FIG. 7-11). When Igor Sikorsky needed more power for his then-giant biplane, he used four engines all strung out along the lower wing. This configuration had its disadvantages under asymmetrical power conditions as previously discussed, but only Sikorsky seemed able to overcome them.

One German copy, the Siemens-Forsman bomber of 1915 and the American Curtiss Model T flying boat of 1916 tried it, but none went beyond the prototype stage. State-of-the-art improvements allowed four-abreast engine installations to become standard for most heavy bombers and large transports of the 1930s and on.

Specifications, Ilya Mourometz 5: Powerplants four 150-hp Sunbeam, wing span 97 feet 8 inches, gross weight 10,150 lb., top speed 755 mph.

Fig. 7-11. The Russian Sikorsky Ilya Mourometz bombers of 1913-17 were the world's first four-engine aircraft and were the only successful ones to use four-abreast mounting until the early 1930s.

The Zeppelin-Staaken Giants

The real pioneer of the multiengine heavy bomber was the German Zeppelin-Staaken Giant series introduced early in 1915 and kept in production as essentially the same airframe to the end of World War I.

The Staaken, so named because it was built in the Staaken (Berlin) Plant of the parent Zeppelin concern, the famous rigid airship manufacturer, introduced many new features and improved on others. Curtiss had developed the installation of single and multiple engines between the wings of biplane flying boats, but Zeppelin improved on this by putting the engines in neat streamlined nacelles. For landplanes, the Zeppelin introduced individual multiwheel landing gear units under each engine nacelle to help distribute the weight. This engine-over-wheels arrangement became standard for most multiengine designs and remains in use to the present day.

The first Zeppelin bomber, designated V.G.O.1 (for Versuchs Gotha Ost, the leased East Gotha Works where the first few were built) was a trimotor, with one 240-hp Maybach airship engine in the nose and two mounted as pushers in the nacelles (FIG. 7-12). This positioning of a nose engine and two side engines at very nearly the same level to minimize trim variations in pitch set the standard for most subsequent trimotor landplanes.

After testing, the nacelles of the V.G.O.1 were modified to place a gunner's position in the front, an innovation in defense armament. A need for more power resulted in the six-engine V.G.O.III (later redesignated R-III in the new German R-for-Reisenflugzeug, or Giant Airplane series). The R-III airframe (FIG. 7-13) was nearly identical to the earlier models. With only three propellers, it appeared to be another trimotor.

The nose now contained two 160-hp Mercedes engines mounted side-by-side, with each connected to the common propeller through a gearbox. Each engine had its own honeycomb radiator mounted on top of the nose. The side engines were paired in tandem in lengthened nacelles, still with the forward gunner. The extended shaft of the forward engine, which was mounted lower than the rear engine, ran under the rear engine and joined its shaft in a gearbox that drove the single pusher propeller.

Again, each engine had its own radiator suspended between the upper wing and the nacelle. This configuration was repeated, with more powerful engines, on the following R-IV and R-VII models. The R-V reversed the nacelle arrangement to use a tractor propeller and put the gunner behind the engines.

Coupled engines proved to have their drawbacks with both mechanical and excess weight problems, so the majority of the production Staaken Giants, the R-VI and R-XVI, plus some seaplanes for the German Navy, used four engines paired in pusher-puller nacelles, with each engine driving its own propeller (FIG. 7-14). This

Fig. 7-12. The most successful giant bombers of World War I were the German Zeppelin-Staakens, which started with the trimotored V.G.O. model in 1915. Note the common practice of posing a small airplane alongside to illustrate the size differential.

Fig. 7-13. With only three propellers, the Zeppelin-Staaken R-III resembled the V.G.O., but two tandem engines in each nacelle drove a single pusher propeller and two side-by-side engines in the nose drove a single tractor propeller.

Fig. 7-14. The four-engine Zeppelin-Staaken R-VI of 1916-18 simplified the power transmission problem by having each engine drive a propeller directly, then grouped them in tandem pairs in nacelles close to the fuselage to minimize asymmetric power control problems.

arrangement has been used by many four-engine designs right up to World War II. The Staaken models R-XIV and R-XV obtained additional power by adding a single engine to the nose, which placed them among the very few five-engined airplanes in the world.

There was work space in all the two-engine nacelles of the Staaken Giants, with some riding mechanics doubling as top-wing gunners by means of a ladder leading from the nacelle to the gun on top of the wing.

The R.VI and R.XVI became the most successful four-engine bombers of WW I and were exceeded in numbers only by the Sikorskys. They largely supplanted the Zeppelin airships for bombing raids over England and several were used for airline service in Germany after the war.

Specifications, Staaken R-VI : Four 245-hp Maybach Mb IV engines; wing span 138 feet 5⁵/₈ inches; wing area 3,595 square feet; gross weight 26,066 pounds; top speed 84.35 mph.

Handley Page HP 42

Other arrangements were also used to bunch the engines of four-engine designs close to the fuselage. The four 550-hp Bristol Jupiter engines of the British Handley Page HP 42 of 1930 put the thrust even closer to the centerline than did the Staaken R-VI. Mounted

on the upper wing, the two top engines were as close together as their propeller blades would allow (FIG. 7-15).

The HP 42 was a standard long-range airliner for Imperial Airways, and eight were built. From 24 to 38 passengers were carried at a cruising speed of 100 mph.

Specifications: Wing span 130 feet; area 2,990 square feet; gross weight 29,000 pounds.

Tarrant Tabor

An early example of a six-engine bomber that combined the engine arrangements of the Staaken R-VI and the later HP 42 was the single Tarrant Tabor built near the end of World War I but not completed until afterward. It too was a giant, with a center wing span of 131 feet 3 inches and a total area of 4,950 square feet. Gross weight was 44,672 pounds.

Power was supplied by six 450-hp Napier Lion engines, four in two nacelles between the lower and center wing and two more in individual nacelles between the center and upper wing (FIG. 7-16). For the first takeoff, made on May 26, 1919, the pilot started his roll mainly on the power of the lower engines. When he gave full power to the upper ones, the added thrust, multiplied by the great distance to the wheels that were rolling on turf, created a force moment that

Fig. 7-15. A variation on bunching four engines close to the fuselage was used by the British Handley-Page 42 of 1930.

Fig. 7-16. The British Tarrant Tabor of 1919. Application of full power to the upper engines caused it to nose over with fatal results on its first takeoff.

was too strong for elevator control to overcome and the Tabor nosed over. This ended development and the airplane was scrapped.

D.F.W. R.I

Some designers sought to obtain the benefits of four engines for large aircraft without having the drag of traditional engine nacelles and their supporting structure by putting the engines inside the fuselage. Usually, these drove two or more side-mounted propellers through shafts and gears, but the mechanical handicaps of the arrangement largely negated the aerodynamic advantage of the centralized engines.

A representative example is the German D.F.W. (Deutsche Flugzeug-Werke, or German Aircraft Factory) R.I of 1916. Four 220-hp Mercedes DIV engines in the fuselage each drove one outboard propeller as shown in FIG. 7-17. The opposite-rotating forward propellers were mounted just under the upper wing while the rear propeller shafts were just above the lower wing. In view of later experience with low-mounted propellers to the rear of the wheels, it would have been better to mount the rear propellers high and the forward ones low.

The R.I was sufficiently successful to serve with the German Army on the Russian front in 1917 and to

win orders for six improved R.II models, only two of which were completed by war's end.

Specifications: Wing span 96 feet 9$^5/_8$ inches; gross weight 18,440 pounds; wing area 1,998 square feet; duration six hours at a cruising speed of 81 mph.

Linke-Hoffmann R.II

The unique German Linke-Hoffmann R.II of 1918 (FIG. 7-18) attempted to improve on the mechanical complexity of the D.F.W. R-models by hooking all four internally-mounted 260-hp Mercedes DIVa engines to a single propeller in the nose. The engines were arranged in two side-by-side pairs, and the propeller had a diameter of 22 feet 8 inches, the largest used on an airplane to that time or since (some airships have used larger ones). Each engine could be disengaged separately through a clutch, and the R.II was able to remain airborne on only two engines.

Only one example of the two prototypes ordered was completed, and that after Armistice Day. After a few test flights, the R.II was scrapped on orders of the Allied Control Commission.

Specifications: Wing span 138 feet 4 inches; gross weight 26,460 pounds; wing area 3,443 square feet; duration seven hours at a cruising speed of 74 mph; maximum speed 81 mph.

Fig. 7-17. The German D.F.W. R-I of 1916 with four engines inside the fuselage. The low-mounted rear propellers were susceptible to damage from gravel kicked up by the wheels ahead of them.

Fig. 7-18. The German Linke-Hoffman R-II of 1918 had four 260-hp engines connected to a single propeller.

Salmson-Moineau

One design that reached limited production with one engine in the fuselage driving two outboard propellers through shafts and gears was the French Salmson-Moineau of 1916. This Army observation plane featured a 230-hp Salmson (formerly Canton-Unne) water-cooled radial engine mounted crossways in the fuselage (FIG. 7-19). The crankshaft extended from both the front and back of the engine and was coupled to the two shafts that extended to right-angle bevel gears on the propeller shafts. This model saw limited production.

A real oddity was the experimental Salmson trimotor, which featured two radial engines back-to-back in the fuselage driving outboard propellers through shafts and gears. A third engine in the nose drove a propeller directly (FIG. 7-20).

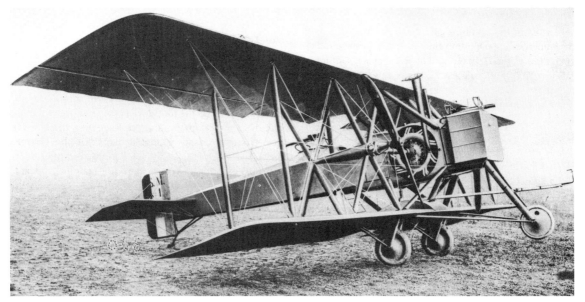

Fig. 7-19. The French Salmson-Moineau of 1916 featured a single radial engine mounted crossways in the fuselage to drive two propellers.

Fig. 7-20. A variation of the Salmson-Moineau design featured three engines, one driving a propeller directly and two others driving propellers through shafts and gears.

Gotha-Ursinus G.W.D.

Most of the bombing planes of World War I were twin-engine biplanes with their engines in nacelles on each side of the fuselage mounted either as tractors or pushers. All of the standard designs suffered from two major problems of the time: the tendency of the airplane to turn in flight because of propeller torque and the difficulty of maintaining yaw control when one engine lost power or shut down completely.

Oskar Ursinus, editor of the German aviation magazine *Flugsport*, was also an engineer and tackled both of the problems at once with a unique new twin-engine design (FIG. 7-21). To eliminate the propeller torque problem, he had the propellers of the 160-hp Mercedes DIII engines rotate in opposite directions so that their torque actions cancelled each other out, the first-known application of this practice to individual engines. (The Wright Brothers and others had used contra-rotating propellers driven by a single engine since 1903). The practice of oppositely-turning engines has been in wide use on twin-engine designs ever since Ursinus.

To minimize the trim problem with asymmetric power, Ursinus placed the engines as close together as their propellers would permit. To do this, he had to make a major rearrangement of the traditional airframe. He put the engines on the lower wing and raised the

fuselage to the upper wing. The lower portion of the nose was then bevelled so that the propellers of the closely-spaced engines would clear it.

Because Ursinus had no manufacturing facility, he was able to prevail upon the established Gotha Waggon-fabriek concern to build his design after the military showed interest. In 1915 Gotha built several for the German Army as the Gotha G.I, the first of the famous line of Gotha bombers, and one seaplane, the U.W.D. (for Ursinus Wasser Doppeldecker) for the German Navy in 1916.

Specifications: Wing span 66 feet $7^{1}/_{4}$ inches; gross weight 6,849 pounds; wing area 855.6 square feet; top speed 86 mph.

Dornier Wal

When the German Dornier firm began building large flying boats in 1915, careful effort was made to keep the thrust as close to the centerline as possible. Dornier's four-engine models of 1917 and 1918 had their engines paired in pusher-puller nacelles, technology transferred from the Zeppelin-Staaken landplanes (Dornier was a wholly-owned subsidiary of Zeppelin). Postwar two-engine Dornier boats, named Wal (German for whale), retained the tandem engine arrange-

Fig. 7-21. The German Ursinus G.W.D. of 1915 with closely-spaced engines to reduce asymmetric power trim problems and turning oppositely-rotating propellers to eliminate torque problems.

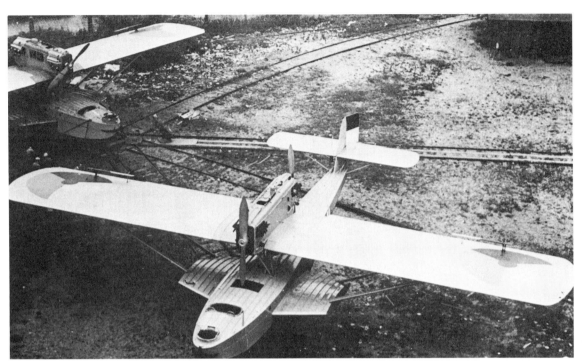

131

Fig. 7-22. A representative German Dornier Wal flying boat of the 1920s with two engines installed in a single nacelle above the wing. Note the sponsors, called Stummelflossen.

ment with both engines neatly mounted directly on top of a parasol monoplane wing (FIG. 7-22). Four-engine versions of the Wal, called Superwal, used two similar nacelles mounted as close to the centerline as propeller clearance would allow.

Besides better control under one-engine-out conditions, there was another good reason for keeping the engines of Dornier flying boats on or close to the airplane centerline. In 1918 Dornier had developed unique stub-floats, or sponsons, called Stummelflossen that projected from each side of the hull to perform the water stabilization function of strut-mounted floats near the wingtips. Besides reducing drag, the aerodynamic shape of the sponsons contributed lift in flight. Because of their short moment arm, however, sponsons lost effectiveness if too much weight was distributed outward on the wing.

The Wal concept was highly successful. It was in production from 1922 into early World War II, was copied by others (mostly without the sponsons), and

was revived, Stummelflossen and all, by a new Dornier company in 1984.

Specifications, 1929 Wal: Two 500-hp Lorraine engines; wing span 73 feet 9½ inches; wing area 1,032 square feet, gross weight 13,640 pounds; top speed 102.5 mph.

Dornier Do.X

The ultimate application of the Wal tandem-engine concept was the huge 12-engine Do.X of 1929 (FIG. 7-23). The wing was high enough off the water, and thick enough, to allow the engines to be carried in nacelles built into the leading edge of the wing as on contemporary German Junkers designs. However, it was not desirable to string the needed 12 engines out along the wing, or to house the engines in elongated nacelles directly on the wing surface as on the Wal. The compromise was to put six pairs of engines close together in short nacelles supported on struts entirely above the upper wing surface.

Fig. 7-23. The German Dornier Do.X of 1929 featured 12 engines in six tandem nacelles above the wing.

Because German aircraft engine development was behind the rest of the world at the time, the Do.X originally used 450-hp British Bristol Jupiter air-cooled radial engines. These were soon replaced by 600-hp water-cooled American Curtiss Conquerors, but still the Do.X was underpowered.

For several years the Do.X was the world's largest airplane in terms of weight and wingspan, and is still the world's only 12-engine airplane. On one flight the Do.X set a world record by carrying 169 people aloft for an hour-150 passengers, 10 crew, and *nine stowaways*! The first Do.X of three built was retired to a Berlin Museum and was destroyed during an air raid in World War II.

Specifications: Wing span 157 feet 5 inches; wing area 4,885 square feet; gross weight 123,200 pounds; top speed 134 mph.

Fokker F-32

When the monoplane configuration became popular for landplane transports and bombers in the late 1920s, the same old problem of placing multiple engines on the largest designs remained. For four-engine designs, the most popular arrangement was push-pull pairs as pioneered by Staaken and Dornier. The American Fokker F-32 of 1929 (FIG. 7-24) and so designated because of its 32-passenger capacity is representative of many high-wing four-engine monoplanes of the time.

However, the F-32 and similar designs with the rear propellers close to the ground encountered a serious problem. With no lower wing to shield them, the rear propellers were very susceptible to damage from gravel and other debris thrown up by the wheels or sucked up by the vortices of the propellers themselves. In spite of this, some tandem-engine designs remained in service until early WW II.

In spite of its 525-hp Pratt & Whitney Hornet engines, the F-32 was underpowered. Of seven built, only two served on an airline route, and then only for a little over a year. Later four-engine Fokker transports built in Holland placed all of the engines in a line, a return to 1913-1917 Sikorsky practice.

Specifications: Wing span 99 feet; gross weight 22,500 pounds; wing area 1,350 square feet; high speed 150 mph, cruising speed 120 mph.

Bleriot 195

In some respects, a low-wing monoplane can be considered a biplane without an upper wing, at least as far as the placement of multiple engines goes. Push-pull pairs of engines mounted between the wings of biplanes were common from 1916 into the 1930s. The French Bleriot Model 195 of 1929 (FIG. 7-25) was a

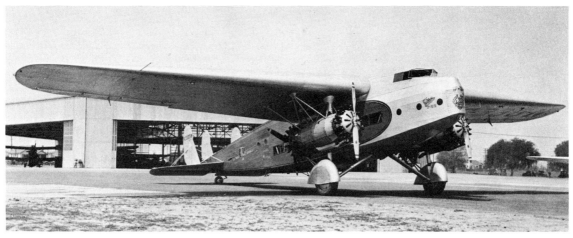

Fig. 7-24. The American Fokker F-32 monoplane of 1929 resembled the Zeppelin-Staaken R-VI of 1916 in that the four engines were installed in tandem in nacelles close to the fuselage.

Fig. 7-25. The French Bleriot 195 paired tandem engines in two nacelles as on the Fokker F-32, but with the low wing, the engines had to be placed above the wing.

monoplane with a full cantilever wing. This could have supported engines along the leading edge, as was becoming popular at the time, but the wing was so close to the ground that there would be no propeller clearance.

The only logical arrangement, therefore, was to put the four 250-hp Hispano-Suiza engines in paired nacelles above the wing as though the low-wing monoplane was a biplane. (Look at the front-view photo; it is easy to visualize an upper wing on it.)

Specifications: Wing span 70 feet 10 inches; gross weight 18,000 pounds; wing area 970 square feet; high speed 120 mph; endurance 18 hours.

Dornier Do.14

A switch on the Salmson that used one engine to drive two propellers was the German Dornier Do.14 of 1936. This otherwise conventional flying boat had one pusher propeller in the traditional location above the

Fig. 7-26. The Dornier Do.14 had two engines in the hull driving a single-pusher propeller above the wing.

wing, but it was driven through a shaft and two gear-boxes by two 690-hp BMW VI water-cooled engines in the hull (FIG. 7-26). These were installed longitudinally in tandem, facing each other. Each was connected to a single gearbox located between them. A vertical shaft from this box turned another gear at the top that drove the propeller shaft. The system worked, but only one Do.14 was built.

Specifications: Span 82 feet; gross weight 25,080 pounds; top speed 169 mph.

Dornier Do.26

Aircraft design involves a great number of compromises—called *tradeoffs* in order to meet certain requirements. In the four-engine Super Wal flying boats, Dornier had a good transport, but it didn't have transatlantic range for the international commercial competition that was shaping up in the late 1930s.

Extending the range (and speed) called for extensive cleanup of the basic design. This was relatively easy to do while retaining the tandem-pair engine arrangement, but it presented the problem of the rear propellers being too close to the water. Since these were already mounted on extension shafts so the rear engines could be further forward for balance purposes, the "fix" was to pivot the shafts at the engine end. This raised the propellers sufficiently for takeoff and landing (FIG. 7-27). The slight loss of thrust due to the upward deflection was more than compensated for by the added speed of the plane in the clean cruise configuration.

The original Do.26s built for the German airline Luft Hansa were used over the South Atlantic just before World War II ended the operation. To enable them to fly with a greater fuel load than they could take off with, they were launched by catapult from special mother ships that are illustrated in Chapter 13. When war broke out, the three airline Do.26s and others still under construction were taken into the Luftwaffe.

Specifications: Span 98 feet 5 inches; wing area 1,291 square feet; powerplants four 880-hp Junkers Jumo 205 diesel engines; gross weight 49,600 pounds; cruising speed 189 mph.

Fig. 7-27. The Dornier Do.26 of 1939 pivoted the extension shafts of the rear propellers upward during takeoff and landing to keep them out of the spray.

Macchi-Castoldi MC-72

The usual way to get more speed out of a single-engine airplane is to put in a bigger and more powerful engine. When one is not available, other means must be found.

For a racing airplane, the added drag of conventional twin-engine design would far overcome any speed that could be gained from the added power. Mario Castoldi solved this problem with his design for the 1931 Schneider Trophy Race, the MC-72, built by the Italian firm of Macchi.

This was in all respects but one a traditional single-seat twin-float tractor racing seaplane. Castoldi got the power of a second 1300-hp Fiat AS-6 engine by installing it backwards, behind and coupled to the first. The two drove contrarotating coaxial propellers (FIG. 7-28).

Various mechanical problems kept the MC-72 out of the 1931 race, but with a new engine pair producing 3,100 hp, it managed to set the world's absolute speed record at 440.8 mph on October 23, 1934. While this speed was surpassed by some experimental German landplanes in 1939, it remains today as the record for propeller-driven seaplanes. The record-setting MC-72 is preserved today in the Museum of Flight in Turin, Italy.

Specifications: Wing span 31 feet 1 inch: area 161.4 square feet; gross weight 6,395 pounds.

Loughead Olympic

Another approach to getting the benefits of twin-engine power and reliability while retaining the streamlining advantages of a single-engine design was taken by the American Alan Loughead in 1931. He used an airframe very similar to the earlier Lockheed (note different spelling than that of the original founder) Vega high-wing cabin monoplane.

Power was supplied by two 125-hp Menasco engines. These were six-cylinder in-line air-cooled types and were mounted on their sides in a single narrow nose cowling separated only far enough to obtain propeller clearance (FIG. 7-29). This experimental model, named Olympic, flew successfully but was unable to attract backers or buyers in the depression years of the early 1930s.

Lockheed Unitwin Starliner

The Loughead/Lockheed idea of two engines in the nose of a single-engine design did not die with the passing of the Olympic. In 1938, the major Lockheed Aircraft Corporation, which had established Vega Aircraft as a subsidiary firm near its main plant in Burbank, California, took a slightly different approach.

Again using two 250-hp Menasco engines, Vega used an old Lockheed Altair airframe as the test bed for

135

Fig. 7-28. The Italian Macchi-Castoldi racer had two engines in tandem in the nose driving the first practical application of coaxial contrarotating propellers.

Fig. 7-29. The American Loughead Olympic Duo Six had two normally inverted Menascos engines mounted on their sides in the nose just far enough apart for the propellers to clear each other.

Fig. 7-30. The Lockheed (note different spelling) Starliner featured a Unitwin engine—two 250-hp Menascos mounted side-by-side and coupled to a single propeller.

an idea that went back to the Linke-Hoffmann R-II of 1918 but on a lesser scale—two side-by-side engines coupled to a single propeller. These were mounted vertically in a much more conventional-appearing nose (FIG. 7-30). This installation was called the Unitwin. Should one engine fail, it could be disconnected and the plane could continue its flight on the other.

The modified Altair flew successfully and encouraged the development of a designed-for-the-purpose model with commercial possibilities, the Starliner. This, too, was successful with the same Menasco Unitwin installation; however, the buildup of military orders for World War II caused it to be abandoned.

Specifications: Span 41 feet; gross weight 6,000 pounds, cruising speed 178 mph at 66 percent power, 155 at 50 percent power.

Dornier Do.335 Pfeil

When Dornier developed its model 335 Pfeil (German for arrow) fighter late in World War II, it obtained the power of two 1750-hp Daimler-Benz 603A engines in a narrow fuselage by combining Castoldi's idea of tandem engines on the airplane centerline with the older idea of a prop-behind-the-tail pusher. The result was a very successful tandem-engine "push-pull" airplane, with one engine in the nose and a second one just aft of the wing driving its propeller through an extension shaft (FIG. 7-31). The front engine had a traditional annular nose radiator while the radiator for the rear engine was housed in an air scoop under the rear fuselage, *a la* P-51 Mustang.

The tail was a true cruciform, with equal-size fins and rudders above and below the fuselage, the lower

Fig. 7-31. The twin-engine Dornier Do.335 Pfeil of 1944 had a propeller at each end. This is a special two-seat trainer version.

one serving as a skid to keep the propeller from touching the ground if the airplane overrotated on takeoff or landing. To keep the pilot from hitting the rear propeller during emergency parachute jumps, an explosive charge would blow off the propeller and the top fin.

Dornier had patented the push-pull arrangement in 1937. He received no encouragement from the government for a fighter, however. Being one of Germany's main suppliers of bombers, he was told to stay in that line of work and not dilute his efforts with a fighter. By 1942, however, the idea of a two-engine bomber-interceptor suddenly became very popular and go-ahead was given for the Pfeil.

Prototypes were flying in September 1943, but the development problems of high-performance aircraft being what they are (and further complicated by politics), it was not until early 1945 that the first production Do.335A-1 models left the factory. As a result, they did not get into combat. Several variants had been developed earlier, including night-fighter and photoreconnaissance models and even a tandem-seat transition trainer.

The Pfeil proved to be a very good airplane, one of the fastest piston-engined fighters ever. It could take off and climb on either of its engines. Naturally, it was big, with a wingspan of 45 feet 3 inches, 414 square feet of area, and a gross weight for the A-1 version of 21,186 pounds. Top speed at 21,000 feet was 474 mph—a bit over the absolute speed record of 469 mph set on April 26, 1939. This record was to stand for piston-engine types until August 16, 1969, when it was raised to 483 mph by Darryl Greenamyer's highly-modified 1946 Grumman F8F Bearcat. No one was seeking official records during the war, so the Pfeil's accomplishment went unsung.

Only one Do.335 survives today, the property of the National Air and Space Museum of the Smithsonian Institution.

Wagner Twin Tri-Pacer

An interesting return to the Loughead Olympic concept of two engines and propellers side-by-side in the nose was made by Harold Wagner of Portland, Oregon, in 1952. However, instead of spacing the two 125-hp Lycoming engines of a standard Piper PA-22 Tri-Pacer far enough apart for the propeller arcs to clear each other, he placed the engines closer. Propeller interference was avoided by putting a propeller hub spacer on the left engine to move the propeller ahead (FIG. 7-32). This allowed the two propeller arcs to overlap by almost one blade length.

Except for the engine installation, which put it on an experimental license, the airplane was otherwise a stock Tri-Pacer that eventually reverted to standard.

Fig. 7-32. The Wagner Twin Tri-Pacer followed the Loughead Duo Six concept but placed the engines closer together and let the propellers overlap.

Caproni-Campini N.1

The introduction of the turbojet engine early in World War II opened up all sorts of possibilities for new powerplant installations and locations. For twin engine types, the jets were usually hung under the wings on early fighter designs and later built into the wings on large bomber types. For single-jet types, burying the jet in the middle of the fuselage, with straight-through flow of air from the nose to the tailpipe, was the preferred configuration.

Oddly, one of the first reaction-propelled airplanes to fly, the Italian Caproni-Campini No. 1 of 1940 (often and erroneously called the CC-2), was not powered by a turbojet engine (FIG. 7-33). It used a 900-hp Isotta-Fraschini piston engine to drive a compressor that fed high-pressure air to a combustion chamber where it was mixed with fuel, ignited, and ejected through the tailpipe as a high-speed jet blast. In this respect, the CC-1 was a two-engine airplane, although only one was used for propulsion.

The first flight was made on August 28, 1940, but was regarded only as an interesting experiment by officialdom. There was no official interest, hence, no follow-up development in wartime.

A two-seater, the CC-1 had a span of 52 feet, area of 387 square feet, and a gross weight of 9,250 pounds. Top speed was only 233 mph—hardly representative of the true jets developed soon afterward by others.

One significant contribution that the N.1 made that is not generally appreciated is the development of an afterburner, in which additional fuel was injected into the jetstream at the tail to provide additional thrust. The British call such a system *reheat*, elsewhere it is an *afterburner*. Prior to its use on the N.1, the top speed was only 205 mph. Afterburners began coming into regular use on high-performance airplanes in the early 1950s so while the N.1 was a failure as a jet plane, it still made a significant contribution to high-speed flight.

The CC-1 survives today in the Museum of Science and Technology in Milan, Italy.

Douglas XB-42

In 1944 the Douglas Aircraft Company rolled out a radical new twin-engine bomber, the XB-42 (FIG. 7-34). It was immediately nicknamed the Mixmaster because its behind-the-tail coaxial propellers resembled the fa-

Fig. 7-33. The Italian Caproni-Campini N.1 of 1940 looks like a jet but the first-stage power was supplied by a conventional piston engine.

Fig. 7-34. The American Douglas XB-42 of 1944 featured two buried engines above the wing driving coaxial contra-rotating propellers behind the tail.

mous kitchen appliance. In the interest of obtaining maximum aerodynamic efficiency by not having the wing encumbered by the traditional engines and nacelles, the two liquid-cooled Allison V-12 engines were buried in the fuselage.

As a switch on the Dornier Do 14 arrangement, the engines were paired side-by-side in the upper fuselage above the long bomb bay and slightly ahead of the airplane center of gravity. Each drove a separate extension shaft to a gearbox ahead of the contrarotating propellers.

At nearly 400 mph, the two XB-42s were the fastest piston-engine bombers ever built, and could carry an 8,000-pound bomb load 1,800 miles. However, the end of World War II and the advent of jet propulsion ended further development of the XB-42. Essentially the same airframe was used for the XB-43, which substituted two buried jet engines for the piston engines. This quickie adaptation was bypassed by newer designs developed specifically for jet engines.

Specifications: Two 1,375-hp (1,900-hp War Emergency) Allison V-1710-129 engines; wing span 70 feet 6 inches; wing area 555 square feet; gross weight 35,700 pounds.

Beech Twin-Quad

Designers of multiengine airplanes with wing-mounted engines have long dreamed of achieving an aerodynamically-clean wing by burying the engines completely inside the wing and driving the propellers by extension shafts. This has nearly been accomplished on a few giants with wings thick enough to contain the engines, but even the huge ConVair B-36 of 1946, with one of the thickest wings ever, could not completely enclose its six pusher engines within the wing. For smaller transport planes in the size range of the popular Douglas DC-3, the idea could not even be considered due to the bulk of engines then in use.

Beech Aircraft Corporation of Wichita, Kansas, finally achieved the long-sought ideal when it introduced its Model 34 Twin-Quad in 1948 (FIG. 7-35). This 20-passenger transport was smaller and lighter than the ubiquitous DC-3 that was due for replacement, but had the same capacity and higher performance. The Model 34 was a unique design on several counts, and its name came from its use of two propellers (Twin) and four engines (Quad).

It was possible to enclose the 375-hp Lycoming S-580 engines completely within the wing because they

141

Fig. 7-35. The Beech Aircraft Corporation Twin-Quad airliner of 1948 featured four flat engines in the wings, each pair driving a single tractor propeller.

Fig. 7-36. The British Norman-Britten Trislander, essentially a twin-engine Islander feeder-airliner with a third engine installed on the tail.

were of the flat, or opposed-cylinder, design with two banks of four air-cooled cylinders facing each other instead of being in the traditional V, or radial, arrangements. Flat engines had been in wide use in lightplanes since the early 1930s, but the Lycoming was the highest-powered of the type to its time.

The two engines in each wing were installed facing each other, their shafts joining in a common gearbox that drove the efficient large-diameter slow-turning propeller ahead of the wing.

The Twin-Quad was also novel in being the largest airplane ever to use the V-type, or butterfly, tail just introduced as a production item on Beech's Model 35 Bonanza (see Chapter 14). However, it never got beyond the prototype stage.

Specifications: Wing span 70 feet; gross weight 19,500 pounds; top speed 230 mph at 8,000 feet.

Britten-Norman Trislander

The British firm of Britten-Norman introduced a 10-passenger twin-engine commuter airliner in 1965 called the Islander. This became very successful over succeeding years and is still in production by a successor firm, Pilatus Britten-Norman.

When greater capacity was desired, the Islander underwent the usual fuselage stretch to accommodate up to 17 passengers. Rather than use two engines with more power to handle the extra weight and bulk, the builders elected to add a third engine and make a trimotor—the Trislander (FIG. 7-36). Because the fuselage was so low to the ground, it was not considered practical to put the third engine in the traditional nose position. Instead, it was put on top of the tail. The far-aft weight of the added engine was balanced by the long extension of the nose and more forward location of the payload.

Specifications: Powerplants, three 260-hp Avco-Lycoming O-540 engines; wing span 53 feet; gross weight 10,000 pounds; cruising speed at 59 percent power 150 mph.

8
CHAPTER

Landing Gear

BY ITSELF, UNCONVENTIONAL LANDING GEAR DOES NOT make an aircraft unconventional, but it can certainly contribute to a notably different appearance. Often, unconventional landing gear is the result of a major departure from conventional configuration on the part of the aircraft itself that requires a major change in the landing gear. In many cases, thoroughly conventional aircraft have been fitted with unconventional landing gear to adapt them to special uses or situations.

In the mid-1930s a number of new civil aircraft designs were regarded as unconventional because they featured *tricycle* landing gear, with the main wheels behind the center of gravity and nosewheel forward. Many people did not realize at that time—or had forgotten—that tricycle gear was in wide use before World War I but had been dropped mainly due to the performance requirements of the war (FIG. 8-1). The extra wheel was a weight and drag penalty, and the more docile ground-handling characteristics, or "safety" features, were unnecessary for pilots trained to handle "hot" military airplanes.

Military considerations dictated most of the aircraft configurations that were standardized in World War I, and it took nearly 20 years for the weight and performance handicaps of tricycle gear to be accepted as valid tradeoffs for the obvious safety and easy ground handling features of the configuration. The term "conventional gear" is still used to describe two wheels in front and a tailwheel aft, but the term is now a misnomer since nearly all production civil and military aircraft use tricycle gear.

The principal advantage of tricycle gear is the greatly reduced tendency to ground-loop during the landing roll, since the main wheels are behind the center of gravity. Also, the level attitude of the fuselage greatly enhances the pilot's visibility during taxiing and the brakes can be applied much more abruptly without risk of nosing the airplane over.

Fig. 8-1. A 1910 Curtiss Model D pusher with the tricycle landing gear that was in common use at that time.

One disadvantage of tricycle gear in the old days was that it was not steerable, but that was hardly a problem before World War I. Planes did very little taxiing; they were usually towed or man-handled to the takeoff point and were similarly hauled back to the hangar when the landing roll ended. From the 1930s on, the nosewheel was made steerable. One minor advantage of the taildragger configuration from WWI to the adoption of tailwheels was that it was relatively steerable by blasting the tail around with full-throttle application. Also, the tail skid was an effective brake on turf airfields.

It is interesting to note that kits have been developed to convert some classic taildragger models to tricycle. In one case, the Piper PA-20 Pacer of 1950-51 offered tricycle gear as an option, but it became so popular that the conventional gear version was abandoned. On the other hand, some pilots who like livelier airplanes have converted tricycle models to taildraggers, and again, conversion kits are available.

Variations on wheel arrangement are quite numerous and only a few are illustrated here.

144

Voisin Quad-Gear

In pre-World War I years, one of the most popular wheel arrangements consisted of four wheels positioned as on an automobile. The fact that they did not have brakes and were not steerable did not seem to deter their use.

The best-known example is the series of French Voisin pusher biplanes that were used as bombers from 1914 into 1917 and as trainers thereafter. Hundreds were built, and the U.S. Army bought eight 220-hp. Voisin Model VIIIs in 1918. The Model V is shown in FIG. 8-2.

Voisin V specifications: Powerplant, Canton-Unne 150-hp; span 48 feet 4 inches, gross weight 2,552 pounds; top speed approximately 70 mph.

Voisin Bicycle Gear

An interesting variation tried by several pre-World War I designers including Voisin was the bicycle arrangement, with two main landing wheels, one ahead of the other. To keep the machine level when at rest or moving at less than flying speed, outrigger skids or auxiliary wheels were installed under the wings. This arrangement was workable but never adopted for regular service until 1947 (see next entry).

The plane shown in FIG. 8-3 is a special French Voisin prototype with a 230-hp Canton-Unne water-cooled radial engine mounted as a pusher. The single lower tail boom was low enough to clear the propeller, but the upper boom was divided from the wing to midway to the tail for clearance. Actually, there were two rear wheels in order to support the weight, but they were so close together that they did not provide tricycle stability; the outrigger skids were still necessary. The rear wheel set was behind but close to the center of

Fig. 8-2. The French Voisin Model V of 1914 with nonsteerable four-wheel landing gear.

Fig. 8-3. An experimental 1915 Voisin with bicycle landing gear and stabilizing outrigger skids.

gravity, so it was easy to rotate the plane during landing and takeoff.

Boeing B-47

At first glance, the Boeing B-47 of 1947 appears to be a repeat of the 1914 bicycle-gear Voisin with such state-of-the-art improvements as a steerable front unit, both units retractable, brakes, and wheels on the outriggers. All of this is true, but the B-47 also had a major difference from the 1914 design.

Because of the size of the bomb bay, it was impossible to locate the rear wheels (two on one strut, but still requiring outriggers for lateral stability) close enough to the center of gravity to allow the plane to rotate for takeoff and landing. As a consequence, the

aircraft had to be built so that its ground angle at rest was also the proper angle of attack for takeoff and landing (FIG. 8-4).

Because stopping such a heavy plane (198,000 pound takeoff weight, well over 100,000 pounds landing weight) on existing paved runways was a major problem, a unique supplement to the braking system was used—a braking parachute. This was another device developed in Germany during the war. As soon as the plane touched down, the chute was deployed from a compartment in the tail (FIG. 8-5). This practice has since become widespread, but the B-47 was the first major production model to have it designed in. After experience was gained, the braking chute was deployed a few seconds before the B-47 touched down.

145

Fig. 8-4. Bicycle landing gear with outriggers reappeared in a big way on the American Boeing B-47 of 1947.

Fig. 8-5. It was necessary to use a braking parachute to help stop the B-47 and other heavy military models after landings.

Jacobs/Schweyer Weihe

For many years, one class of aircraft got along nicely with no wheels at all—the gliders. Through the 1920s, even the largest ones were quite light. They were launched by shock cord from hillsides and later towed aloft by a winch or an airplane. For takeoff and landing on turf, a single skid under the forward fuselage was adequate. For ground handling, the gliders could be towed by a car or even lifted bodily by two or three people.

As the gliders and sailplanes (high-performance gliders) got bigger and heavier and takeoffs were made from harder surfaces, it was hard to get the ship moving. Also, the wear on the skid was considerable and it became difficult to move the ship around on the ground. Wheels were the logical answer, but permanent wheels on the glider were undesirable from a weight and drag standpoint. Since they were needed only on the ground, a detachable two-wheel dolly was used.

This remained attached during the takeoff and was dropped as soon as the glider was airborne (FIG. 8-6). The landing was then made on the skid. This system was also used successfully on the German Messerschmitt 163 rocket-powered interceptor of World War II. It remained a feature on some high-performance German sailplanes produced into the 1950s, but with light weight no longer a consideration, the high-performance types now utilize retractable wheels and have

even deleted the skid in the quest for aerodynamic cleanliness.

Specifications: Span 59 feet, area 191.5 square feet; aspect ratio 17.8:1; gross weight 781 pounds; best glide ratio 29:1 at 42.7 mph.

Arado 234A

A different form of takeoff dolly was used to allow the twin-jet German Arado 234A bomber of 1943 to get airborne before landing on a retractable skid. At first it was like the gliders—a simple dolly attached to the airplane that was dropped right after takeoff (FIG. 8-7). For such a heavy plane, however, this had to be a pretty substantial structure. If dropped from too high, it was destroyed on hitting the ground. It was therefore replaced by an even larger dolly that stayed on the ground, with the airplane simply lifting off when it reached flying speed.

The landing gear was the unique feature of the airplane. The world's first purpose-designed jet bomber was so small in the interest of reducing weight and drag that it was a single-seater that had no room in which to retract a conventional wheeled gear. A heavy retractable skid was built into the belly, with smaller skids under the engine nacelles. The system worked, but no one seemed to give serious consideration to the postlanding problems of getting a dozen or more wheel-less airplanes back to the hangar after a sortie. They would have to be hoisted by heavy equipment so that dollies

146

Fig. 8-6. Some heavy gliders needed wheels to ease the takeoff run, but then dropped them to reduce aerodynamic drag. Landing was made on the skid. This is the author's 1939 German Weihe.

Fig. 8-7. The prototype versions of the German Arado Ar.234 of World War II took off from three-wheeled dollies and landed on skids as shown on the experimental Ar.234-V6.

could be put under them again, and then towed in. They could not taxi under their own power when mounted on the dollies.

The realities of the recovery problem were finally appreciated, so the airplane was redesigned as the improved Ar.234B model with a wider fuselage that could accommodate a wheeled tricycle landing gear. The following figures are for the production Ar.234B model but FIG. 8-7 shows one of the early A-type airframes modified to the Ar.134V-6, (V for Versuchs, German for experimental), an experimental four-jet variant.

Specifications: Powerplant two Junkers Jumo 004B, 1,980 pounds thrust; span 46 feet 3 1/2 inches, area 284 square feet; gross weight 21,715 pounds; top speed 461 mph at 26,250 ft.

Schweizer and Frankfort Gliders

When training gliders got heavy enough that the weight of a wheel was not a significant handicap, a single wheel was built into the belly close to the center of gravity as shown in the flight view (FIG. 8-8) of an American Schweizer 1-19 utility glider. If the wheel was ahead of the loaded CG, the glider rested on the mainwheel and a tail skid. If the wheel was behind the CG, it rested on the nose skid when the pilot was aboard. He had to be careful when getting out to ease his weight off the nose gradually, because once free of his weight ahead of the CG, the glider rested on its tail skid. The tail could bang down surprisingly hard if he just stepped out.

How do gliders keep from crashing when landing on such an unstable device as a single wheel? The answer is in the long wings. When headed into even a slight breeze, the long wings generate lift to help the opposite wing panels balance each other. When taking off, most glider operations utilize a "wingman" to hold the wingtip level and to give arm signals to the tow operator. As the glider starts to roll, its wings will stay level and the wingman, after running a few steps, lets go.

148

Fig. 8-8. Most American gliders from 1930, like this 1946 Schweizer 1-19, used a single wheel projecting from the fuselage and protected the wingtips with skids or rollers.

Fig. 8-9. The long wings of most gliders enable them to balance on their single wheels and keep their wings level when headed into a breeze. Here the author instructs a student in a motionless Frankfort TG-1A Cinema.

When landing into the wind, most gliders can keep the wings level until fully stopped, after which one wingtip, which is protected by a small skid or wheel, settles slowly to the ground. As a training exercise, student pilots sometimes "fly" motionless gliders headed into the wind, keeping the wings level or rocking them by means of the stick as shown in FIG. 8-9, a Frankfort TG-1 war surplus two-seat training sailplane.

A utility glider such as the 1-19 shown has a wingspan of 36 feet 8 inches, aspect ratio of 7.9, and an L/D or glide ratio of 17:1. The TG-1 has a span of 46 feet 3 inches and an L/D of 20:1. War surplus trainers like the TG-1, the Schweizer TG-2 and -3, and the Laister-Kauffman TG-4 were the mainstays of the American soaring movement for nearly 15 years after World War II.

Dayton-Wright TA-5

A variation of the monowheel landing gear was tried by the U.S. Army Air Service Engineering Division in 1924. As a possible weight and drag reduction, they tried a land-going equivalent of the Navy's single-float seaplanes. A single main wheel was located in the normal forward position with smaller wheels under each wingtip (FIG. 8-10). A major difference from the seaplane operation was that the landplane rested on its tailskid in a nose-high altitude while the seaplane stayed level.

While the span of the TA-5 was as great as some gliders, the wing loading was much higher and the

wings would not hold level at low speed. The idea was quickly abandoned, but other designers have reinvented it since with equal lack of success.

The Dayton-Wright Airplane Company that had an Army contract to build the TA-5 (Trainer, Air Cooled, Model 5, in the pre-1924 Army system) was absorbed by the new Consolidated Aircraft Company, which refined the TA-5 into the tandem-seat and very popular PT-3 (Primary Trainer, Model 3) for the Army and the NY (N for Trainer, Y for Consolidated) for the Navy.

TA-5 specifications: Powerplant, 200-hp Lawrance (later Wright) J-1; span 34 feet 9 inches; area 285 square feet; gross weight 2,235 pounds; top speed 104 mph.

Piper Super Cub with Treaded Wheels

Ever since World War I, designers have tackled the problem of landing airplanes on rough or uneven terrain. One popular approach that has been tried several times—and shown to work—was tractor-like tread around two or more wheels on each side of the plane. The Italian-owned Piper PA-18 Super Cub shown in FIG. 8-11 is a 1950s experiment representative of many before it. It used oversize wire wheels attached through a yoke to the axles of the standard Cub landing gear. Brakes were fitted to the front wheels but not the rear. While the tread-gear Cub could land on rough ground and stop much more quickly than one with standard gear, it was difficult to steer.

The Piper Super Cub is a development of the

Fig. 8-10. The idea of a single main wheel on the centerline and outrigger wheels under the wings didn't work out for powered airplanes like this Dayton-Wright TA-5.

150

Fig. 8-11. An American Piper PA-18 Super Cub fitted with tractor-tread landing gear in Italy.

famous J-3 that was introduced in 1937. The PA-18 Super Cub version appeared in 1950 with 108-hp Lycoming 0-235 engine in place of the original 65-hp model. With various improvements and increases of power to a 150-hp Lycoming 0-320, it remained in production by Piper until 1982.

PA-18-150 Super Cub specifications: Powerplant Lycoming 0-320 150-hp; span 35 feet 2 1/2 inches; area 178.5 square feet; gross weight 1,750 pounds; top speed 135 mph.

Boeing B-50 with Treads

The various landing gear gimmicks tried for soft or rough-ground operations didn't work well enough to be practical for military airplanes, particularly those with

Fig. 8-12. A Boeing B-50B fitted with experimental tractor-tread landing gear in 1949.

retractable landing gear. During World War II and subsequently, the problem was pretty well taken care of by laying down pierced steel mats (PSP, for pierced steel planking) in linked sections.

These didn't handle heavy bombers very well, however, so experiments continued after the war. The airplane shown in FIG. 8-12 is a Boeing B-50B, the postwar version of the famous B-29. It had 75ST aluminum structure instead of 24ST, bigger engines, and a notably taller tail. This one was fitted briefly with tread-type landing gear similar to others tried on high-performance Army airplanes over several previous years. Instead of the treads running around two oversize wheels as on the Cub, the treads ran over much smaller bogie-wheels in the manner of a tractor or tank.

B-50B specifications: Span 141 feet 3 inches; area 1,720 square feet; gross weight 168,708 pounds; top speed 385 mph at 25,000 ft.

Piper PA-11 Cub with Tandem Wheels

After all the trials of various tread-type landing gear for multi-wheeled light airplanes, the best proved to be tandem wheels with no treads or tracks at all. The gear shown on a Piper PA-11 Cub (FIG. 8-13) was developed by Art Whittaker of Portland, Oregon, in 1949.

This gear used two of the regular balloon tires normally used on Cubs in tandem on each side. Between them, these made a soft enough "footprint" that the plane wouldn't sink into soft ground; the yoke pivoted

on the regular axle to follow the contours of the rough ground. The added weight and drag was a minor handicap for planes in the Cub class, but again, it was hard to make tight turns. For example, it could not lock the brake on one wheel and pivot around it as was common practice when taxiing on a road or other narrow area.

Arado 232

An alternative approach to tractor treads for rough-field landing gear was taken by the German Arado Ar. 232A assault transport of 1941. This used conventional

Fig. 8-13. A Piper PA-11 Cub fitted with four standard-size airwheels paired in frames that pivot on the axles of the standard landing gear.

151

Fig. 8-14. The Arado Ar.232A with coventional retractable tricycle landing gear plus 22 smaller wheels under the center of gravity of the short fuselage.

tricycle gear for takeoff and for landing on smooth terrain or runways. For other landings, it had two rows of 11 small non-retractable bogie or crawler wheels beneath the fuselage and close to the center of gravity. The main gear retracted, but only far enough for the bottoms of the main wheels to be even with the bottoms of the small wheels (FIG. 8-14). This put most wheels on the ground in rough terrain, with a long enough wheelbase to bridge some of the low spots.

The original Ar. 232As were twin-engine models with 1,200-hp Bramo Fafnir engines. The principal production model was the heavier four-engine Ar. 232B shown.

Specifications: Span 109 feet 10³/₄ inches; area 1,535 square feet; gross weight 44,080 pounds; top speed 191 mph at 13,120 ft.

Piper Super Cruiser with Tundra Tires

After all the different landing gear developed for operations on rough or soft ground, the method favored by the Alaskan and Canadian bush fliers is to use greatly oversized low-pressure tires, called "tundra tires," on otherwise standard landing gear. These are easy to install and give the airplane the same ground maneuverability of standard gear.

The airplane shown in FIG. 8-15 is a Piper PA-12 Super Cruiser, an enlarged version of the Cub. Ordinarily, this (and the Cub) uses 8.00 × 4 wheels and tires; this one is fitted with 29 × 13 × 5.00 tires. It also features "booster" wingtips, extended fiberglass

units that increase the span and area slightly and reduce wing loading and wingtip vortices to reduce landing speed and shorten the takeoff run.

Specifications, standard PA-12: Powerplant 107/115-hp Lycoming O-235C; span 35 feet 5 inches; area 179 square feet; gross weight 1,750 pounds; top speed 115 mph.

HELICOPTER LANDING GEAR

The VTOL capability of the helicopter enables it to use notably different types of landing gear. Some make use of airplane-style wheels for rolling takeoffs (which require less power than vertical) and taxiing. Since small utility helicopters can fly right into their parking spots, they do not really need wheels. Many use simple skids, with small manually lowered wheels that allow the copter to be pushed into the hangar, etc. (FIG. 8-16).

A non-rolling gear peculiar to some copters is a set of balloonlike air bags that serve both as soft shock absorbers for land operation and pontoons for water operation (FIG. 8-17). Since the copter can lift off the water vertically instead of having to reach flying speed by planing forward on the surface, the floats can be of simple circular cross-section instead of the hydrodynamically efficient stepped design of the conventional seaplane.

FLOATPLANES

Airplanes that could operate from water developed almost in parallel with those that operated from land.

Fig. 8-15. A Piper PA-18 Super Cruiser with oversize "tundra tires" for landing on soft Alaskan terrain.

Fig. 8-16. A U.S. Navy Bell HUL-1 with skid-type helicopter landing gear. The small wheels can be lowered for manual ground-handling.

Fig. 8-17. A civil Bell 47J helicopter with inflatable rubberized cloth pontoons that are amphibious without needing wheels.

154

The first successful seaplanes were landplane designs that had pontoons substituted for the conventional landing gear. The flying boat, with the fuselage doubling as a hull, was a separate line of development.

Early pontoons (commonly called "floats") were tried in various arrangements, but only two became standardized. One was a large central float with smaller floats under each wingtip to stabilize the plane on the water (FIG. 8-18). The other used two equal-size floats in parallel that gave stability on the water in the manner of conventional paired wheels (FIG. 8-19). The single-float arrangement has been favored for small military types; the twin-float type, with its much better stability and steering on the water, is the standard for civil types. Actually, no single-float civil seaplane has even received a full U.S. approved type certificate.

Fig. 8-18. The single main float with wingtip floats was favored by the U.S. Navy from 1911 until floatplanes were phased out in 1962. The airplane is a Curtiss SOC-3 Seagull, normally based on a cruiser.

Fig. 8-19. Twin floats, as on this Luscombe 8E, are used universally for civillian floatplanes and were used on large Naval types when a torpedo was carried under the belly.

Another float arrangement, used briefly before and during WWI and not seen since, uses three very simple floats in the form of stepless "sea sleds" with two installed forward to replace normal wheels and one under the tail to replace a tail skid (FIG. 8-20). This arrangement now offers interesting possibilities for seaplane conversions of homebuilt landplane designs.

A major disadvantage to adding pontoons to a standard landplane is the increased weight and drag and the corresponding loss of payload and performance. These are prices that must be paid for the benefit of operating from water. In some designs—particularly flying boats—the drag of wingtip floats has been reduced somewhat by having them retract against or partly into the wing, or swing up to form wingtips.

Civil and military seaplanes are still being built, but in very small numbers. Seaplane operations throughout the world began to decline during World War II, when airstrips were built in many areas formerly accessible only be seaplane. At the same time,

the development of reliable long-range landplanes with superior performance pushed the big military patrol bomber flying boats out of the picture. Similarly, landplane airliners with transoceanic range and better performance put the big civil flying boats out of business almost immediately after the end of World War II.

AMPHIBIANS

The addition of wheels to an established flying boat design or a pontoon seaplane is simply a means of adding versatility to the particular design at the cost of added weight and reduced performance. Their presence on the seaplane does not make it unconventional.

Loening Amphibian

Until 1924, most amphibians were either flying boats or pontoon seaplanes to which retractable wheels had been added. Grover Loening, the first person to

Fig. 8-20. A British Sopwith Baby seaplane with the three-float arrangement that was popular to the end of World War I.

receive an aeronautical engineering degree, came up with something new. He cleaned up the traditional single-pontoon seaplane by moving the float much closer to the fuselage and then filled in the space with structure to create a deep and roomy hull (FIG. 8-21).

He was able to raise the float thanks to the U.S. Army's development of an inverted model of the famous 400-hp wartime Liberty engine. This enabled the propeller shaft to be raised significantly above the usual position of the thrust line. This distance, plus the use of a small-diameter four-blade propeller, made the new arrangement workable. The higher float put the lower wing closer to the water, so Loening was able to clean the design up still further by attaching the wingtip floats directly to the wing instead of using the usual maze of struts and wires.

Knowing that conservative-minded pilots would be distrustful of a strange-looking machine, Loening used some applied psychology. He used the most conventional wing design possible so that pilots would have a view of familiar structure from the cockpit. This paid off, and Loening amphibians sold well to the Army,

Navy, and civil markets. The basic design was carried on by Grumman with the JF/J2F (J for Utility, F for Grumman) duck series from 1934 to nearly the end of World War II.

1924 Loening COA-1 (Corps Observation Amphibian) specifications: Span 45 feet; area 500 square feet; gross weight 5,560 pounds; top speed 122 mph.

SKIS

For operation on ice and snow, skis are a direct substitute for wheels. To increase versatility and allow a plane to fly from a snowy area to bare ground, combination gear has been developed and is in wide use; the original wheel projects through a hole in the center of the ski for ground operation and the ski can be lowered for snow operation. See Chapter 15 for use of such skis on water.

A minor disadvantage of skis is that they have no brakes, so tight turns cannot be made while taxiing and the plane may not be able to stop if landing on a downward slope.

Fig. 8-21. The Loening COA-1 of 1924 filled in the space between the fuselage and float of conventional single-float biplanes and added retractable wheels.

Shortly after World War II, experiments were conducted with retractable *hydroskis* as a means of reducing the hull drag of flying boats for takeoff. Hydroskis were also tried as a way of making some Air Force cargo landplanes amphibious (FIG. 8-22). Their fuselages were made watertight, but since these pre-existing structures did not have hydrodynamically efficient bottoms, retractable hydroskis were used to provide the

Fig. 8-22. A retractable hydroski was used to convert this landplane Chase YC-123E cargoplane to a flying boat. The normal landing gear was retained to make it amphibious.

Fig. 8-23. In World War I and the early 1920s, landplanes that were expected to ditch at sea were fitted with hydrovanes ahead of the wheels to prevent nose-overs. Inflatable flotation bags are mounted above the wheels. The airplane is a U.S. Navy Hanriot HD-2.

necessary planing surfaces. No production resulted from this. See Chapter 14 for another hydroski installation.

Hydrofoils, which are oriented spanwise of the aircraft instead of lengthwise like skis, have been tried as an aid to seaplane takeoffs since before World War I, but nothing has come of these. During and shortly after World War I, some conventional military landplanes were fitted with *hydrovanes* ahead of the standard landing gear to keep the plane from nosing over during a deliberate descent on water (FIG. 8-23). (Seaplanes do "land" on water—a contradiction of terms, but in common use.)

FLOTATION BAGS

While not actually landing gear, flotation bags are intended to keep a landplane afloat after a forced landing on water until rescue can be effected (FIG. 8-24). The system was developed in England in 1918. Folded rub-berized bags, to be inflated by bottled gas after ditching, were added to some existing airplanes by means of external frames added above the landing gear. The initial applications were used in conjunction with the previously described anti-noseover hdyrovanes. The hydrovanes were soon deleted, but the add-on bags, usually stowed in more refined bolt-on containers on the sides of the fuselage or on the wings, were retained for several years.

In the late 1920s the U.S. Navy ordered flotation bags to be built into single- and two-seat landplanes that operated over water and the U.S. Army issued similar requirements for certain fighters. For most, the bags were kept in compartments built into the undersurface of the upper wing of biplanes (FIG. 8-25).

By the middle 1930s both services had abandoned built-in flotation bags, supplying the crew members with inflatable rubber rafts instead of trying to keep the airplane afloat.

Fig. 8-24. The U.S. Navy Hanriot of Fig. 8-23 kept afloat by the flotation bags that were inflated after a successful ditching.

Fig. 8-25. Flotation bags stowed in the upper wing of the U.S. Navy Boeing F4B-2 fighter of 1931 pop out of the compartments and inflate automatically when the system is activated by the pilot.

9

Twin Fuselages

OVER THE YEARS, A NUMBER OF SUCCESSFUL AIRCRAFT have made use of two fuselages rather than one. Some of these structures are really complete fuselages, containing engine, crew, and payload, and support one half of the tail surfaces and landing gear. Others are in sort of a shadow area and are much lesser structures that may carry some, but not all, of the foregoing items. Usually, these have evolved from the booms that support the tail surfaces on classic pusher designs in which the propeller of a center-line engine is behind the wing instead of ahead of it.

160   There are no significant inherent disadvantages to the twin-fuselage concept other than the obvious ones of the cost, weight, and drag of two structures rather than one. There has been some concern expressed about the occupants being subjected to vertical accelerations as the plane rolls about the longitudinal axis, but the distances involved are far less than those between the cockpit of a modern jet airliner and the main wheels, in which the pilots are moved quite a distance vertically as the plane rotates on takeoff with no noticeable ill effect.

Spacing of the fuselage or hulls is usually determined by the need to keep two propeller arcs apart, or for propellers to clear a central pod. No one seems to have taken advantage of propellerless jet engines to build a modern twin-fuselage design. Some have been seen in recent paper proposals for giant heavy cargo or tanker planes, but nothing has come of these so far.

Fokker M.9/K-I Battleplane

Necessity is said to be the mother of invention, and in 1915 the need for an airplane capable of shooting down other airplanes resulted in the Fokker K-I *Kampfflugzeug,* German for battleplane. The synchronizer gear that allowed a speedy single-seater to shoot forward along the line of flight had not yet been perfected, so another high-performance design that could fire forward was needed.

The K-I is an outstanding example of Dutch-born Anthony Fokker's ability to adapt major components of existing designs into a new one. The K-I (actually M.9 in Fokker's own model numbers; the K was for the official German battleplane class) used the outer wing panels of existing Fokker biplanes on a new wide center section that supported a center pod with a cockpit for the pilot and two 80-hp Oberursel-Gnome rotary engines, one a pusher and the other a tractor. Two fuselages from other M-models, each complete with its own tail surfaces, were then added. There were cockpits for machine gunners where the engines used to be (FIG. 9-1).

The hurriedly conceived and assembled K-I flew poorly. No further development or refinement was undertaken because Fokker had just come up with a gun synchronizer that made the existing M.5 Eindecker series into the world's first effective pursuit planes, or fighters.

Caproni Trimotors

The Italian Caproni firm became famous in World War I for a series of twin-fuselage trimotor bombers. Unlike the Fokker K-I, these were carefully designed from scratch and were notably successful. The British used some, and others were built under license in the U.S. While many other designers tried twin-fuselage models, the Capronis of 1915-18 were the only ones to reach significant production for many years.

Like the Fokker, the Caproni (Model 32 of 1915 shown in FIG. 9-2) had a pod or nacelle centered between two fuselages. The pod was fitted with a 100-hp Fiat engine mounted as a pusher while two other

Fig. 9-1. The tandem-engine German Fokker K-I of 1915 used two fuselages with completely separate tail surfaces.

Fig. 9-2. The Italian Capronis of World War I had a single horizontal tail surface connecting both fuselages.

Fiats were in the noses of the fuselages. The horizontal tail connected both fuselages at the rear and projected a distance outboard from each. There were no personnel in the fuselages; the crew all rode in the pod.

The span of the CA-32 was 74 feet 10 inches and it had a top speed of 71 mph. The 1918 CA-46 model had a total of 1,200 hp, spanned 76 feet 10 inches, and had a top speed of 103 mph.

Although not built in numbers as great, the most publicized model over subsequent years was the giant CA-40 triplane, featuring the same layout except for three wings. This had three 400-hp American Liberty engines, spanned 96 feet 6 inches, and had a gross weight of 17,700 pounds. Top speed was only 98 mph, however.

Siemens-Shuckert R-III

While most twin-fuselage airplanes had the structures side-by-side, a few used an over-and-under configuration. The German Siemens-Shuckert R-I to R-III bombers of 1916 should probably be classed as a "split fuselage" design rather than a twin fuselage because the double structure was only used aft of the wing. One object of the feature was an improved field of machine gun fire from positions at the intersection of the two triangular structures.

Another novel feature of the representative R-III shown in FIG. 9-3 was the powerplant installation, with three 220-hp Benz engines inside the forward fuselage driving two outboard propellers through shafts and gears connected to a common gearbox.

One really advanced feature of the R-III was the use of small auxiliary surfaces between the wings; these acted as boosters for the ailerons, which were notoriously "heavy" on large airplanes. The use of servo tabs did not come into general use for another 15 years.

Although they flew, and were accepted by the German Air Force, the seven original Siemens R-models (R stood for reisenflugzeug, or giant airplane, in WW-I German designations) were not very effective offensive machines, and only one of each was built.

R-III specifications: Span 112 feet 8 inches; gross weight 15,004 pounds; top speed 82.5 mph.

162

Fig. 9-3. The 1916 German Siemans-Shuckert R-III featured double fuselage structure aft of the wings.

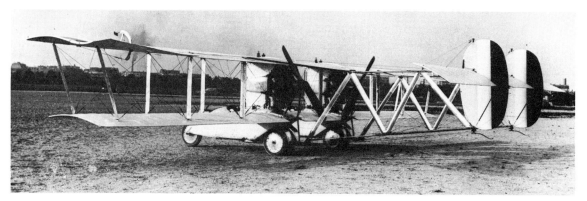

Fig. 9-4. The Twin Voisin of 1915 was created by joining two of the bicycle-gear models shown in Chapter 8.

Double Voisin

Some twin airplanes were designed from scratch as a single unit, but others were created by actually combining two examples of previously existing models.

Such was the case of the unique French Double Voisin of 1914. It used the complete fuselages of two of the bicycle-landing-gear Voisins joined by a new wing center section and a connecting horizontal tail. One complete set of outer wing panels from one of the "bicycles" completed the assembly (FIG. 9-4).

Needless to say, only this single prototype was built and no technical data other than the photograph is available.

Thomas-Morse MB-4

In 1919, the American Thomas-Morse Aircraft Company of Ithaca, N.Y., responded to a U.S. Post Office Department request for a twin-engine mail-plane. The resulting MB-4 was virtually an update of the 1915 Fokker K-I, although the T-M engineers were obviously unaware of it.

The same concepts prevailed, however, with minor differences. The mail compartment was in the pod between the engines while two pilots sat at duplicated and cross-connected controls in the two fuselages (FIG. 9-5). One wonders how the pilots communicated with each other over the distance between them in those days

Fig. 9-5. The American Thomas Morse MB-4 of 1919 differed from the Fokker K-I in that the pilots rode in the fuselages instead of the pod.

before the development of electronic communication systems. Certainly the famous Gosport speaking tube used between the tandem cockpits of some training planes of the time would not have been suitable.

Like the Fokker but unlike some other twin-fuse-lage designs, the B-4 did not connect the rear ends of the fuselages. The two separate sets of tail surfaces were from the earlier Thomas-Morse MB-3 fighter. The powerplants were Wright Model Hs, American-built versions of the 300-hp French Hispano-Suiza then being used in the MB-3.

The Post Office bought the MB-4 prototype but did not order production models.

Specifications: Span 48 feet 6 inches; gross weight 5,564 pounds; top speed 122 mph.

Savoia-Marchetti S-55

In 1925, the Italians again took the lead in twin-fuselage aircraft, this time with a twin-hull flying boat, the twin-engined Savoia-Marchetti S-55 with 400-hp French Lorraine engines. The novelty of the design was not so much in the use of roomy twin hulls but in the fact that the hulls were very short to save on weight and drag (FIG. 9-6). The horizontal stabilizer connected the rear ends of the two tubular-truss booms that projected from the rear of the hull. S-55s were widely used by the Italian Air Force and civil airlines and remained in service through 1938.

Although the hulls were roomy, the pilot and copi-lot sat in an open cockpit on the centerline of the thick cantilever wing beneath the forward engine of the tandem pair. This was a poor location for visibility; the distance back from the leading edge severely reduced downward visibility forward and the high dihedral angle of the wooden wing blocked visibility directly to the sides.

S-55s made some famous flights. Commander Francesco de Pinedo had reached Arizona on a 1927 westward flight around the world when a careless smoker ignited some spilled gasoline alongside the wooden hull and the plane was destroyed. De Pinedo had another S-55 shipped to the U.S. from Italy, completed a U.S. tour, and flew back to Italy via the Azores.

The most famous S-55 operations were the mass flights of improved S-55 models with a covered cockpit and other refinements. Air Marshall Italo Balbo led a flight of twelve across the South Atlantic to Rio de Janiero and back in 1930; he also led a really spectacular flight of 24 from Italy to the Chicago World's Fair in 1933.

Specifications, 1930 S-55A: Powerplants two 700-hp Fiat engines; span 79 feet 11 inches; area of 990 square feet; gross weight 16,940 pounds; top speed 147 mph.

Fig. 9-6. The twin-hull Italian Savoia Marchetti S-55 flying boat of 1925.

Fig. 9-7. The six-engine Russian Tupolev ANT-22 of 1935 was the largest twin-hull or twin-fuselage airplane ever built.

Tupolev ANT-22

The Russian Tupolev ANT-22 of 1935 differed from the Marchetti S.55 in using full-length twin hulls and being of greater size, with six 950-hp engines in three tandem nacelles above the wing (FIG. 9-7).

Little is known of this one-only prototype other than it was a heavily-armed military model that on December 8, 1936, set a world weight-to-altitude record by lifting a payload of 22,000 pounds (10,000 kilograms) to an altitude of 6,300 feet (5,000 meters).

Specifications: Span 167 feet 4 inches; length 79 feet; gross weight 73,832 pounds; top speed 142 mph.

Lockheed P-38 Lightning

By far the best known of all twin-fuselage aircraft, and the one built in the greatest numbers (10,036), is the U.S. Army's Lockheed P-38 Lightning introduced in 1938 and produced until 1945(FIG. 9-8). As a daring new concept in pursuit plane design, it had several years of teething troubles before becoming a very effective combat model in 1943. It quick earned the respect of German pilots, who named it *Der Gabelschwanz Teufel,* or "forked-tail devil."

The P-38, with two Allison V-1710 engines of 1,150- to 1,600-hp driving counter-rotating propellers, was adaptable to other roles besides fighting. When camaras were installed in the nose, in place of the formidable battery of four .50-caliber machine guns and one 20mm or 37mm cannon, it became the F-4 and F-5 photoplane. Later, nose sections were made inter- changeable so the same airplane could fly in either configuration, usually with the P-38 designation. A few were even converted to "pathfinder" bomb leaders, with a bombardier riding in a transparent nose. On his signal, other (single-seat) P-38s, carrying bombs instead of auxiliary fuel tanks, would drop their bombs.

The fuselages of the P-38 were almost too slim to be called that, so should probably be called booms. In any case, they were tightly packed with engine, turbo-supercharger, radiators, and main landing gear. The pilot rode in a center pod as on the old Capronis. Late in the war, a two-seat night fighter (P-38M) was developed that squeezed a radar operator into a raised seat behind the pilot. Earlier, a two-seat version had been tried with the second seat in the left-hand fuselage.

Specifications P-38L: Powerplants two 1,475-hp Allison engines; span 52 feet; area 327.5 square feet; gross weight 21,600 pounds; top speed 414 mph at 25,000 feet.

Heinkel He.111Z

When Messerschmitt produced the world's biggest cargo glider in 1941, with a wing span of 180 feet and a gross weight of 86,860 pounds, there was no existing towplane capable of pulling it. A *Troica* of three Junkers JU-52 trimotors—pulling on separate ropes— worked, but a single tug was still needed. This was obtained by physically joining two examples of the Luftwaffe's standard Heinkel He. 111H twin-engine bomber into the five-engined He.111Z model, the Z standing for zwilling, or "twin."

165

Fig. 9-8. Because of its performance in World War II, the Lockheed P-38 is probably the best-known of all twin-fuselage aircraft. This is an early YP-38 service test model in 1941.

Fig. 9-9. The German Heinkel He.111Z was created by actually joining two pre-existing He.111 bombers through a new wing center section that also carried a fifth engine.

Like the Fokker K-I and T-M MB-4, each fuselage had its own set of tail surfaces. The right-hand unit of the pair had its left wing removed outboard of the engine and the left-hand one had its right wing removed. The two were then joined by a flat center wing section that was fitted with the fifth 1,350-hp Jun-

kers Jumo engine at the center point. The centerlines of the fuselages were 42 feet apart, making the He.111Z the widest twin-fuselage model ever (FIG. 9-9).

Twelve Zwillings were assembled and saw limited use, mostly in the Russian campaign. The problem of towing the Me-321 glider was resolved when it was fitted with six 750-hp captured French Gnome-Rhome engines and became the Me-323 cargo plane, but some Me-321s remained gliders and still needed their zwilling tugs.

Specifications: Span 116 feet 1.66 inches; area 1,587 square feet; gross weight 63,052 pounds; towing speed with one Me-121, 137 mph; 155 mph with two smaller Gotha Go-242 gliders.

North American P-82 Twin Mustang

The North American P-82 Twin Mustang that appeared in 1946 has long been regarded as simply two standard P-51 fuselages joined to create a new model. This is not so. While the fuselages have high commonality with the P-51H, they were designed for the twin installation, not merely adapted.

The P-82 (F-82 after July 1948) was intended as a

long-range escort fighter. Early models were powered with the American-built version of the British Rolls-Royce Merlin engine, but the P-82E and on used the 1,600-hp Allison V-1710-143/145. The double dash numbers indicate opposite rotation of otherwise identical engines in the same airplane, as on the P-38.

The P-82 was like the MB-4 and the He-111Z in having crew in each fuselage, but the fuselages were joined at the rear by the horizontal tail surfaces (FIG. 9-10). While both cockpits were fitted with flight controls, the designated pilot flew from the left. In most fighter operations, a radar operator was on the right. Armament consisted of six .50-caliber machine guns in the center section of the wing, plus others in an optional centerline pod. The night fighter variants carried a large radar pod under the center section. Twin Mustangs recorded some notable firsts and lasts. It was the first USAF plane to down a North Korean aircraft in

Fig. 9-10. The North American P-82 Twin Mustang of 1945 used fuselages similar to those of the famous P-51 Mustang, but they were not actual P-51 components.

that conflict and it was the last piston-engined fighter model acquired by the U.S. Army/Air Force. A total of 272 were built, the last being the P-82G night fighter.

Specifications: Span 51 feet 3 inches; area 408 square feet; gross weight 25,591 pounds; top speed 461 mph at 21,000 feet.

Twin Ercoupe

An example of two stock model airplanes being combined for a special purpose is the 1948 effort that resulted in the twin Ercoupe showplane (FIG. 9-11).

The Ercoupe was built by the Engineering and Research Corporation, or ERCO. The stretching of this acronym into Ercoupe for a two-seat side-by-side personal airplane was logical and easy. The all-metal design, initally with a 65-hp Continental engine and later with as much as 90 hp, went on the market in 1940 and became famous as a non-spinnable "safety" design for inexperienced pilots due to its unique two-control system and limited elevator travel to prevent spinning. It was also the first mass-produced private airplane in the U.S. with tricycle landing gear. Production was suspended during WWII, but was resumed afterward until curtailed again by the Korean War. The design rights were then sold. Since then, a variety of new owners introduced various changes and kept the basic design in production until 1969.

The Twin Ercoupe was put together as an air show novelty by joining two fuselages at the ends of the center section stubs and at the inner ends of the standard

tail surfaces. With the elevator restriction removed, it put on excellent aerobatic demonstrations at air shows.

No specifications are available for this one-of-a-kind machine.

Wagner/Piper Twin Cub

One oddity of the Wagner/Piper Twin Cub of 1949—other than being a marriage of two standard Piper Cubs—is that the two airplanes, FIG. 9-12, were not identical to start with. One was the famous J-3 that had been introduced in 1937 and improved until production ended in 1947; the other was the refined PA-11 version produced during 1947-49. The J-3 was fitted with the enclosed cowling and 85-hp Continental engine of another PA-11 to balance the power and drag.

The two fuselages were closer together than on any other twin, even the Twin Ercoupe (on which the spacing permitted the propeller arcs to clear each other). Harold Wagner, who also developed the Twin Tri-Pacer, used the same propeller-overlap trick to get his closer spacing. A short section of the standard Cub horizontal tail joined the fuselages at the rear, while the fronts were joined by a short center section and a steel tube truss beneath the fuselage that distributed the loads between the two landing gear units, one outboard unit from each airplane. Again, the left-side propeller was fitted with a spacer hub to move it ahead of the other to allow the overlap.

Like the Twin Tri-Pacer, the Twin Cub was a short-lived one-only. The Piper PA-11 of 1948, known

Fig. 9-11. Two Ercoupe lightplanes were joined in 1948 to create this twin-fuselage design for airshow work.

Fig. 9-12. Two Piper Cubs were joined to create the Wagner Twin Cub. Close spacing of the fuselages was made possible by overlapping the propellers.

as the Cub Special, was a slightly cleaned-up J-3 Cub and started with the same 65-hp Continental engine. Power was soon increased to 95 hp.

Fougia Twin Jet

One of the rare examples of a twin-fuselage jet is the Gemeaux I built in 1951 by the French firm of Fougia et Cie. This was created by joining two pre-existing Fougia CM 8R-15 Cyclone single-jet research models, themselves adaptations of an earlier Fougia glider design.

In the late 1940s the firm produced, in addition to twin-engine transports, a series of single-seat sailplanes. The CM 8-15 Sylphe model (for 15-meter wing span, or 49 feet 2½ inches) was interesting in that it featured one of the earliest applications of a V-tail to a glider (FIG. 9-13). With small jet engines becoming available, Fougia found it very easy to install a 220-pound thrust Turbomeca jet on top of a CM 8-15 fuse-

Fig. 9-13. The French Fougia Gemeaux I joined two single-jet research models into a twin-jet four-wheel two-seater.

lage and let the jet blast blow through the V section. This was strictly a research project; the combination would have made a dandy little sportplane with a smaller wing but was far too expensive for an average sportsman-pilot.

Joining two CM 8R-15s to take advantage of twin-engine safety and a two-man crew was relatively easy and resulted in a new model, the CM88R Gemeaux I.

The inner end of each V-tail was shortened slightly to reduce the fuselage spacing, the span was reduced, and the individual landing gears wing modified to make a single four-wheel steerable unit.

Gemeaux I specifications: Span 35 feet 3³/₄ inches (published figure, but appears to be greater in the photo); gross weight 2,416 pounds; top speed 177 mph.

10
CHAPTER

Monoplane-Biplane Convertibles

OVER THE YEARS, MANY ESTABLISHED AIRPLANE designs have undergone major configuration changes to acquire certain desired characteristics and have become new models in the process. Most often, the basic fuselage, engine, tail, and landing gear were retained; the significant changes were made in the wings. Sometimes a monoplane design got a second wing to become a biplane because more lift or maneuverability was needed. In other cases, established biplanes were converted to monoplanes, usually to get more speed. In either case, the changes usually resulted in a new model designation in spite of the high percentage of component commonality.

In a very few cases, the airplane was designed to fly as either a monoplane *or* a biplane according to the requirements of the moment. Most of these were basically monoplanes with provision for the addition of a second wing. Care had to be taken to have the centers of pressure of both wings line up with the center of gravity so that proper balance would be maintained whether one wing or two was installed. On such designs, the additional wing was seldom the same size as the original, so the wing area was not doubled.

While all of the examples presented have worked, their versatility was not as great as expected and none got beyond the prototype stage and into production.

The other approach to bi-mono convertibles is to have two entirely different sets of wings instead of one add-on wing. This allows different placement of each set and a greater change of appearance. The only known operating example is my own homebuilt design, the Fly Baby.

The best-known bi-mono convertibles are illustrated in this chapter, along with a few nonreversible conversions that were made for special purposes.

Curtiss-Cox Texas Wildcat

One airplane that first flew as a monoplane but ended up as a biplane was the Texas Wildcat racer built by Curtiss to the order of a rich Texan, Mr. S.E.J. Cox. This (and its sister ship, the Cactus Kitten) was to represent the United States in the 1920 Gordon Bennett Trophy Race that was being held in France. They had some very advanced features for the time, the most notable being an enclosed cockpit, with the canopy sliding on tracks to allow pilot access. This was to become a standard feature of racers and high-performance military airplanes starting in the early 1930s. The wing struts anchored to the ends of the landing gear axles, and the shock absorbers were built into the wheels (FIG. 10-1).

The Cox racers were designed to be flown as either monoplanes or biplanes. The strut bracing to the high monoplane wing remained the same for both installations. The smaller lower wing attached to the bottom of the fuselage and was supported outboard by unique box struts that were devoid of the traditional incidence wires (FIG. 10-2).

Design and construction of the 400-hp racers was rushed (as so often has been the case of racers) and they suffered from lack of time for careful testing and debugging. Only the Texas Wildcat was flown in the U.S. before the race, and then only with an oversize

171

Fig. 10-1. The American entry in the 1920 Gordon Bennett Race, the Curtiss-Cox Texas Wildcat. On its only test flight in the U.S., it had used a large monoplane wing. The first flight with the smaller racing monoplane wing, shown here, was made after the airplane reached France.

Fig. 10-2. An alternate set of biplane wings was fitted to the Texas Wildcat at the factory, but the airplane did not fly with them in the U.S. These wings were not sent to France with the airplane because another set of biplane wings was hastily built there.

test monoplane wing. With this, it had a top speed of 183 mph and was expected to turn in 214 with the "fast" wing.

Both planes, as monoplanes, were hastily crated and shipped to France, where frustrating delay was encountered with French Customs officials, so there was little time for assembling and testing the racers. The Wildcat was the only one assembled. It made its first flight with the racing monoplane wing in France and proved to be almost uncontrollable. Apparently the biplane wings had not been shipped, as Curtiss pilot Roland Rohlfs reports that the nearby Morane-Saulnier Aircraft factory was called on by the Curtiss team to build a new set of biplane wings.

After one quick hop as a biplane showed that the wildcat had been tamed, Rholfs took off for the short flight to the race site, but damaged a wheel on takeoff. The wheel collapsed on landing, flipping the plane on its back and wrecking it beyond repair. Ironically, the Wildcat would have done well to retain the original "slow" wing—the winning time for the race was only 168 mph.

The Cactus Kitten wasn't even uncrated in France, because there was no time to build another lower wing

for it. To tame it for the 1921 Pulizer Trophy Race in the U.S., it was fitted with *three* wings and placed second at 170 mph, the world's fastest-ever triplane (FIG. 10-3).

Wildcat biplane specifications: Powerplant Curtiss CD-12 of 400 hp; span 25 feet; wing area 145 square feet; gross weight 2,407 pounds; top speed (calculated) 214 mph.

Cactus Kitten triplane specifications: Span 20 feet; wing area 210 square feet; best speed on closed course 170 mph.

Junkers T-26

In 1922, the Junkers Flugzeugwerke A.G. of Dessau, Germany, introduced a unique parasol monoplane sporting model, the T-19. The engine was an 80-hp British Armstrong-Siddeley radial. This enjoyed limited sales in the depressed postwar market. A similar T-23 model with an 80-hp Le Rhone rotary engine was introduced in 1923, but this had a new feature—a lower wing could be added to make it a biplane. With one wing it was the T-23E (*Eindecker*—monoplane) and as a biplane it was the T-23ED (*Doppeldecker*—biplane).

173

Fig. 10-3. The Cactus Kitten, sister ship of the Texas Wildcat, never flew as a monoplane or biplane, only as a triplane.

Because wings were of cantilever construction, no interplane bracing was needed other than struts to connect the two wings near the tips. The idea was not popular at the time, and only the one example was built.

Junkers did not give up on the idea, however, and tried again with the T-26 of 1925. The basic airframe was nearly identical to the T-19 and T-23, but the engine was changed to an 80-hp Junkers L-1a six-cylinder in-line. The different powerplants were responsible for the different model designations of otherwise identical airframes (FIGS. 10-4, 10-5).

The T-26E had a span of 43 feet 2 inches and 231 square feet of wing area. Gross weight was 1,720 pounds and the top speed was 81 mph. The T-26D had

Fig. 10-4. The German Junkers T-26 in its E (for eindecker or monoplane) form.

Fig. 10-5. The same Junkers T-26 airframe with a lower wing added to make it the T-26D (doppeldecker or biplane).

360 square feet of area, gross weight of 1,775 pounds, and a top speed of only 71 mph. Again, only one was built.

Fokker F-V

In the early 1920s, the Fokker Aircraft Company was the leading European producer of single-engine transports (Mr. Fokker had returned to his native Holland after building warplanes in Germany during World War I). These were monoplanes at a time when the biplane was still predominant in all fields. These had their limitations in some areas, however, so Fokker developed the F-V in 1922 as an eight-passenger parasol monoplane with provision for the optional installation of a lower wing (FIGS. 10-6, 10-7). Because the

Fig. 10-6. The Dutch Fokker F-V of 1922 as a monoplane.

Fig. 10-7. The Fokker F-V with lower wing added.

wings were full-cantilever, as on the Junkers, there was no need to add the usual flying and landing wires to the biplane. (In fact, it was a wartime association with Junkers that sold Fokker on cantilever wing construction in the first place.) The engine was a 360-hp British Rolls-Royce Eagle.

Span of the monoplane wing was 52 feet 6 inches, with 480 square feet of wing area. The lower wing added another 260 square feet. Cruising speed as a monoplane was 118 mph and 112 mph as a biplane. The useful load as a biplane was 2,650 pounds, but only 2,000 pounds as a monoplane.

The F-V was successful in both configurations, but not enough to win production orders. The single example was sold to a Russian airline that operated it as a biplane.

Curtiss XF13C-1/2

The U.S. Navy was reluctant to adopt monoplane fighters for operation from its aircraft carriers for several years after the Army had moved into the monoplane age. The reason given was that the higher landing speed and longer takeoff runs of monoplanes made them less suitable for carrier operations.

In December 1933, Curtiss flew the XF13C-1, a new experimental fighter built on a Navy contract (FIG. 10-8). Preliminary calculations showed that this landed too fast to suit the Navy, so a lower wing was designed for quick addition to make the aircraft a biplane (actually, a sesquiplane, since the area of the lower wing was less than half that of the upper), the XF13C-2. Because the wings were not cantilever, it was necessary to remove the struts of the monoplane and replace them with the flying and landing wires of conventional biplanes, so the change could not be made as quickly as on the Junkers and Fokker designs (FIG. 10-9). The upper wing had a span of 35 feet and 204 square feet of wing area. The lower wing spanned only 24 feet 3 inches and had an area of 77 square feet.

The plane was completed in the -1 configuration but was first flown as the -2 without changing the -1 designation on the rudder. Performance was unsatisfactory, as might be expected of such an afterthought arrangement. With a 700-hp Wright R-1510 radial engine, the top speed of the -2 was only 210 mph at 10,000 feet. The landing speed figure is not available. The -1, at 4,141 pounds gross weight, topped 242 mph at 10,000 feet.

After other modifications that resulted in a desig-

Fig. 10-8. The U.S. Navy Curtiss XF13C-1 in its original monoplane form, December 1933.

Fig. 10-9. Conversion of the XF13C-1 monoplane to the XF13C-2 biplane required extensive revision of the wing bracing system and replacement of the diagonal struts with wires.

nation change to XF13C-3, the monoplane continued its Navy tests but was rejected. The Navy did not put monoplane fighters into its carrier squadrons until 1939.

Hillson Bi-Monoplane

War encourages the development of all sorts of special-purpose configurations that would not get serious consideration under normal circumstances. One of these was the British Hillson Bi-Monoplane of 1941, which was unique in that it was intended to be both a biplane and a monoplane on the same flight!

The object was to combine the short takeoff and fast climb characteristics of the biplane with the greater top speed of the monoplane. The advantages of having all of these capabilities in an interceptor fighter were obvious, but getting them all into one airplane under the existing state-of-the-art would take a long period of development.

The Hillson design was not intended to be the desired interceptor, but merely to show how the performance could be obtained through demonstration of a low-powered proof-of-concept prototype. The bi-mono was built as a small but complete low-wing cantilever monoplane generally similar to the fighters of the day

(FIG. 10-10). To obtain the biplane characteristics, a 30-foot cantilever upper wing without ailerons was attached to the top of the canopy and stabilized with a pair of short struts on each side (FIG. 10-11). After takeoff and climb to the desired altitude, the upper wing was jettisoned and the plane proceeded as a fast monoplane.

The idea worked, and the performance differentials made it look worthwhile enough to try on an existing fighter. A disadvantage, of course, was that the upper wing could be considered a loss each time, but this was justifiable for a wartime mission.

Slip-Wing Hawker Hurricane

The Hillson Bi-Mono worked well enough to encourage trials with an established fighter plane, so an old Hawker Hurricane Mark I that had been used in Canada and returned to Britain was selected. The 1,025-hp 325-mph Hurricane, which first flew in November 1935, had been the mainstay of the 1940 Battle of Britain. In spite of the appearance of newer designs, updated versions with 1,280 hp were to remain in production through September 1944.

An upper wing, equal in span, area, and planform to the standard monoplane wing, was built. This was

Fig. 10-10. The British Hillson Bi-Mono of 1941 as a cantilever low-wing monoplane.

Fig. 10-11. The Hillson proof-of-concept prototype in its biplane configuration.

installed on struts directly over the regular wing for balance purposes (FIG. 10-12). It was well above the cockpit for two reasons—one, to give the pilot room to get in and out; and, two, to maintain an efficient gap/chord ratio between the two wings. If biplane wings are too close together, the aerodynamic efficiency of the pair falls off significantly. That's why most biplanes maintain a ratio of one or more, the gap begin equal to (or preferably exceeding) the chord.

The Slip-Wing Hurricane was tested, but was obviously not worth considering for production. In spite of its novelty, it has received very little mention in the many extensive histories of the Hurricane that have been written.

Hurricane MKI specifications: Powerplant Rolls-Royce Merlin II 1,030-hp; span 40 feet; wing area 257 square feet; gross weight 8,050 pounds; top speed 318 mph.

Bowers Fly-Bi-Baby

When I designed my homebuilt Fly Baby, I took a different approach to using the same airplane as both a biplane and a monoplane. I intended from the beginning for the airplane to be flown as one or the other, but not by simply adding a wing to a monoplane.

First flown in 1960, the 65-to-85-hp Fly Baby is a conservative low-wing single-seat monoplane (FIG. 10-13). It was an entrant in the Experimental Aircraft Association Design Contest of 1959 and 1960, which was postponed until 1962 for a shortage of contestants. The Fly Baby won in 1962.

Adding a second wing to a low-wing monoplane with straight wings presented several problems. One was that an upper wing smaller than the lower would look odd, because it was not necessary to double the original wing area as an equal-size upper wing would do. Second, the upper wing would have to be directly over the lower to maintain lift location and balance. Because the pilot was seated directly on the center of gravity—and therefore right on the middle of the wing—an upper wing right over his head would, because of the small size of the Fly Baby, leave him no room for getting in and out of the cockpit.

It was necessary to move the center section of the upper wing forward so that, with the aid of a center section cutout, the pilot could get in and out behind the wing instead of under it. The problem with this, however, was that moving the upper wing forward moved all of its lift area forward and put the existing center of gravity too far behind the new center of lift to be workable.

179

Fig. 10-12. A standard British Hawker Hurricane fitted with a jettisonable upper wing for faster climb.

Fig. 10-13. The author's Fly Baby in its standard monoplane form.

180

Fig. 10-14. The Fly Baby biplane does not merely add a wing, it uses a completely different interchangeable set. Note the equal sweepback on both wings.

This situation called for the adoption of one of the oldest tricks in the business—sweeping the outer panels of the wing back to put the lift in proper relationship to the center of gravity. Because it had already been decided that the upper wing didn't have to be the same size as the lower, and had to have sweep, why not build a new and interchangeable lower wing of matching size! This would make the plane look like a biplane that had been designed as such instead of being a mere add-on.

Because the upper wing was so far forward, it would require excessive sweep to correct the lift dislocation with this surface alone, so, both wings were swept back equally, 10 degrees (FIG. 10-14). This gave the Bi-Baby a strong resemblance to those biplane classics, the British De Havilland Tiger Moth and the German Bucker Jungmann. Being non-cantilever, both sets of wings require their own wire bracing systems.

Because there are no performance benefits involved, a natural question is, "Why go to all that effort?" The answer is simple: For recreational flying, some pilots just like biplanes better than monoplanes.

Stinson L-5 Sprayers

All sorts of modifications are made to stock-model airplanes to adapt them for special purposes. In most cases, these compromise the conditions of the standard airworthiness certificate under which the standard model operates and forces it into a Restricted or even an Experimental license.

Such is the case of one World War II surplus Army liaison plane, the two-seat, 185-hp Stinson L-5. While many of these were acquired by private owners and used in their original configuration, others were put to work in such specialized jobs as dusting or spraying crops. The modifications required for this work, plus operating under overload conditions, put them on Restricted licenses.

It was easy to put spray rails and tanks on the L-5 (FIG. 10-15), but the 185-hp Lycoming engine under its tight cowling was not too well suited to the work. The desire for a bigger load, slower speed, and more power was met in some L-5s by installing a 220-hp war-surplus Continental radial engine, extending and squaring off the wingtips, and adding a lower wing (FIG. 10-16). Because the original monoplane lift struts were retained, the conversion was conceivably reversible and

the biplane L-5 could revert to a monoplane, thereby qualifying for inclusion in this chapter.

Unmodified L-5 specifications: Lycoming O-435 engine of 185 hp; span 34 feet; wing area 155 square feet; gross weight 2,020 pounds; maximum speed 130 mph.

Winters-Ryan PT-22

Another example of converting a standard monoplane to a special-purpose biplane is the World War II surplus Ryan PT-22 trainer modified by air show pilot Cliff Winters.

The stock PT-22 was a low-wing monoplane with a closed-loop system of wire bracing anchored at the top to the fuselage at the upper longerons and at the bottom to the landing gear trusses (FIG. 10-17). In converting to a biplane, Winters shortened the span of two sets of PT-22 wings, joined the upper panels on cabane struts added to the fuselage, and replaced the 160-hp Kinner radial engine with a 220-hp Continental (FIG. 10-18).

As a biplane, the Winters Special required standard biplane wire bracing between the wings. Because the original wires to the landing gear were now gone, the landing gear legs were now unstable, so required additional struts to stabilize them in a classic example of the statement that there is seldom such a thing as a simple change to an airplane structure—there have to be other changes to accommodate it.

The Winters-Ryan Special had a short airshow career—Winters tried to perform an airshow standard, a snap-roll on takeoff, but it turned into a snap-and-a-half. Winters was killed when his plane hit the runway upside down.

Unmodified PT-22 specifications: Kinner R-540-1 engine of 165 hp; span 30 feet; wing area 135 square feet; gross weight 1,860 pounds; maximum speed 125 mph.

Curtiss XF6C-6

Reversing the more common practice of converting an existing monoplane to a biplane, the Curtiss XF6C-6 of 1930 was a standard U.S. Navy Curtiss F6C-3 Hawk fighter (FIG. 10-19) cleaned up extensively for the Navy's entry in the 1930 National Air Races. Because of its mishap, this marked the end of U.S. military participation in civil air racing.

181

Fig. 10-15. A World War II surplus Stinson L-5 monoplane in standard configuration with spray rails attached.

182

Fig. 10-16. An L-5 converted to a biplane, with extended upper wingtips and a 220-hp radial engine replacing the 185-hp horizontally opposed model.

The first of two major changes to the XF6C-6, called the Page Navy Racer because it was flown by Marine Corps Captain Arthur Page, was removal of the lower wing and relocation of the upper wing slightly farther aft to maintain the lift location (FIG. 10-20). Second, a special Curtiss V-1570* Conqueror engine, normally rated at 600 hp but boosted to over 770, replaced the standard 435-hp Curtiss V-1150, or D-12. Other refinements were a new single-leg landing gear and replacement of the "chin" radiator beneath the engine with surface radiators laid on the top and bottom of the wing (as used briefly on the Curtiss service racers and the Curtiss PW-8 fighter of the early 1920s).

The XF6C-6 was leading the field with record lap times of 219 mph when Capt. Page was overcome by carbon monoxide fumes and crashed fatally.

---

*In U.S. military designations, the letter identifies engine cylinder arrangements; V for V-type, R for radial, and O for opposed. The number is piston displacement to the nearest five cubic inches. Some commercial aircraft engines employ the same system of identification.

Fig. 10-17. Standard configuration of the Ryan PT-22, a World War II U.S. Army primary trainer.

Fig. 10-18. Cliff Winters' special biplane conversion of a PT-22 for airshow work.

Fig. 10-19. A Curtiss F6C-3 Hawk, a standard U.S. Navy carrier-based fighter of 1926-30.

Fig. 10-20. The XF6C-6 monoplane racer of 1930, converted from an F6C-3 biplane.

Comparative Specifications

	F6C-3	XF6C-6
Powerplant	Curtiss V-1150 435 hp	Curtiss V-1570 Spl. 770 hp
Span	31 feet 6 inches	31 feet 6 inches
Area	252 square feet	158 square feet
Gross Weight	2,963 pounds	3,130 pounds
High Speed	153 mph	250 mph (calculated)

Bristol Bullfinch

Although not exactly in the "add-a-wing" category of the other convertible mono/biplanes in this chapter, the British Bristol Bullfinch of 1923 does qualify as a convertible with a unique exception: to become a biplane the fuselage of the Bullfinch had to be stretched to make the airplane a two-seater.

Three Bullfinch fighters were ordered from the Bristol Aeroplane & Motor Corp. The first two were strut-braced parasol monoplane single-seat fighters powered with 400-hp Bristol Jupiter radial engines (FIG. 10-21). These (Bristol Model 52) were the first monoplanes ordered by the biplane-minded R.A.F. since 1915. Unconventional features were the use of two underfins with small auxiliary rudders at the rear of a fuselage that ended in a horizontal, rather than a vertical, knife-edge, and a double taper in thickness for the wing, which put a very thin center section at the pilot's eye level for improved visibility.

Bristol had also suggested a two-seat version of the Bullfinch, so the third article on the contract was completed as such, Bristol Model 53 (FIG. 10-22). As provided for in the original design, the rear portion of the steel-tube fuselage unbolted just behind the pilot's

185

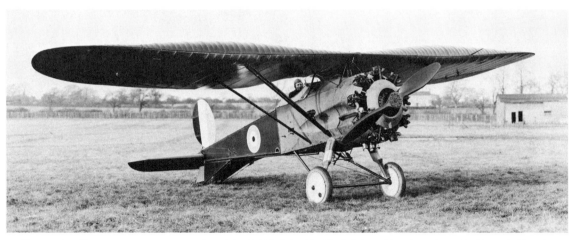

Fig. 10-21. Single-seat monoplane version of the British Bristol Bullfinch fighter. Note the unique double underfins, the double taper of the parasol wing, and the dividing line between two fuselage sections just behind the pilot.

Fig. 10-22. Two-seat biplane version of the Bullfinch, with a new straight section of fuselage containing a rear cockpit bolted in between the original fuselage sections. Added lower wing aligns center of lift with the new center of gravity.

cockpit. A new straight section containing a complete gunner's cockpit was then bolted in between the two separated sections.

To accommodate the rearward shift in the center of gravity that the new crew position caused, a slightly shorter full-cantilever wing was added below the bolt-in rear cockpit. This put the overall lifting area in proper relationship to the relocated center of gravity. Needless to say, there were no production models of the Bullfinch.

11
CHAPTER

Convertaplanes

CONVERTAPLANES ARE AIRCRAFT THAT COMBINE THE vertical takeoff and landing capability (VTOL) of the helicopter with the faster level flight capability and longer range of the airplane. Since it is neither one nor the other, the convertaplane does not have to look like either. As a result, configurations vary greatly. Also, since it is a vehicle that operates in two separate flight modes, it is of necessity a compromise. Some of the features that are useful in one mode may be useless dead weight or drag that must be carried along in the other, and therefore a handicap.

The dreams of vertical takeoff and descent combined with fast forward flight is as old as the dream of flight itself. The helicopter, originally conceived by Leonardo da Vinci in 1500 , is not a true convertaplane in that its rotary wing provides *all* the support during both the forward and vertical flight modes. The successful convertaplane is a recent phenomenon that had to wait for the development of turbine powerplants capable of delivering thrust that exceeds the gross weight of the aircraft in order to lift it by power alone.

ZERO AIRSPEED CONTROL PROBLEMS

All convertaplanes have a control problem not shared by the airplane. On airplanes, with their forward speed, such conventional controls as ailerons, elevators, and rudder move in the airstream; the reaction of the airstream alters the attitude of the airplane. Convertaplanes may have these conventional flight controls for the forward flight mode, but they are useless during vertical takeoff/landing attitudes and hover, when there is no airflow over them.

The convertaplanes must have a second control system for use during low or zero airspeed. Depending on the configuration and powerplant of the craft, this can consist of jet streams initiated by quick-acting valves at wingtips and other points that are activated through the regular control system, variable thrust from multiple direct lift rotors or propellers, or control surfaces located in the slipstreams of propellers or rotors.

CONFIGURATIONS

Convertaplanes are of two basic types, each with its own special problems of power transmission and conversion. The designs shown here have all worked, but most have not attained a sufficiently satisfactory relationship between cost and effectiveness to justify production and use.

Level-Rising Convertaplanes

These remain horizontal in both flight modes. They use the thrust of propellers, rotors, or jets for takeoff and then vector that thrust to the rear for horizontal flight. In the forward-motion mode, the necessary lift is usually provided by the air flowing over fairly conventional wings. In a few, the thrust generators are tilted forward only enough to provide forward motion; they must still provide the lift as well.

Vertical-Rising Convertaplanes

These, called "tailsitters" are aligned vertically for takeoff and landing and rotate through 90 degrees for level flight in which their wings become effective. Needless to say, this type has major disadvantages for commercial operation. The few built have been single-seat military types with either fighter-plane or straight research model designations.

Many convertaplane designs have flown successfully since the late 1940s, but only one—the British Harrier—has gone into mass production because of high cost, technical complexity, or limited range and payload.

An Exception

Some craft that lift vertically and then move forward are in commercial use, however. These are *hovercraft*, not convertaplanes. They lift off the ground or water only to the height where the volume of air escaping beneath the bordering skirt equals the volume being taken in at the top. The are not truly aircraft, so are not detailed in this book.

The following descriptions of significant convertaplanes are grouped by their basically different configurations and are arranged chronologically within these groups following brief introductory remarks.

COMPOUND HELICOPTERS

Before the terrific thrust available from gas turbine engines was successfully applied to direct lift for convertaplanes, the simplest approach was to start as a helicopter for vertical takeoff and then revert to a propeller for forward propulsion. Power was then taken off of the rotor, which continued to rotate as on an autogyro, but pitched to generate minimum lift. Much of the lift for high-speed forward lift came from a conventional wing. Two examples follow.

McDonnell XV-1

In 1952, the U.S. Army and Air Force established a short-lived V category for aircraft capable of vertical takeoff and landing that were not true helicopters (which were covered by the R-for-Rotorcraft designation until 1948 and then became H-for-Helicopter). In 1956, the V category was expanded to include production aircraft capable of merely Short Takeoff and Landing (STOL) as well as VTOL types. The first design tested in this new category was the four-place McDonnell XV-1 (FIG. 11-1). Two prototypes were built. They were designed for specific personnel missions, not as a research experiment. They could carry a pilot and three passengers or two litter patients and a medical attendant.

Fig. 11-1. The McDonnell XV-1 successfully combined the functions of a helicopter and a fixed-wing propeller-driven airplane.

The XV-1, which flew on April 29, 1955, combined helicopter and airplane characteristics in having a rotor plus wings and a pusher propeller. The prop was driven by a 550-hp Continental R-975-19 air-cooled radial airplane engine, but the rotor was not driven mechanically as on other helicopters. High-pressure air from a compressor connected to the engine was ducted to small McDonnell jet units at the tips of the small-diameter rotor. For fast forward flight, the jets were shut down and the rotor auto-rotated in a low-lift setting. After early test flights, two small helicopter-type tail rotors were added aft of each rudder to improve control during hover. Even when the propeller was not used for propulsion, the XV-1 could attain 200 mph as a pure helicopter. Span of the small wing was 26 feet.

Fairey Rotodyne

The heaviest helicopter/airplane combination, the British Fairey Rotodyne, was actually a compound helicopter, not a true convertaplane (FIG. 11-2). The 90-foot rotor supplemented the lift of a 580-square foot wing during forward flight.

First flown on November 6, 1957, the prototype was a 40-passenger airliner and cargoplane powered by two 3,000-hp Napier Eland turboprop engines. In addition to driving propellers, the Elands drove compressors that fed high-pressure air to jet units at the rotor tips. Fuel was injected and burned there. The tip jets were shut down during forward flight and the rotor functioned as on an autogyro.

With 6,000 hp available for lift and thrust, the 33,000-pound Rotodyne was fast, and set a helicopter speed record of 191 mph. Orders were taken for several civil production versions, but these were cancelled and the two prototypes were scrapped in 1960.

TAILSITTERS

The rotation of the tailsitter creates serious orientation problems for the pilot. If his seat is fixed, he is on his back for takeoff and landing. Landing while looking over one's shoulder can be very tricky. Some designers tried pivoting the pilot's seat so that he sat upright with his seat remaining level relative to the horizon regardless of the attitude of the aircraft.

The three outstanding U.S. tailsitter designs are described.

189

Fig. 11-2. The British Fairey Rotodyne, at 33,000 pounds, was the largest and heaviest of the compound-helicopter type of convertaplane.

ConVair XFY-1 Pogo

The first workable tailsitter was the highly unorthodox single seat fighter developed by ConVair for the U.S. Navy as the XFY-1. This was to be a convoy protection fighter, a plane that could operate from a small clear space on the deck of a ship and not need the long deck of a regular aircraft carrier. After a long series of tethered tests, the XFY-1 made its first free flight on August 2, 1954, to become the first successful true VTOL aircraft other than a helicopter (FIGS. 11-3, 11-4).

For the first time, a propeller powerplant was installed in an aircraft having a gross weight less than the available thrust. Because of the necessary smallness of the airframe and the tremendous power of the 5,850-hp Allison YT-40-A-14 turboprop engine, it was necessary to use coaxial propellers to neutralize torque effect. (Actually, the XFY-1 was a twin-engine airplane, but each engine did not drive a separate propeller.) Two T-38 turbine engines were coupled through a gearbox and common shaft to create the YT-40; either T-38 drove both propellers together, but not one alone.

The plane, nicknamed Pogo because its up-and-down movement could be likened to that of a pogo-stick, was a delta-wing type with two large vertical fins. The tips of the wings and fins were equally spaced and were fitted with long-stroke shock absorbers and small rollers that formed the landing gear. Conventional rudder and ailerons were effective during hovering, as they were located in the propeller slipstream.

In anticipation of the orientation and operational problems of the pilot, his seat was mounted on gimbals so that he was nearly level at all aircraft attitudes. While this simplified some of his problems, that of landing an airplane backwards while looking over one's shoulder was extremely difficult. The first flight that transitioned from the vertical to horizontal and back to the vertical was made on November 2, 1954. The Pogo flew successfully, but not well enough to justify continuation of tailsitter development.

Fig. 11-3. The U.S. Navy's delta-wing ConVair XFY-1 Pogo tailsitter convertaplane in flight.

Fig. 11-4. Pogo sitting erect in its two-piece portable hangar.

Of the two XFY-1s, built, one is preserved at the U.S. Naval Air Station, Norfolk, Virginia.

Lockheed XFV-1 Salmon

An interesting contrast to the XFY-1 Pogo is the Lockheed XFV-1 Salmon designed by Lockheed to the same U.S. Navy specification for a vertical takeoff turboprop fighter. It was named Salmon in honor of Lockheed test pilot Herman "Fish" Salmon.

The XFV-1 used a straight wing and had a cruciform tail oriented 45 degrees to the wing to support a tailsitter landing gear (FIG. 11-5). For its initial flights in March 1954, however, the Salmon was fitted with a bolt-on conventional landing gear unit forward; the two lower tailwheel assemblies were modified to accommodate rolling takeoffs.

The XFV-1 did not perform as well as expected and only rolling takeoffs were made. The second of two ordered was scrapped before completion and the development of turboprop-powered VTOL fighters was abandoned.

Ryan X-13 Vertijet

A pair of tailsitters that didn't really sit were built by Ryan for the U.S. Air Force in 1955. A delta wing design powered by a British Rolls-Royce Avon turbojet

Fig. 11-5. The Lockheed XFV-1 Salmon had a cruciform tail assembly oriented 45 degrees to the wing.

engine of 10,000-pounds thrust, the Vertijets were X-13 in the Army/Air Force X-for-Experimental series.

Since there was no propeller slipstream passing over the conventional control surfaces for control at zero airspeed, the Vertijet used a movable tailpipe to deflect the jet and keep the plane properly aligned. For the initial test flights, starting in December 1955, a bolt-on tricycle landing gear was used to allow conventional rolling takeoffs and landings.

For vertical operation, the Vertijet used what was undoubtedly the world's most unusual airport. The plane did not rest on the ground like a bird, it took off from and landed on a wall like a fly. The "airport" was a trailer on which the flat bed could be elevated by hydraulic jacks to the vertical position. Near the top was a heavy cable stretched between two posts. The Vertijet was attached to the cable by a hook under the nose. Since this was "under" the plane, the pilot could not see it. He was guided into position for his hook-on landing by a controller at the top of the wall who talked him in by radio. There was also a 20-foot wand that projected outward from the top of the wall. Proper alignment with the wand kept the plane centered and reference to the number of stripes on the wand told the pilot how far out he was (FIG. 11-6).

The first flight was made on December 10, 1955,

Fig. 11-6. Because of its jet engine, the Ryan X-13 Vertijet could not take off vertically from the ground. It operated from a hook projecting from a wall.

Fig. 11-7. For test purposes, the Ryan Vertijet made rolling takeoffs on a conventional landing gear.

194 using a bolt-on tricycle landing gear for a rolling take-off and conventional flight (FIG. 11-7). The first vertical/horizontal/vertical flight was made on April 11, 1957. With a thrust-to-weight ratio of 1.3:1, vertical operations were successful, but further development of tailsitter jets was abandoned. One of the Vertijets was put to good use for several subsequent years as a traveling static Air Force exhibit at major air shows. It is now preserved at the Air Force Museum in Dayton, Ohio. The other is owned by the National Air and Space Museum.

Approximate Vertijet specifications: Span 21 feet; length 24 feet; gross weight 7,500 pounds. Accurate specifications and performance figures were not published.

TILTING WINGS

Tilt-wing aircraft combine the VTOL capability of the helicopter with a relatively conventional multi-engine airplane on which the engines are mounted on the wing and are fixed relative to the chord. The objective is to achieve the speed, range, and cargo capacity of the airplane with helicopter takeoff and landing capability.

For takeoff, the wing is aligned vertically and the propellers lift the plane on sheer power. The wing is gradually lowered to the level position for transition to level flight; all lift then comes from the wing and the propellers provide propulsion only.

Several U.S. manufacturers and one Canadian built experimental tilt-wings; the heaviest and most successful is presented here.

Hiller-Ryan-Vought XC-142A

The unique four-engine XC-142A, jointly developed by Vought, Ryan, and Hiller, was designated in the regular Air Force C-for-Cargo series. It also marked the end of the line for the Army/Air Force C-series that originated in 1925; rather than go to higher numbers, the new combined services system of 1962 started over again with a new C-1.

Except for somewhat distorted proportions, the XC-142A resembled a conventional transport airplane. The entire wing, which supported the four 2,850-hp General Electric T-64-1 turboprop engines, rotated from the normal horizontal position to full vertical (FIGS. 11-8, 11-9). As the wing tilted up, the horizontal tail tilted down at the trailing edge. Low-speed trim control was by a tail rotor in a horizontal plane.

Fig. 11-8. The four-engine Hiller-Ryan-Vought XC-142A with its wing tilted to the vertical takeoff position.

Fig. 11-9. A composite photograph of the XC-142A in full transition from vertical to horizontal flight.

With first flight on September 29, 1964, the XC-142A worked well—better than many other convertaplanes. Although five were eventually built, the design was not placed in production; it was more economical to simply build bigger and faster helicopters for the mission.

XC-142A specifications: Span 67 feet 6 inches; wing area 534 square feet; gross VTOL weight 37,474 pounds; gross STOL weight 44,500 pounds; top speed 431 mph at 20,000 feet.

TILTING ROTORS

The tilting rotor (or propeller) type of convertaplane has proven to be the most-used configuration, at least among the experimental models. A disadvantage of some, when competing with helicopters in small takeoff and landing areas, is the necessarily wide span resulting from two large-diameter rotors mounted side-by-side.

Many convertaplanes use multiple engines driving individual rotors or propellers, so the loss of power from one engine to its corresponding rotor while in flight could be disastrous. To prevent this, some multiengine convertaplanes resort to cross-shafting, in which if one engine cuts out, the affected rotor can be driven by an engine other than its own.

Curtiss-Wright X-100

Instead of tilting wing-mounted engines as on the XC-142A, the privately funded Curtiss-Wright X-100

used two of what are called *lifting propellers* rather than rotors for direct lift; it then rotated them forward to provide propulsion. The single-seat X-100 (no relation to aircraft in the Army/Air Force X-series) was a low-cost test vehicle to determine the feasibility of a tilting rotor system (FIG. 11-10).

Power was provided by a single 825-hp Lycoming YT-53L-1 turboprop engine in the fuselage driving the tilting propellers. Trim at hover and low speed was by means of the turbine exhaust through a controllable nozzle in the tail.

First flight was in March 1960. Performance was marginal and the tail duct control was barely adequate, but the X-100 proved its concept to be workable and encouraged the development of the much larger C-W X-19A. The X-100 is presently preserved by the National Air and Space Museum of the Smithsonian Institution.

Specifications: Span to tips of propellers 25 feet; gross weight 3,729 pounds; top speed 240 mph.

Curtiss-Wright X-19

The limited success of the Curtiss-Wright X-100 encouraged the development of a larger design with potential service use, the X-19. Two were ordered under a U.S. Air Force contract, but only one was delivered. This had a six-seat airplane-like fuselage fitted with two short-span tandem wings, each having a tilting lift-propeller at the tip.

The X-19 was powered by two 2,000-hp Lycoming T-55 turboprop engines. Each drove two 13-foot pro-

Fig. 11-10. Curtiss-Wright X-100 was a low-cost proof-of-concept design with two lifting propellers.

196

Fig. 11-11. The Curtiss-Wright X-19 featured four tilting propellers at the ends of short fixed wings.

pellers, but cross-shafting made it possible for one engine to drive all four if one engine failed (FIG. 11-11). Propeller speed was 1,203 rpm for vertical flight and 955 rpm for cruise. Control was by lift modulation at low speed—pitch change on the propellers (but not to full force reversal as on a helicopter tail rotor) and by rudder and ailerons in level flight.

The first flight was made on June 26, 1964, but as with the X-100, the performance was not notably successful. The X-19 crashed on August 25, 1965, to close the era of aircraft development for the famous Curtiss-Wright Corporation that resulted from the 1929 merger of the Curtiss and Wright organizations.

Specifications: Wing span 34 feet 6 inches; length 44 feet 5 inches; area of forward wing 5,511 square feet; area of rear wing 9,815 square feet; gross weight 14,750 pounds.

Bell X-22A

The Bell X-22A is another four-tilt-propeller convertaplane that is included here to show state-of-the-art advances over the C-W X-19. Instead of two engines, the X-22A used four 1,250-hp General Electric YT-58-8 engines, one for each propeller but cross-shafted so that any one could be driven by other that its own engine. Two were built on a joint U.S. Army/Navy/Air Force contract.

As with the X-19, control was by means of thrust modulation through propeller pitch change, but the efficiency of the propellers was greatly enhanced by surrounding them with shrouds (FIGS. 11-12, 11-13). Controllability was improved further by installing elevons in the slipstreams of all four propellers. First flight was on March 17, 1966.

Specifications: Wing span 39 feet 3 inches; gross weight 15,980 pounds; estimated top speed 325 mph.

Bell XV-3

The first really workable follow-on to the two-tilting-rotors C-W X-100 was the four-place Bell XV-3, which was built for a U.S. Army/Air Force research program. In its design stages, it had been designated H-33 in the helicopter series, but was switched to the V category. Like the X-100, the XV-3 derived lift and propulsion from two rotors driven by a single engine (FIG. 11-14). These were bona fide rotors, with a diameter of 33 feet, not lifting propellers. The engine was a 500-hp Pratt & Whitney R-985 air-cooled radial airplane unit. There was no cross-shafting as on multiengine tilt-rotor designs. In event of an engine failure, the rotors automatically reverted to the vertical position and the XV-3 could descend in autorotation like an autogyro or a regular helicopter.

The rotors tilted forward to provide propulsion, but some lift was obtained from the 31-foot wing during forward flight. Conventional airplane-type tail surfaces were provided but there was no auxiliary control by air blast as on the X-100. First flight was on August 23,

Fig. 11-12. The Bell X-22A also used four tilting propellers but enclosed them in shrouds to increase their efficiency. Auxiliary control surfaces were installed directly behind/below the propellers.

Fig. 11-13. The Bell X-22A in level flight with shrouded propellers in the full-forward position.

Fig. 11-14. The Bell XV-3 with large-diameter helicopter-type tilting rotors.

1955. The XV-3 worked quite well, but was underpowered with the R-985 engine.

Specifications: Rotor diameter (two) 33 feet; length 30 feet 3¹/₂ inches; gross weight 4,800 pounds; top speed 181 mph.

Bell XV-15

Bell carried on the XV-3 tilt-rotor concept with the XV-15 of 1977, which featured two 1,550-hp Lycoming LTC1K turboshaft engines (FIG. 11-15). While the tilt-rotor principle remains the same as for the XV-3, the application is notably different in that the engines are mounted on the ends of the short fixed wing instead of being in the fuselage, and the complete power packages tilt instead of just the rotors. Cross-shafting permits both rotors to be turned by either engine.

The first of two XV-15 prototypes made its first hover flight on May 3, 1977, and the first transition to full airplane flight was made by the second prototype on July 24, 1979. The test program was highly successful.

In view of the high cost of developing entirely new aircraft, Bell teamed up with Boeing Helicopters to develop the Bell/Boeing V-22. At 60,000 pounds with two 6,150-hp Allison T-406 engines turning 38-foot

Fig. 11-15. The Bell XV-15 tilt-rotor convertaplane with the wingtip power packages in an intermediate position between helicopter lift and forward thrust for flight as an airplane.

rotors, the V-22 is the largest tilt-rotor so far (FIG. 11-16). Capacity is 24 armed troops or equivalent cargo. U.S. armed forces ordered a total of 957. First hover flight was on March 19, 1989.

XV-15 specifications: Rotor diameter (two) 25 feet; length 42 feet 1 inch; gross weight 13,000 pounds; high speed 382 mph.

DEFLECTED PROPELLER OR JET SLIPSTREAM

This type of VTOL aircraft, in which the slipstream of horizontally aligned propellers was deflected downward by large wing flaps, was short-lived. The concept worked, but there were more efficient ways of using the available power to do the job. Only one example is presented here.

Ryan VZ-3

The first successful example of a deflected-slipstream VTOL was the Ryan VZ-3, a design for the U.S. Army and Air Force in the new VZ series for VTOL research inaugurated in 1956.

The single-seat VZ-3 was a pure research design. Power was supplied by a 785-hp Lycoming YT53-L-1 turboprop engine in the fuselage driving two large outboard propellers; their arcs extended beyond the tips of the wing. The wing was fitted with full-span double flaps that could be lowered 90 degrees to deflect the propeller slipstream. To avoid slipstream spillage under the wingtips, large fences were installed (FIGS. 11-17, 11-18). For control during hover and low-speed flight, compressed air ducts were installed in the tail.

First flight of the VZ-3 was on February 7, 1958, and the program continued for several years, during which minor modifications were made to the airplane. With nearly 800-hp available and an aircraft gross weight of only 2,600 pounds, one wonders if the VZ-3 wouldn't have worked better if the propellers were changed to tilting rotors for direct lift instead of using deflected thrust. However, the purpose of the design was to evaluate that particular configuration, not to develop an efficient VTOL aircraft as such.

Specifications: Span 23 feet 5 inches; length 27 feet 3 inches; gross weight 2,600 pounds. Performance figures not published.

Fig. 11-16. First-flight photograph of the Bell/Boeing V-22, the world's first production-model, tilt-rotor convertaplane.

Fig. 11-17. The Ryan VZ-3 deflected-slipstream VTOL with flaps fully extended.

Fig. 11-18. The VZ-3 in level flight with flaps retracted. Note the upward orientation of the propeller thrust lines.

DIRECT JET LIFT

Convertaplanes using pure turbojet power instead of tilting rotors or propellers still followed the same principle—vectoring the thrust after takeoff to obtain forward motion. This was accomplished in two ways—by rotating the jet engines or by deflecting the jet blast of a rigidly-mounted jet or jets through movable nozzles. One significant example of each, plus a milestone intermediate design, is presented here.

Bell Jet VTOL

The first VTOL aircraft to fly successfully on jet propulsion alone was the unnamed Bell VTOL of 1954. This is a prime example of a simple proof-of-concept prototype assembled from available components. The metal fuselage and vertical tail were from a Schweizer 1-23 glider, the wing was from a Cessna 140A lightplane, and the landing gear came from a Bell Model 47 helicopter (FIG. 11-19). The powerplants were two 1,000-pound thrust Fairchild J-44 jets borrowed from the U.S. Air Force.

The jets were pivoted on each side of the fuselage for lift and propulsion. Control at hover and low speed was by compressed air from a separate turbo compressor ducted to discharge nozzles at the wingtips and tail.

First flight was on November 16, 1954. The thrust of the jets was barely over the gross weight of the plane for vertical flight, but was excessive for horizontal flight—it was difficult to throttle down enough to keep from exceeding the airspeed limitation on the hybrid airframe. The Bell VTOL proved its point; the company then abandoned that approach to VTOL flight and tried other approaches (see XV-3 and X-22).

Rolls-Royce Flying Bedstead

While it is hard to visualize the British Rolls-Royce Flying Bedstead of 1958 as any kind of a recognizable aircraft, it was very important to the development of later jet-powered convertaplanes. It was built to prove or disprove just one thing—that deflected jet thrust could raise an aircraft vertically. As such, it is an excellent example of a simple proof-of-concept test vehicle.

Fig. 11-19. The twin-jet Bell VTOL was assembled from existing aircraft components to serve as a low-cost, proof-of-concept prototype for direct jet lift.

Officially, it was called a Thrust Measuring Rig, or TMR, and was powered by two Rolls-Royce Nene turbojet engines in the 10,000-pound thrust class with their axes horizontal. The vertical thrust was obtained by deflecting the jet blast downward. It was known that direct thrust could lift an aircraft of the proper weight; the question was whether the jet blast could be mechanically deflected as much as 90 degrees without significant loss of thrust and still do the job. The TMR proved that it could on October 25, 1958 (FIG. 11-20).

The Bedstead was not intended to fly high, but when off the ground it needed effective control. This was provided by four ducts and nozzles utilizing bleed air from the compressor stages of the jets—two for pitch control and two for roll.

Hawker/BAC Harrier

The first deflected-jet VTOL aircraft to enter regular service, and the most famous, is the British Aircraft (formerly Hawker) Harrier. This single-seat fighter has had a long history of development prior to service and

is representative of the long development time required to design and perfect modern high-technology aircraft. The use of the new vectored-thrust system of lift and propulsion further complicated the development problems.

Development started in 1958 with the first of six Hawker P.1127 prototypes. This used a single 11,500-pound thrust Bristol-Siddeley turbojet engine fitted with four deflection nozzles. The position of the engine in the fuselage dictated the use of a tandem landing gear with outriggers on the wing similar to the Boeing B-47 arrangement. Control at hover and low speed was by "puffer jets" in the nose, tail, and wingtips.

The first hover flight was on October 21, 1960, and the first transition from hover to full forward flight was in September 1961. Thanks to the range of the deflector nozzles, the P.1127 could not only take off vertically, it could fly backwards even sideways like a helicopter (FIG. 11-21). The subsequent performance encouraged the building of additional test and development models with increased power (15,500-pounds thrust) that were named Kestrel. These were followed

204

Fig. 11-20. The British Rolls-Royce Flying Bedstead proved the practicability of deflected jet thrust for direct-lift aircraft.

Fig. 11-21. The British Hawker Harrier fighter is the best-known aircraft to use deflected jet thrust for lift. This is the U.S. Marine Corps' AV-8 version hovering.

by production models named Harrier and Sea Harrier that became operational on April 1, 1969. The Hawker firm had since been absorbed by British Aerospace, so the airplane became the BAC Harrier. The Harrier is still in production in England and is being built in the United States as the AV-8 for the U.S. Marines (A for Attack; Model Eight; the V was added to show similarity to, but not inclusion in, the V for S/VTOL series). The British carrier-based model acheived world-wide fame from its performance in the Falkland Islands War of 1982.

While the Harrier can make vertical takeoffs from small clear areas, its gross weight must be kept below the thrust of the engine. This puts a severe limit on range (because of fuel) and military load. Greater loads can be carried when the Harrier makes a rolling take-off, so the Sea Harriers are normally based on aircraft carriers.

This operation is unique in itself. At the end of the rolling start, the Harrier is deflected into an increased nose-up attitude by means of a curved "ski-jump" ramp at the bow of the carrier.

Specifications, Harrier Mark 3: Powerplant Rolls-Royce Pegasus 103 21,500-pound thrust; span 25 feet 3 inches; wing area 201 square feet; maximum rolling takeoff weight 25,000 pounds; top speed 737 mph; climb to 40,000 feet 2 minutes 22 seconds.

Dornier Do.31E

Dornier introduced an experimental VTOL transport in 1967, the Do.31E (FIG. 11-22). This was a two-pilot military transport with accommodation for up to 36 fully-equipped troops or a variety of military cargo. The Do.31E utilized both vectored-thrust and direct-lift jets for vertical takeoff. The main powerplants, carried in two nacelles under the wing, were 15,500-pound-thrust British Siddeley Pegasus jets with vectored thrust nozzles as on the Harrier. These were used for both vertical takeoff and for cruising flight. To assist the vertical takeoff and landing, eight 4,400-pound-thrust Rolls-Royce RB.162 direct-lift jets were installed in two streamlined pods on the wingtips. Once the Do.31E was aloft and had the 153 mph forward speed necessary to sustain it on the lift of its relatively small wing, the wingtip jets were shut down and carried along as dead weight.

The two Do.31Es proved to be successful but costly experiments and no production was undertaken.

Specifications: wing span 59 feet 3 inches; gross weight 60,600 pounds; wing area 613.5 square feet; cruising speed at 20,000 feet 400 mph.

CONVERTIBLE AUTOGYRO: *205*

Herrick Vertaplane

Unlike compound helicopters, the rotors of which continue to turn when the aircraft are propeller-driven, the Herrick Vertaplane was an autogyro with wings; it could convert its rotor into a second fixed wing, and vice versa (FIG. 11-23). An American, Gerald Herrick, first tried the idea on his HV-1 Vertoplane in Novem-

Fig. 11-22. The 10-engine German Dornier Do.31E, with two lift-thrust engines in nacelles near the fuselage and eight lift-only engines in pods at the wingtips.

Fig. 11-23. The upper wing of the American Herrick Vertaplane also doubled as an autogyro rotor.

ber, 1931, after extensive wind tunnel tests. It flew as a biplane first, with the rigid rotor serving as a cantilever upper wing, and then as an autogyro. Herrick knowingly departed from Cierva's basic flexible-blade principle and cyclic operation. His rigid rotor was moderately successful thanks to a symmetrical airfoil section on the rotor coupled with a tilting rotor head which generated equal lift around the full circle. The HV-1 was lost on its first attempt to convert from a biplane to an autogyro in flight.

Herrick's second venture was the HV-2A, now called the Vertaplane, with a notably smaller rotor/upper wing. This flew in 1937. It was able to successfully convert from biplane to autogyro, but had other aerodynamic problems that interfered with perfection of the concept. World War II ended development of the HV-2A, which is now preserved in the National Air and Space Museum.

12
CHAPTER

Flying Automobiles

ONE OF THE MAJOR DRAWBACKS TO WIDER USE OF THE small airplane for business or pleasure is the need to keep it at an airport that is a long way from both home and the desired destination. Getting the plane to either of these places from the airport has long been a subject of concern. In fact, the U.S. Army's 1908 specification for its first airplane required that it be easily dismantled for transportation on a standard horse-drawn Army wagon.

Two basic approaches have been made to the problem since the airplane became a practical vehicle in World War I. The first is to build a vehicle that is primarily an automobile and fit it with wings and tail; the second is to make a relatively conventional airplane "roadable." Each has its advantages and disadvantages. Being a compromise vehicle, however, the flying car or roadable airplane sacrifices some desirable characteristics of one mode to acquire needed characteristics of the other.

ADVANTAGES

By keeping his airplane at home, the owner is able to save on hangar cost and the need for a separate vehicle in which to drive to the airport. Also, if bad weather is encountered on a trip, he can land (presumably on or adjacent to the highway) and continue on the ground if he has the type of machine that retains its wings during ground operation.

DISADVANTAGES

These far outweigh the advantages. One, of course, is the mechanical complexity and cost of combining the functions of two basically different vehicles.

Two, the weight problem becomes serious and, for most designs built so far, the useful load is quite small relative to the power and cost of the vehicle. Performance is also low relative to the power available, and neither vehicle performs nearly as well nor as economically as its "pure" equivalent of the same weight or horsepower.

Another disadvantage is the necessarily light structure as a car and overweight condition as an airplane. Without the heavy frames of automobiles, the hybrids can suffer extensive damage in accidents that would merely be "fender benders" in a car. The light structure also offsets roadability, especially on designs where the wings stay with the vehicle on the ground. Strong winds can easily blow the vehicle off the road.

An area that few people consider when discussing such vehicles is the legal end. The licensing requirements are terrific, combining *all* of the federal and state licenses and paperwork required for *both* vehicles.

Further, one still has to fly from established airports these days; it is illegal to land on roads and highways. Any off-airport landing has hazards, and one can even get into trouble by landing in a farmer's field these days if the farmer wants to make something of it.

Other disadvantages are the fact that the mechanic at the corner garage cannot make even simple repairs to the airframe of a certificated aircraft engine or system, and you cannot teach your kids to fly it without having a flight instructor rating on your pilot license. Also, the leave-the-wings-at-the-airport types can't simply land when the weather gets bad, drive on for a while, and then fly again when the weather breaks. They must eventually return to where they left the wings. Few of the flying automobiles developed so far have the capability for road trips of several hundred miles.

WINGED AUTOMOBILES

The earliest approach (and still a popular one) involved putting wings on a lightweight car. The wings were a part-time auxiliary, not a permanent part of the vehicle. As such, they were removed and stayed at the airport when the car was driven home. This of course is a handicap in requiring airport storage space, plus the time and effort involved in attaching the wings and tail. If significant rigging and adjustment is involved, a mechanic's sign-off may be required.

Some of these use two powerplants, one for ground operation and another for flying. This of course is both a weight and cost handicap, and requires two types of gasoline—regular or premium for the auto engine and and aviation-grade for the certificated airplane engine. The two-fuel problem is being minimized somewhat by the current movement to permit older airplane engines to operate on autogas because of the difficulty in obtaining 80-87 octane aviation fuel.

A few designs have used one engine for both operations, disconnecting the propeller and transmitting the engine power to the wheels. This is a problem because the aircraft power requirement is so much higher than that for the car. Further, an air-cooled airplane engine has serious cooling problems when buried in a car body and idling in traffic with no ram-air cooling.

ROADABLE AIRPLANES

This approach is to modify a relatively conventional airplane so that the wings can be folded for road travel. Other things must be added, such as more effective brakes and steering, brake lights and turn signals, a horn, and bumpers. Additionally, the propeller is not only very inefficient for surface travel, it is also a multiple hazard. Some builders have put temporary wire guards around them, but the wind blast is a menace to pedestrians, litter on the road, and other vehicles. Some designs bypass the propeller and direct the power to the wheels, thereby adding to the complexity and cost.

While many different winged automobiles and roadable airplanes have been built—and some even certificated—none have gotten into production.

Curtiss Autoplane

The first serious effort toward producing an automobile that could fly was made by the American Cur-

tiss Aeroplane & Motor Company. The Autoplane was exhibited at the Pan-American Aeronautic Exposition, held in New York City in February 1917.

The three-seat automobile body was built of aluminum. The pilot/chauffeur sat alone at the front of the cabin with two passengers side-by-side behind him. A 100-hp Curtiss OXX airplane engine in the car-like nose drove the rear wheels through a gearbox and shaft. An extension shaft from the engine turned pulleys at the rear of the body that drove a high-mounted four-blade propeller through belts or chains. An oddity was the reappearance of small canard surfaces, not used by Curtiss since 1912, above the front wheels (FIG. 12-1).

Curtiss' talent for adapting major components of one aircraft for use on another was reflected in the use of standard Model L triplane wings. Because of the pusher propeller, the tail surfaces were carried on two wire-stabilized booms.

The Autoplane, Curtiss Model 11, flew briefly but not well, and was quickly abandoned.

Specifications: Wing span 40 feet 6 inches; speed range as an airplane 45-65 mph.

Waterman Arrowbile

American interest in flying automobiles lagged from Curtiss's 1917 effort until 1938, when Waldo Waterman, a long-time airplane designer of note, introduced his new Arrowbile. This was a minor redesign of his original 1935 tailless Arrowplane pusher entry in the government's design contest for low-cost personal airplanes.

Waterman's entry did win, so he developed something more versatile, the very similar Arrowbile with a fuselage that could be separated from the wings to function as an automobile. This one even had an automobile engine, a 100-hp Studebaker, behind the two-seat cabin (FIG. 12-2).

Besides weight, one of the long-standing problems of using automobile engines in airplanes has been the usually higher running speed of the auto engine—much too high for efficient use of a direct-drive propeller. Waterman took advantage of Curtiss' old Autoplane system of a propeller offset from the drive shaft to "gear down" his propeller to the ratio of 1:1.94 through the belt drive.

The fuselage was more like an airplane component than a car, with tricycle landing gear—at most, some-

Fig. 12-1. The Curtiss Autoplane of 1917 had a special automobile-like body fitted with standard model L triplane wings.

Fig. 12-2. The Waterman Arrowbile of 1937, a roadable version of the tailless Arrowplane of 1935.

Fig. 12-3. Waldo Waterman and the automobile component of his Arrowbile.

thing to use for getting to town from the airport, not general automotive use (FIG. 12-3). Six Arrowbiles were built. Waterman refurbished one in 1961 and presented it to the Smithsonian Institution.

Specifications: Span 38 feet; gross weight 2,500 pounds; top speed as as airplane 120 mph.

Pitcairn Whirlwing Roadable Autogyro

The first significant American aircraft manufacturer after Curtiss to build a flying automobile or roadable aircraft was Pitcairn Aviation of Willow Grove, Pennsylvania. This firm had been the leading U.S. manufacturer of autogryos in the U.S. since 1928 and had made many technical contributions to the type through its partnership with the original inventor, Juan De La Cierva.

In 1939 Pitcairn introduced its Model PA-36 Whirlwing, which looked like a conventional autogyro in that the propeller was in the nose. The engine, how-

ever, was buried in the all-metal fuselage behind the cabin and drove the propeller through an extension shaft (FIG. 12-4). One power takeoff went to the rotor to pre-spin it prior to takeoff and another went to the rear wheel that drove the Whirlwing, with its rotor blades folded, along the road.

The outbreak of World War II ended Pitcairn's work with the so-far-successful roadable autogyro.

Spratt Wing/Stout Skycar IV

Since 1930, famous American designer William B. Stout had been trying to develop an easy-to-fly "everyman's airplane" through his series of Skycars. At the end of World War II he teamed up with George Spratt of the Stout Research Division of ConVair, who had been developing airplanes with movable wings for several years. The Spratt/Stout collaboration, identified as Skycar IV, was built by ConVair when that firm became interested in flying automobiles in 1946.

Fig. 12-4. The Pitcairn Whirlwing, an autogyro with folding rotor blades, that could be driven on the ground by power to the tailwheel.

Fig. 12-5. The Stout/Spratt Skycar IV built by ConVair in 1946.

The Spratt wing was similar to that of the Mignet Flying Flea in being the primary pitch control for the airplane, but did much more in that it was also pivoted in such a way that it could be banked to put the plane in a turn. The wing was mounted above an elongated auto-like body with a buried engine driving a pusher propeller at the rear through an extension shaft (FIG. 12-5). The fixed end fins were used for stability only, not control. With the movable wing, there was no need for elevators, rudder, or ailerons.

This proof-of-concept prototype concentrated more on the aerodynamic details than the automotive. Although this one, for which technical data is conspicuously absent, was abandoned, Mr. Spratt is still developing aircraft with his wing at this writing.

Fulton Airphibian

The first American flying automobile since the 1917 Curtiss Autoplane to have a ground unit that actually resembled an automobile was the Fulton Airphibian introduced in 1946. Robert E. Fulton Jr.,

founded Continental, Inc., in Danbury, Connecticut, to develop and hopefully manufacture it.

As with the Curtiss and the Waterman, the flying unit was left at the airport. A 165-hp Franklin airplane engine was in the front of the two-seat car. For road use, the three-blade propeller was removed and hung on the side of the airplane fuselage. The two units were joined by quick-disconnect fittings; separation could be accomplished in three minutes and hookup could be made in seven (FIGS. 12-6, 12-7). Small outrigger wheels under the wing struts stabilized the air unit after the car was driven away. The first flight was made on Novem-

Fig. 12-6. The Fulton Airphibian with wings attached, ready to fly.

Fig. 12-7. The Airphibian showing the outriggers used to stabilize the airframe when the automotive unit is driven away.

212

ber 7, 1946. After a refined second prototype was built, it received the first Approved Type Certificate (ATC) ever awarded to a flying automobile.

In spite of this milestone achievement, the Airphibian did not find a market. The design was sold to a major lightplane manufacturer, Taylorcraft, but no further development or production was undertaken.

Specifications, FA-3 Airphibian: Span 36 feet 5 inches; wing area 180 square feet; gross weight 2,100 pounds; cruising speed 110 mph.

ConVairCar

Several major U.S. aircraft firms looked into the prospects of diversifying their product lines after World War II, and this included building automobiles. By far the most serious was ConVair, which tested prototypes developed by other organizations as well as building two prototype ConVairCars of its own in addition to the Skycar IV.

These were built by the company's Stinson Division but carried the ConVair model number 118. This had by far the most conventional car unit yet, a complete little two-seater powered by a 26-hp water-cooled Crosley automobile engine (FIG. 12-8). The all-metal air unit was a nearly-complete airplane that fastened to the top of the car through three load-carrying fittings plus

self-connecting control hookups. Powerplant for the air unit was a 180-hp Lycoming O-435 airplane engine.

A novelty of the combination was that the two units came separately. ConVair announced a price of $1,500 for the car, based on a production run of 160,000. The air unit was to be available on a rental basis—drive to the airport in the car, rent the wings there, then leave them at the destination airport, much like a rental trailer.

The first ConVair flew well on November 15, 1947, but crashed on its third flight after the pilot took off with a nearly empty fuel tank. (It is a violation of Federal Aviation Regulations, incidentally, to run out of gas in an airplane.) ConVair lost interest in the car project after this setback. The Stinson Division was sold to the Piper Aircraft Company, which soon liquidated it.

Plane-Mobile

Little is known of the 1947 Plane-Mobile other than the photos and the memories of some who have seen it. It was more airplane than car, with welded steel tube fuselage and fabric covering. An old (pre-1937) 37-hp single-ignition Continental A-40 airplane engine was in the nose and a power takeoff through a shaft drove the oversized tail wheel for road travel. The Plane-Mobile overcame the "wings-at-the-airport"

Fig. 12-8. The 1947 ConVairCar was primarily a small automobile with a separate airplane bolted on top of it.

problem by making them foldable so that the vehicle would always be complete (FIGS. 12-9, 12-10).

One surviving photo, taken in April 1947, shows the Plane-Mobile involved in a ground-loop accident during a test flight. No further information is available.

Taylor Aerocar

By far the most successful of the flying automobiles was the Aerocar developed by Molton B. Taylor of Longview, Washington. His approach was notably different—a complete car unit that carried the wings, rear fuselage, and tail along on road trips in the form of a trailer (FIG. 12-11). The first flight was in October 1949, and seven were built over the next several years. Full FAA certification as a standard-licensed airplane was received in 1956.

The first Aerocar 1 used a 125-hp Lycoming O-290 airplane engine, but the improved 1C used a Lycoming O-320 derated to 143 hp. The propeller was behind the Y-tail at the end of a long shaft (FIG. 12-12). Taylor scored a major breakthrough here, not only for his Aerocar but for all airplanes with long extension shafts. He licked the age-old torsional vibration problem by installing a dry-fluid clutch between the engine and the shaft. This allowed the shaft to slip a little during the load reversals. Some designers in the past, including the Wright Brothers for their chain drives, had eliminated the problem by the use of flywheels that kept the engine end of the shaft "ahead" of the propeller end, but the weight of a flywheel was unacceptable for practical small airplanes.

Aerocar 1C specifications: Span 34 feet; wing area 190 square feet; gross weight 2,100 pounds; top speed as an airplane 117 mph, as a car 67 mph; cruising speed 110 mph; landing speed 50 mph.

Bryan Roadable

An interesting roadable airplane built by an amateur for recreational flying combined with the convenience of home storage was the Bryan II Roadable of 1960. Some major components of a standard Ercoupe airplane were used.

214

Fig. 12-9. The 1947 Plane-Mobile was more a roadable airplane than a winged automobile. It was driven on the ground by power to the tailwheel.

Fig. 12-10. The Plane-Mobile with wings folded. There is no information as to how the propeller was disconnected for ground travel.

Fig. 12-11. The Taylor Aerocar with the airframe component set up for road travel as a trailer for the car.

Fig. 12-12. The Aerocar ready for flight. This was the first consistently successful design with a behind-the-tail propeller driven by a long extension shaft.

216

Fig. 12-13. The homebuilt Bryan Roadable was a roadable airplane that used its protected pusher propeller for propulsion on the ground.

The basic design was a twin tailboom pusher. The modified Ercoupe wing folded upward 90 degrees just outboard of the landing gear and 90 degrees again near the tips. The combination of a pusher propeller inside the booms, plus the box the formed by folded wing, was considered to be a sufficient safeguard for using the propeller to move the Bryan II down the road (FIG. 12-13).

13 CHAPTER

Getting Airborne

FROM MAN'S EARLIEST ATTEMPTS AT FLIGHT, GETTING the machine off the ground and into the air has been a major problem. The early inventors realized that their aircraft could not simply leap up in the air and into instantaneous flight like a bird. Except in the case of helicopters, or hang gliders launching into a stiff wind, the machine had to be brought up to flying speed by a run into the wind—called a *rolling takeoff* as compared to a direct liftoff.

Attaining the necessary speed took some doing, and various approaches were made to the problem. The principal types used by the pioneers, and those still in use today, are detailed in the following paragraphs.

MANUAL LAUNCH

Pilot's Feet The first person to get into the air consistently on man-made wings was the German Otto Lilienthal. He made over 2,000 flights in seven different gliders between 1891 and 1896, all of them from his feet. He would lift his lightweight hang gliders and run down a slope into the wind before taking off. If the wind was in the wrong direction for the slope, he couldn't fly. To overcome this restriction to his experiments, he built the world's first specialized flying site, a 50-foot high mound of earth. From the top of this he was always able to launch downhill into the wind (FIG. 13-1).

The running start down a slope, or a simple step-off from the top of a cliff into a strong upslope wind, is standard procedure for today's hang gliders.

After the evolution of ultralight powered airplanes from hang gliders, the FAA decided they could operate without licenses if they were capable of being foot-launched. One demonstration flight was about the most that some models needed to qualify; after that they used wheels. The foot-launch rule was abandoned in 1982 after the unlicensed types were designated *ultralights* by empty weight—under 254 pounds.

Hand Launch The Wright Brothers made major advances over Lilienthal's designs, notably by going to a much longer wing span. They realized that they could not control such a machine in roll by simply shifting the pilot's weight, so they developed mechanical control, one of their major contributions to flying.

Fig. 13-1. Otto Lilienthal and one of his hang gliders at the top of the artificial hill he had built so that he could always launch into the wind.

They also recognized the need to get up to flying speed, but had no means of achieving it, and so sought a windy site where they could be practically motionless relative to the ground yet have the necessary flying speed because of the steady wind. Their request to the U.S. Weather Bureau for information on such a site resulted in their choice of Kitty Hawk, North Carolina.

Although light in weight, their long-winged gliders were difficult for one man to handle, so they relied on helpers. The procedure was simple: The helpers simply picked the glider up by the wing struts and walked it into the wind (FIG. 13-2).

Wingtip Ropes For those gliders that were bigger than the little foot-launched hang gliders, there had to be something better than lifting them by the wingtips. Again, because of human limitations, a good wind had to be blowing as two helpers pulled on ropes permanently attached to the wingtips (FIG. 13-3). This method was popular in post-WWI Germany during the first year or so of the new sport gliding movement. One disadvantage appeared if one wingman let go before the other—the pull on one wingtip not only could, but often did, pull the glider into a turn that the pilot could not over-control. The glider then slewed into the slope, often suffering damage in the process.

Shock Cord Launch A logical development of the two-ropes-at the-wingtips system was the use of a single attach point on the nose and a few more people pulling. However, instead of four to 10 pulling on one rope in a straight line, the launch crew was divided into two halves, each at the opposite end of a long rubber rope (FIG. 13-4). This was called *shock cord* because of its use for shock absorbers on old-fashioned airplanes. (The British called the rope a *bungee* or *bunjie*.)

This system was quite efficient as long as there was sufficient unpaid manpower available, as in a flying club or a military training operation. A ring at the center of the rope engaged an open hook on the nose of the glider, and did not fall off as long as tension was on the rope. On the command "walk," the two groups walked out ahead of the glider at opposite 45 degree angles while others held the glider back (or it was secured by a rope tied to the tail). At the command "run," they ran and put tension into the rubber rope. At the command "Release," those holding the glider let go (or the tail rope was cut). The glider was then snapped into the air as though launched by a slingshot—which the system actually was. As the rope slacked off, the ring fell from the open hook.

This method was widely used throughout the world right up to World War II and even beyond, but only rarely in the United States. It has now been supplanted almost entirely by auto, winch, or airplane tow.

Fig. 13-2. Wilbur Wright in the 1902 glider being launched by helpers lifting on the wing struts and walking into a strong wind.

Fig. 13-3. Two helpers pull on ropes attached to the wingtips of this 1921 German glider to launch it down hill and into the wind.

Fig. 13-4. Shock cord launching became the most popular method of launching gliders at hillside sites from the early 1920s until World War II.

MECHANICALLY ASSISTED LAUNCH

Catapults Even after aircraft acquired suitable powerplants and could attain flying speed on their own, many still needed help with the initial acceleration. The most logical form of assistance was a minor variation of the age-old catapult. Samuel P. Langley used one to successfully launch his 1896 and 1902 models, but failed to get the full-scale Aerodrome airborne in two attempts (October and December 1903: FIG. 13-5).

The first powered flight of the Wright Brothers had an unassisted takeoff, with the Flyer riding on a dolly that rolled along a wooden monorail laid on the sand. The wind was strong enough to lift the machine when it had very little ground speed. When the Brothers moved back to Dayton, where there was less wind, they retained the monorail system but boosted the takeoff by raising a heavy weight inside a pyramid-like tower behind the monorail. A cable ran from the weight, around pulleys at the rear and front of the rail, and back to the dolly. As the weight fell, the rope pulled the dolly and the airplane forward. The Wrights used this system until they added wheels to their planes in 1909 (FIG. 13-6).

Shipboard Catapults After the U.S. Navy got involved in aviation in 1911, it looked for ways to launch airplanes from ships, and began experiments with catapults in 1912. Nothing came of this until shortly after World War I, when a suitable gunpowder-propelled catapult was developed for use on battleships and cruisers. These could be pivoted to launch a two-seat observation plane into the wind. The planes based on these ships were seaplanes, and could be recovered after landing and relaunched without having to land ashore (FIGS. 13-7, 13-8).

Shipboard catapults were used by the world's major navies until shortly after the end of World War II, when helicopters took over the observation role. Catapults are still used, however, on aircraft carriers. These are under the deck at the bow, with only the bridle that engages the hook on the airplanes projecting through a slot in the deck. These are usually steam-powered (FIG. 13-9).

Jet-Assisted Takeoff The idea of using small rockets to give a short burst of additional power during takeoff was tried in Germany in the mid-1920s, but it was not until 1940 that the Jet Propulsion Laboratory of California developed a practical system of solid-propellant rocket motors that could be attached to the airplane for takeoffs and then dropped after burnout. This was called JATO, for Jet-Assisted Takeoff, and became very

220

Fig. 13-5. The unsuccessful Langley Aerodrome during its first catapult launch on October 7, 1903.

Fig. 13-6. From 1904 through 1908 the Wright Brothers used a falling weight and pulley arrangement to pull their Flyer along a launching rail.

Fig. 13-7. A U.S. Navy Curtiss SOC-3 Seagull being launched by shipboard catapult during World War II.

222

Fig. 13-8. A four-engine German Dornier Do.26 flying boat being launched by catapult for the South Atlantic mail run in 1939. This ship is at anchor.

Fig. 13-9. A U.S. Navy Vought F7U Cutlass being launched by catapult from an aircraft carrier. The carriage is beneath the deck, with only a single cable running through a longitudinal slot and connected to the airplane.

Fig. 13-10. Most spectacular user of the JATO technique was the Boeing B-47, which had 36 solid-powder units built into the fuselage. These were jettisonable on later versions.

popular on both sides in World War II for launching over-loaded airplanes.

After the war, the Boeing B-47 scored another first by being the first airplane with JATO designed in. Eighteen 1,000-pound thrust units were built into the fuselage behind the wing in three rows of three on each side (FIG. 13-10). After takeoff, the burned-out units were carried along as dead weight. Later B-47 models mounted up to 36 units on an external rack that was dropped in a safe area after burnout.

For jets, the need for JATO was largely overcome by the development of the afterburner, but piston-engine models retained JATO for many years (FIG. 13-11). Some civil airliners use it for certain undesirable takeoff conditions at high-altitude airports. The early JATO units emitted great quantities of white smoke; later units were smokeless.

Zero-length Launch The combination of rocket power and catapults was used for instantaneous launch systems for interceptor fighters in Germany late in World War II. Some experimental manned rocket models were launched vertically along guide rails. The system was modified in the U.S. after the war to launch standard jet fighter models such as the Republic F-84 and North American F-100 (FIG. 13-12) at angles considerably less than vertical. Powerful rockets attached to the plane pushed it out of a cradle that held it at the proper launch angle. The rocket motor, in effect a king-size JATO unit, was jettisoned as soon as the plane was safely airborne.

Fig. 13-11. Many Allied and Axis aircraft of World War II were provided with fittings for jettisonable solid-fuel JATO units. This is a ConVair PB2Y-3 Coronado patrol bomber.

224

Fig. 13-12. A North American F-100A taking off from a zero-length launcher with the aid of a jettisonable solid-fuel booster rocket.

TOWED LAUNCH

Auto/Winch Tow for Gliders As gliders got bigger and heavier, and it became desirable to operate from flat ground as well as hillsides, additional means of launching were found. One sill in wide use (mainly in Europe) is by winch. A high-speed drum, usually mounted on an old automobile chassis, winds in two or more thousand feet of steel wire or cable to pull the glider into the air. Altitudes of up to 1,000 feet above the ground can be obtained this way. The glider end of the wire is lowered by an integral parachute after the glider opens its release hook. The winch operator keeps winding in after glider release to keep the falling wire from kinking. A car then returns the glider end of the wire to the starting end of the runway for the next launch.

A minor variation of the winch system is the automobile tow. A car at one end of a thousand or more feet of wire tows the glider into the air, much like a child running with a kite (FIG. 13-13). Again, a parachute is used and retrieved in the same manner as for winch tow. Sometimes short ropes are used for straight-ahead low-altitude training tows along a long runway, with the landing straight ahead. At other times, a short rope is used to launch a glider for a short flight to another point on the airport or gliderport.

Airplane Tow for Gliders After winches and cars became standard items for glider launching, it was logical to consider airplanes for the job. Their major advantage was range and altitude—they could take the glider from a flatland base to a mountain soaring site, or to a higher altitude than an auto-tow or winch-launch could get it (FIG. 13-14).

It was easy to do, and the first known aero tow was made in Germany in 1927. People soon envisioned commercial capabilities, with "trains" of gliders dropping off single passenger-carrying gliders at cities along a long aerial route. This never came to be, nor did the concept of towing several gliders in tandem. Multiple tows were not only successful but commonplace, especially in the large troop glider operations of World War II. Each glider, however, was on its own rope connected to the towplane. In rough air, the glider pilots had enough trouble fighting surges and slacking

225

Fig. 13-13. A Bowlus Baby Albatross sailplane on a short-rope auto tow. Up to 2,000 feet of steel wire were laid out for highwire auto tows on long runways.

Fig. 13-14. A Cessna 170B towing two Bowlus Baby Albatross sailplanes into the air simultaneously. The lighter wing loading of the gliders allows them to get airborne first.

of the towrope; in a tandem hookup, the slack/surge problems were simply multiplied by the number of gliders on the line.

As a variation on one airplane towing two gliders, two, and sometimes three towplanes have been teamed to pull one heavy glider. Two Douglas C-47s were used in tandem for a short time to tow the U.S. Army's XCG-17 glider (see page 255), but the best-known example of multiple towplanes is the troika of three Junkers Ju-52/3M transports, each with a separate towline, used to tow the giant German Messerschmitt Me.321 glider that weighed 75,840 pounds and had a wing span of 180 feet. The Germans soon gave up on the Me.321 and put six 1,140-hp engines on it to create the Me. 323 powerplane.

Although aero tow is now the most popular form of glider launch worldwide, it has not completely replaced the older (and lower-cost) methods—nor is it expected to.

Glider Snatch-launch A variation on an airplane-towed launch of a glider was developed during WWII for retrieving military gliders from areas where the towplane could not make a normal takeoff. The procedure evolved out of a pre-war system whereby airmail planes picked up sacks of airmail from small towns where the plane did not land.

The airplane end of the glider towline was supported by a pair of poles set up about 50 yards ahead of the glider (FIG. 13-15). The towplane then approached at

low altitidue and low speed from behind the glider. As it passed the poles, a grapnel suspended below the plane snagged the towline and the pilot immediately applied full power. An inertia reel inside the plane played out additional towline against the increasing drag of a hydraulic brake to absorb the shock of accelerating a 7,500-pound mass from zero to 100 mph in a few seconds.

AIRBORNE LAUNCH

For various reasons, it has often been desirable to carry an aircraft aloft on or under a larger one prior to launching it into flight. The practice is nearly as old as aviation itself and is still in use.

From Balloons The first practical application was by Professor John L. Montgomery for his tandem-wing gliders of 1905. He adopted the then-popular county fair attraction where an acrobat went aloft in a hot-air balloon, did his tricks on the trapeze, and then dropped to earth by parachute (FIG. 13-16). Montgomery hired an acrobat, Daniel Maloney, to pilot his glider after it was raised to a suitable altitude by the balloon.

Although Maloney's flights could be considered research and development (R & D) of an aircraft, it was also show business, and Maloney wore acrobat's tights when performing. This work came to an end when the glider snagged on the launching equipment and was damaged. It collapsed after release from the balloon and Maloney was killed.

Fig. 13-15. A U.S. Army Douglas C-47A making a snatch pickup of a Waco CG-4A troop glider during World War II.

Fig. 13-16. The 1905 Montgomery tandem-wing glider being carried aloft by a hot-air balloon during a public demonstration.

From Airplanes During World War II, some research into the aerodynamics of high-performance airplanes that could not be conducted in wind tunnels was accomplished by dropping large-scale models from bombers. Preset controls would put the models into a dive and radio transmitters aboard would send data to the ground station before the model crashed.

When research into supersonic flight began in the U.S. right after World War II, the rocket-powered Bell X-1—soon to be the first airplane to exceed the speed of sound—was carried aloft several times under the belly of a specially-modified Boeing B-29 and released to fly as a glider (FIG. 13-17). It was also dropped for most of its supersonic powered flights, as were many subsequent supersonic research planes.

FLY-OFF AIRBORNE LAUNCH

On other occasions, conventional powered airplanes, fully capable of making ordinary takeoffs, were carried aloft on the backs of larger planes and flew off under their own power.

The first such event was a one-only test in 1916. There were no aircraft carriers then, but the British

228

Fig. 13-17. The Bell X-1 rocket-powered research plane carried aloft by a modified Boeing B-29 in 1947.

wanted to send fighter planes after the German Zeppelins that were patrolling the North Sea, far beyond normal landplane range from British shore stations. A single-seat Bristol Scout was rigged to the top of a Felixstowe flying boat, which had the range to get the fighter close to the Zeppelins. The test launch was successful, but the scheme was never put into operation (FIG. 13-18).

It was revived again in 1938 and put into commercial operation. Full-distance transatlantic service with airplanes hadn't started, but the Germans had been using mailplanes catapulted from ocean liners to save a full day near the end of the ship's voyage. England beat that by air-launching a fast Short Model S.20 seaplane from the back of a Short Model S.23

Empire class flying boat (FIG. 13-19). The smaller plane, named Mercury, could fly with mail and enough fuel for the England to-New York run, but couldn't take off with that load. The transatlantic operation started on July 21, 1938. When long-range flying boats could finally make it all the way across, the Mercury operation was redirected to Africa.

Mercury specifications: Four Napier-Halford Rapier V 370-hp engines; span 73 feet; wing area 611 square feet; gross weight 15,000 pounds; top speed 207 mph; cruising speed 180 mph.

Test and Ferry When the U.S. space shuttle was tested in 1977, it was carried aloft on the back of a specially modified Boeing 747 airliner for glide tests. Because the shuttle couldn't lift off from the 747 under

Fig. 13-18. A British Bristol Scout perched atop a Felixstowe flying boat in 1916. The intent was to carry the scout far beyond its normal range to a release point from which it could attack German Zeppelins.

Fig. 13-19. Practical use of the 1916 Bristol/Felixstowe system was made by the British Mayo composite of 1938. A small Short S-20 floatplane flew from the top of a Short S-23 flying boat.

Fig. 13-20. Ordinarily, the U.S. Space Shuttle rides atop the Boeing 747 transport for point-to-point ferry flights. For early test flights, it was released to fly as a glider.

its own power, the 747 went into a shallow dive to a speed greater than the minimum flying speed of the shuttle, which then released its fastenings and glided off (FIG. 13-20).

For trips into space, the shuttle is launched vertically by two auxiliary rocket boosters of 2,900,000-pound thrust each, and is maneuvered in flight by its own liquid-fuel rocket engines (FIG. 13-21). After landing from orbital flight at air bases in the western U.S., the shuttle is returned to the Cape Canaveral launch site on the east coast on the back of the 747.

OVERHEAD CABLE

In 1911, French pilots sought to get a conventional Bleriot Model XI landplane into the air without having to use a conventional smooth surface for a rolling take-off. The plane was suspended from an overhead cable; it ran along the cable under its own power and lifted free when it had flying speed (FIG. 13-22). With the light

Fig. 13-21. The space shuttle is launched and boosted to orbital altitude by two solid-fuel rocket motors. The large object between them is the auxiliary liquid-fuel tank for the shuttle, containing 224,458 pounds of liquid hydrogen and 1,337,358 pounds of liquid oxygen.

Fig. 13-22. A 1911 French Bleriot IX taking off from an overhead cable.

wing loadings and short takeoff runs of the day, the cable didn't have to be very long, so there was no problem of it sagging in the middle.

Although the procedure was successful, nothing came of it until it was revived in World War II as the Brodie Device. For this, a cable was rigged along the side of a ship a sufficient distance out to allow wing clearance for a light airplane of the Piper Cub type. The plane was fitted with an overhead hook that engaged the cable for takeoffs and return hook-ons. Runs could be quite short when the speed of the ship and a headwind were combined.

14
CHAPTER

Slightly Unorthodox

MANY DESIGNS OVER THE PAST YEARS HAVE BEEN thoroughly conventional in most details, but have incorporated some relatively minor deviation from standard that made them distinctive. In most cases, the differences were designed in and the airplanes were built that way. Those that were successful then went into production and their differences came to be accepted as regular features. Others did not survive the prototype stage and are recognized now only as historical curiosities.

232   In some cases, standard production aircraft were and still are modified for special purposes, as for crop dusting/spraying (see Chapter 15) or special cargo as illustrated here. Some of these modifications are reversible—the planes can be returned to standard configuration with little trouble—while other changes are permanent. A broad selection of unorthodox configurations is presented in this chapter.

INCREASED PROPULSION EFFICIENCY:

Ducted Propellers   For years, the engineers have known that the efficiency of the propeller could be improved by surrounding it with a close-fitting shroud. However, the weight and drag penalties of the shroud itself more than overcame the gain in propeller efficiency. Some sought to overcome this by making the shroud a tunnel that comprised the fuselage of the airplane. Although quite a few of these have flown, none have gone into production.

Bertrand Monoplane   This 1910 French "tunnel plane" had several unique features. A single 30-hp engine drove two propellers, one at each end of the tunnel (FIG. 14-1). Further, it was a canard that also had conventional tail surfaces. The ailerons were not on the

Fig. 14-1. The two propellers of the French Bertrand monoplane of 1910 were of slightly larger diameter than the tunnel between them.

42-foot span wings, but at the ends of the canard surface.

Jourdan Monoplane This 1911 French design was less of a "tunnel" than the Bertrand. The propeller, located behind the 50-hp Gnome rotary engine, had a greater diameter than the tunnel, which was above a relatively conventional fuselage (FIG. 14-2). No other details are available.

Stipa-Caproni Barrel Plane In 1940 the Italian designer Luigi Stipa revived the Bertrand tunnel concept and got the famous Caproni firm to build it, hence the name Stipa-Caproni. The engine was a 120-hp de Havilland Gypsy III driving a single propeller. As a tunnel, the fuselage had no room for the two crew members, so they sat in a superstructure on top (FIG. 14-3). The plane flew successfully in 1932, after which the

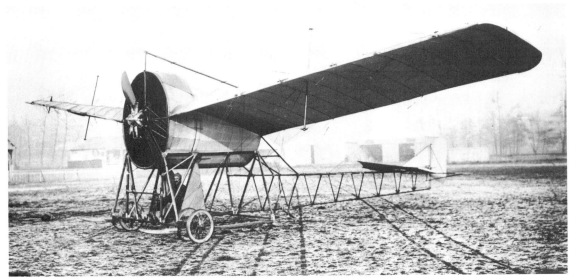

Fig. 14-2. The 1911 French Jourdan had a tunnel behind the propeller that diminished in diameter toward the rear. Note the further oddity of the rotary engine being installed ahead of the propeller, a detail duplicated by several other designs of the time.

Fig. 14-3. The Italian Stipa-Caproni of 1932 had the propeller almost touching the inner walls of the full-length tunnel.

design rights were sold to France. However, the requirements of the war left little time or finances for such far-out experiments and it was shelved.

Bede BD-3 There have been several post-WWII experiments with shrouded propellers in the U.S. Pusher designs seem to be the most suitable configuration for the device, and the Bede BD-3 shown in (FIG. 14-4) is representative. A further oddity of the BD-3 is that two engines in the fuselage were connected by clutches and belt drives to a single extension shaft that drove the three-blade propeller.

All of the shrouded propeller installations so far have been experiments; there are no production examples.

Different Propellers: Cyclogyro A different approach to the propeller problem was taken by the Cyclogyro, which was built in San Francisco about 1930. This paddle-wheel-like arrangement, called a cycloidal propeller, was expected to generate lift as well as thrust (FIG. 14-5). Such propellers, with their blades in a vertical plane, have been successful in boats but not in airplanes.

Fig. 14-4. The American Bede BD-3 had a shrouded propeller just ahead of the tail surfaces.

Fig. 14-5. The American Cyclogyro of 1930 used this paddle arrangement, called a cycloidal propeller.

Fig. 14-6. This 1918 Curtiss Model F flying boat is serving as an ambulance, with the patient on a stretcher strapped to the top of the hull.

235

SPECIAL CARGO MODIFICATIONS

Ambulance Planes   Other than bombs and air-mail, the first specialized cargo for conventional airplanes was a stretcher patient (FIG. 14-6). Since he could not be placed upright in a conventional cockpit, the fuselage of the airplane was modified slightly to accept the prone patient. The practice started in World War I, when the turtledecks of conventional two-seat biplanes were removed to allow the patient to be strapped down on top, but in the open. This was soon changed with the addition of a removable cover. Later, compartments were built into the sides of the fuselage.

De Havilland 4   A more suitable modification for patient comfort was on the De Havilland 4 observation plane shown in FIG. 14-7. There were two litter compartments, one on each side of the fuselage. Several DH-4s were modified by the Army and Navy for this work.

Piper HE-1   The same idea was followed in World War II with the smaller Piper HE-1 (H for Hospital, E for Piper in Navy designations), a minor modification of the three-seat Piper J-5 Cub Cruiser. The turtledeck hinged upward to allow the patient to be placed part way into the regular cabin, where the attendant rode, but his space also extended into the rear

fuselage area (FIG. 14-8). One hundred AE-1s were delivered to the Navy.

Lockheed Constellation   In the old days, cargo that was too big to go through the door of a cabin airplane was sometimes tied on the outside of the plane. Prime examples are canoes carried externally on Canadian bush fliers' planes. If there was no room in the cockpit for the pilot's suitcase in an open-cockpit biplane, he tied it on the lower wing alongside the fuselage.

In post-WWII years, the carriage of external cargo was made common practice through the use of belly cargo pods. These have been used on airplanes from small single-engine types right up to four-engine airliners like the Lockheed Constellation shown in FIG. 14-9.

Fairchild XC-120   The single XC-120 Packplane of 1950 was a modification of a standard U.S. Air Force C-119 Flying Boxcar to evaluate the concept of carrying large preloaded containers without having to load the airplane crate-by-crate. A special podlike container corresponding to a removable fuselage section was developed. This could be wheeled in place from the front of the twin-boom airplane, beneath the pilot's

Fig. 14-7. This 1918 ambulance conversion of an American-built de Havilland 4 has one stretcher in a superstructure on top of the fuselage and another in the fuselage proper with the opening on the far side.

236

Fig. 14-8. The patient occupied the rear portion of the cabin of this World War II U.S. Navy Piper HE-1 after access through the hinged turtledeck.

Fig. 14-9. An external cargo carrier installed beneath a post-World War II Lockheed Constellation airliner.

Fig. 14-10. The Fairchild XC-120 Packplane of 1950 with its removable cargo unit.

cabin (FIG. 14-10). The airplane could fly with or without the pod. Since the removable pod feature eliminated the normal nosewheel previously used, the two main gear units in the boom had to be augmented by two more units in a new quad gear.

Burnelli Lifting Fuselage From 1922 to 1950, the American designer Vincent Burnelli promoted a unique design featuring a widened fuselage built in an airfoil form to provide additional lift as well as increased cabin volume for cargo. He managed to get several prototypes built over the years as he was able to find new backers and firms that would build the planes (FIG. 14-11). None got into production, but one capitalized on the large cabin to carry an automobile on a publicity tour. The last of some seven different Burnelli lifting fuselage airplanes built was completed in Canada in 1947 as the Canadian CBY-3 (FIG. 14-12).

Aero Spacelines/Boeing Pregnant Guppy In the extreme case of modifying a standard airplane to take oversized cargo, Aero Space Lines Corporation modified some Boeing model 377 Stratocruisers by greatly enlarging the upper portion of the double-lobe

Fig. 14-11. The American Remington-Burnelli lifting body RB-2 of 1922. Note that both engines are within the wide airfoil-shaped fuselage.

238

Fig. 14-12. A later form of the Burnelli lifting-body concept, built in England by Cunliffe-Owen in 1939.

Fig. 14-13. In the late 1950s, Boeing 377 Stratocruisers were retired from the airlines and replaced by jets. Some then underwent very unusual modifications, as noted below.

Fig. 14-14. Some Stratocruisers were converted to Pregnant Guppy cargoplanes by rebuilding their fuselages to greater diameter. This version, called the Super Guppy, is powered by turboprop engines.

fuselage (FIGS. 14-13, 14-14). These were used to carry spacecraft components from the factory to the assembly site, and fuselage sections of the French Airbus jetliner from subcontractor plants to the main factory.

Side cargo doors could not be cut into the cargo compartment, so the fuselage was opened up for end-loading. On early models, the rear fuselage section was unbolted aft of the wing and rolled away from the plane on a special cradle for clear access. On another, fitted with 5,700-hp turboprop engines in place of the original 3,500-hp piston models, the forward section (including the complete control cabin) swings to one side on the nosewheel while the forward fuselage rests on a special support cradle (FIG. 14-15).

Fig. 14-15. The nose section of the Super Guppy swings to one side to allow straight-in loading of the cargo.

240

Fig. 14-16. The German Kondor D-VI fighter of 1918 had the center section of the upper wing cut away to improve the pilot's upward visibility.

IMPROVED VISIBILITY

Improving the view of the pilot or observer has always been a prime objective of military airplane designers, and two unorthodox approaches are shown here.

Kondor D-VI This German fighter of 1918 was a conventional design in all respects but one. To improve the pilot's visibility upward and forward, the center section of the upper wing was deleted (FIG. 14-16). This greatly improved the visibility but introduced great aerodynamic handicaps that the designers were not fully aware of at the time. For one, the gap put a big dent in the spanwise lift distribution curve, which normally has its high point right over the fuselage. In addition to the loss of lift, the effective addition of two more wingtips added tip losses and the drag of the additional tip vortices—definitely not one of the better design-improvement ideas.

Blohm & Voss Bv 141 This 1938 German plane was designed specifically to provide an observer with the best field of view possible in a single-engine tractor airplane. To achieve this, he was placed in a separate pod, or nacelle, to the right of the fuselage. To avoid interference with visibility to the rear, the right side of the normal horizontal tail was eliminated (FIG. 14-17). To keep the whole plane in balance, the fuselage was offset to the left of the wing centerline.

The design was not very successful, and only 13 were built for test by the factory and for the Luftwaffe between 1938 and 1943.

STRUTLESS MULTIPLANES

With the advent of cantilever wings, some designers thought they could clean up the classic biplanes and triplanes by eliminating the drag-producing struts and wires. The theory was fine, but in practice it didn't work too well. It turned out that there is considerable force reaction between adjacent wings that puts loads on them that are not present where one wing is working alone. Some new designs that started without struts went into production with them. Four of the relatively few strutless designs are illustrated.

Fokker V-3 Triplane The unique Fokker V-3 prototype of 1917 featured full-cantilever wings (FIG. 14-18). Torsional stiffness was obtained by bridging two closely-spaced box spars with plywood. The plane flew well, but the absence of traditional struts was a psychological problem for the pilots. To satisfy them, thin single struts were installed in the production F-I and Dr-1 models made famous by Manfred von Richthofen, the Red Baron. The struts didn't detract from the performance and it was not necessary to add wires. The Fokker "Tripe" went on to become one of the most maneuverable fighters of World War I.

The Junkers J-I The only strutless biplane to get into actual production was the German Junkers J-I of late 1917, with 227 built. While it had a lot of struts, they only supported the center section and transmitted

241

Fig. 14-17. The German Blohm & Voss Bv141B reconnaissance airplane of World War II featured an asymmetric layout to improve the observer's field of view.

Fig. 14-18. The original Fokker triplane of 1917 had the cantilever upper wing attached by the center section struts only.

landing gear loads; the outer wing panels were true cantilevers (FIG. 14-19).

The J-I (factory designation J-4) was also first all-metal combat plane. The only non-metal items were the fabric on the rear fuselage, vertical fin, and wheel covers, and the wooden propeller.

The primary mission of the J-I was low-altitude attack of front-line troop positions. Because of the small-arms fire that this work drew, the plane was also armored (the letter J identified armored planes in the German World War I system). However, instead of the armor plate around the engine and cockpits being bolted onto the structure after completion, it was designed in as an integral part of the structure.

Specifications: Powerplant Benz Bz IV 200-hp; wing span 52 feet 6 inches; area 533 square feet; gross weight 4,787 pounds; top speed 97 mph.

Christmas Bullet   One of the novel U.S. designs of late 1918 was the strutless Christmas Bullet sesquiplane. It was expected to achieve high speed on only 200 hp with a combination of variable camber, inci-

dence, and dihedral on the upper wing. The spars at the center section were spring steel, which let the wings droop 18 inches at the tip when on the ground and ride 18 inches above the straight position when in flight (FIG. 14-20). The two Bullets each flew only once and managed to crash each time with disastrous results before the idea was abandoned. It seems the torsional flexibility allowed the wing to twist right off.

Darmstadt D.18 and D.22   The German Akaflieg Darmstadt (Darmstadt University Aviation Society) built two interesting two-seat biplanes in 1932 that reflected the latest German high-performance glider technology as then practiced by Darmstadt (FIG. 14-21). The Model D.18 had a 100-hp British Armstrong-Siddeley Genet radial engine and the D.22 had an inverted 150-hp German Argus As.8. As on contemporary sailplanes, the wooden wings were full cantilever, with a plywood-covered D-tube leading edge for torsional stiffness. Struts were used only to attach the upper wing to the fuselage.

Strutless biplanes were not exactly novel at the

Fig. 14-19. The Junkers J-I of 1917-18 was an all-metal airplane with cantilever wings that did not require the traditional interplane struts connecting the outer wing panels.

Fig. 14-20. The American Christmas Bullet of 1919 had flexible cantilever wings that did not require struts.

time, but the little Darmstadts did exhibit one notably unconventional feature—the wings had an extreme stagger angle of 45 degrees. Performance of the D.22 was good, with a top speed of 149 mph at a gross weight of 1,476 pounds and a wing span of only 24 feet 3 inches. The little biplanes were actually design and construction projects for the students at the university and no production was intended.

Fig. 14-21. The sleek German Darmstadt D.22 strutless biplane featured an uncommonly high-wing stagger of 45 degrees.

SPECIAL SEAPLANES

Seaplanes have always had their inherent problems of increased drag due to the floats. Some flying boats have managed to reduce the drag a bit by retracting their wingtip floats, but the conventional pontoon types have been pretty well stuck with the drag of their big "canoes" and the supporting struts. Some attempts to overcome this are shown here, along with some other innovative seaplanes.

Ursinus retractable-float fighter This 1917 effort by the German designer Oskar Ursinus sought to reduce the drag of standard twin pontoons by making them retractable (FIGS. 14-22, 14-23). This quickly reaffirmed the truism that there is no such thing as one major modification to an airplane; other changes have to be made to accommodate it. Since the bows of the floats on floatplanes are normally ahead of the propeller because buoyancy volume is needed that far forward, pulling the floats straight up would cause them to hit the propeller. On the LTG, the propeller was moved forward by putting an extension shaft on the 150-hp Benz engine that was in the standard location.

Dornier RS-IV This German 1918 flying boat, and its 1917 predecessor the RS-III, was unique in the arrangement of its components. It could be called a pontoon seaplane because it had a conventional fuse-lage, but it was also a flying boat because the pilots rode in the flotation component (FIG. 14-24). The RS-IV also introduced the famous *stummelflossen,* short sponsons that projected from each side of the hull to stabilize the plane on the water in place of traditional wingtip floats. These became a virtual trademark of subsequent Dornier flying boats to the end of World War II and were used by such other famous big boats as the Martin China Clipper and the Boeing Model 314.

The location of the four push-pull engines in two nacelles between the hull and the low monoplane wing was a feature unique to the RS-III and the RS-IV. Both models survived the war, but were scrapped by order of the Allied Control Commission.

Besson Quadruplane The French Besson H.5 Quadruplane of 1923 was a conventional flying boat except for the unusual arrangement of its four wings and four engines. The wings were staggered as shown in FIG. 14-25 instead of having their leading edges in the traditional straight line. The four 250-hp water-cooled Salmson radial engines were paired in pusher-puller nacelles built around the next-to-bottom wing. The staggered wing arrangement showed its advantage here in that the rear propellers were ahead of the lower wing trailing edge and were therefore protected from spray during takeoff and landing. The quadruplane was big,

Fig. 14-22. The German Ursinus seaplane fighter of 1917 tried retracting the twin floats as a means of reducing the aerodynamic drag handicap of floatplanes.

Fig. 14-23. Ursinus Seaplane fighter with floats retracted.

with a wing span of 95 feet 1³/₈ inches, but top speed was only 80 mph.

Piaggio-Pegna P.c.7 In the late 1920s the fastest airplanes in the world were the seaplanes built for the prestigious Schneider Trophy Races. Competition among nations was intense, and the accepted way to get more speed out of basically similar designs was to increase the power (see Macchi Castoldi MC-72, in Chapter 7). The only alternate way to get more speed from a given power was to decrease the overall aerodynamic drag of the airplane. On the twin-float monoplanes of the period the only way to accomplish this was to eliminate the bulky floats, with their associated struts and wires. Reverting to the flying boat configuration was ruled out—the type had vanished from the racing scene by 1926.

Fig. 14-24. The Dornier RS IV of 1918 could be regarded either as a single-pontoon floatplane or as a flying boat.

Fig. 14-25. The giant French Besson H.5 of 1923 was a conventional flying boat except for the unique staggering of its four wings. Note the use of a small Nieuport 11 for size comparison.

The Italian Piaggio firm tried something really innovative for the 1929 race. It deleted the pontoons entirely and let the water-tight airframe of its Model P.c.7 provide the flotation (FIG. 14-26). The takeoff run was to be accomplished on hydrofoils, one each where the wheels would normally be on a landplane, plus another under the tail (FIG. 14-27). A 970-hp Isotta-Fraschini engine in the nose was hooked to a conventional airplane propeller through a clutch; the air propeller was not used for the first part of the takeoff because of its proximity to the water.

The engine drove a second shaft from its rear end that turned a small marine propeller below the tail. The idea was for the marine propeller to get the P.c.7 up to near takeoff speed, riding high enough on its foils for the air propeller to be engaged and take over the job.

During trials the P.c.7 got high enough on the foils for the air propeller to be cut in, but the interesting experiment never got airborne.

Specifications: Wing span 22 feet 2 inches; length 29 feet $^3/_4$ inch; gross weight 3,832 pounds; wing area 105.8 square feet; estimated top speed 360 mph.

Blackburn B-20 The British Blackburn B-20 of 1940 was an attempt to produce an extra clean flying boat without resorting to a deep hull or putting the engines above the wing to ensure proper clearance between the propellers and the water. To do this, the bottom of the hull was made a separate structure. This could be lowered on struts, making the plane in effect a large single-pontoon seaplane (FIG. 14-28). The wing floats were retractable and became the wingtips when the one-only B-20 was in flight.

Arado 231 V1 Small pontoon scout seaplanes with various degrees of demountability have been built experimentally for stowage aboard submarines since 1918, but other than a few used by the Japanese in World War II, they have not become production items. One of the most novel, from the point of view of packaging, was the German Arado 231 V1 of 1939 (FIG. 14-29). To enable the two wing panels to fold aft flat without hitting each other, the center section was built on a slant so that the right wing was lower than the left and slid under it when the tiny scout was folded up to fit into a waterproof hangar on the deck of the submarine (FIG. 14-30). Only the single prototype was built.

Convair XF2Y-1 Sea Dart When seen in the air, the ConVair XF2Y-1 of 1954 looked like a conventional delta-wing jet fighter. There was no visual indication such as floats or a boat hull to indicate that it was a seaplane. It did not need these traditional flotation devices because it used watertight wings and the lower fuselage for flotation. At rest on the surface of the water, it looked like a delta fighter that had just ditched and was about to sink.

The drag of the standard V-bottom with hydroplane step was eliminated by omitting these features. Instead, the Sea Dart planed for takeoff and landing on a broad retractable hydroski (FIG. 14-31).

247

Fig. 14-26. No, the Italian Piaggio P.c.7 racer of 1929 has not sunk in shallow water. It was designed to float this way instead of using traditional pontoons.

Fig. 14-27. Ashore, the Piaggio racer displays the hydrofoils that enable it to rise above the surface of the water and the marine propeller that gets it up to planing speed.

Fig. 14-28. The British Blackburn B-20 of 1940 was really a flying boat in that the retractable pontoon formed part of the body when it was retracted. In other respects, it was a floatplane with retractable main and wingtip floats.

Fig. 14-29. The tiny Arado Ar.231 V1 was designed to fold up quickly for stowage aboard World War II German U-Boats.

Fig. 14-30. Arado AR.231 VI folded up. Note the canted center section and the small diameter of the stowed package.

By fighter standards, the XF2Y-1 performed well. Five were built, all on experimental or service test contracts. There was no production.

TINY MITES

People are always striving to achieve the extremes in almost any field of endeavor. In aviation we have not only the fastest airplanes, but also the largest and the smallest. Building the largest is a frightfully expensive operation that can take many years and billions of dollars to complete. Building the smallest is something that a dedicated hobbyist can hope to achieve at little cost.

The term "smallest," however, is open to interpretation. There is the smallest in terms of actual wing span, or smallest in the sense of the least weight or horsepower. Two legitimate claimants to the title with different approaches are presented here.

Coward Wee Bee Designed by professional aeronautical engineer Ken Coward, the Wee Bee of 1948 was proclaimed at the time to be the "World's Smallest Airplane," and by some standards it was. Of conven-

Fig. 14-31. The delta-wing jet-powered ConVair XF2Y-1 Sea Dart running on a pair of retractable hydroskis.

tional all-metal construction and proportions, it was scaled down so far that the pilot could not sit in it—he lay prone on top of it (FIG. 14-32). Wing span was 18 feet and the empty weight was 210 pounds. The size and unique pilot position made the Wee Bee a successful airshow attraction.

Power was supplied by a 20-hp two-stroke-cycle engine as used by small unmanned military antiaircraft targets. This was more than 25 years before even smaller two-cycle engines were added to established hang glider designs to start the new ultralight category, bringing the empty weight to record lows that no man-carrying plane scaled down from conventional structures can hope to match.

Stits Sky Baby Unchallenged claimant to the title of "World's Smallest Airplane" is the Stits Sky

Fig. 14-32. The all-metal Coward Wee Bee of 1948 with the pilot operating it from a prone position on top of the fuselage.

Fig. 14-33. From the point of view of wingspan, the Stits Sky Baby of 1951 is still the world's smallest man-carrying airplane. The 6′ 1¹/₂″ author emphasizes its small size.

Baby (FIG. 14-33). Built by Ray Stits of Riverside, California in 1951-52, the Sky Baby utilized conventional welded steel tube fuselage and tail and wooden wings, all fabric-covered. Powerplant was an 85-hp Continental C-85, and the pilot sat in a conventional cabin. The stubby 7 foot 2 inch biplane wings were so short and stiff that they did not need struts or wires for bracing. In fact, if conventional struts had been used in their normal positions, the pilot could not open the cabin door!

With only 36 square feet of wing area and an empty weight of 452 pounds, the Sky Baby was "hot." Top speed was 185 mph, cruise speed was 165 mph, and it landed at 80.

OTHER UNORTHODOX DETAILS

There have been many other basically conventional aircraft with one or more unorthodox features—far too many to describe here. Seven of particular interest are presented.

Spad A-2 Pusher-Puller By 1916 the Allies had not yet developed a synchronizer gear to allow a machine gun to be fired forward through the propeller of a high-performance plane and match the lethal German Fokker monoplanes that were then ruling the skies. In an attempt to develop a fighter that combined the forward field of fire enjoyed by the clumsy pusher designs of the era with the higher performance of the tractor type, the French Spad firm put a gunner in a pod *ahead* of the propeller in an otherwise conventional tractor design. The pod was supported by struts from the landing gear and a double boom assembly from the upper wing that cleared the propeller (FIG. 14-34).

Widely called the pusher-puller because of the pod ahead of the propeller, the Spad A-2 was actually put into limited production. Its career ended as soon as a successful Allied synchronizer gear appeared and the basic airframe evolved into the famous Spad VII and XIII single-seaters.

Amiot 140M Traditionally, the crews of most military airplanes built into the early 1930s were seated

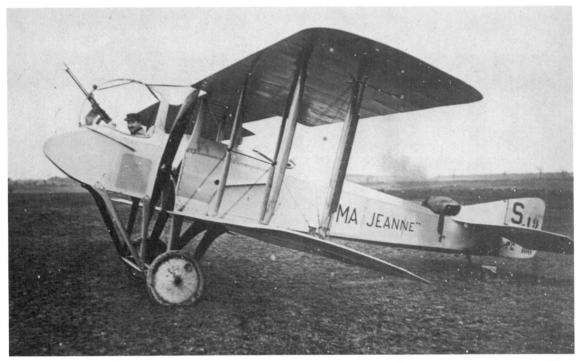

Fig. 14-34. The French Spad A-2 of 1916 was developed to combine the forward field of fire of the pusher design with the performance advantages of the tractor. Solution: put the gunner ahead of the propeller.

in the upper portion of the fuselage, usually in open cockpits. The advent of cabin-type airplanes put them entirely inside a conventional fuselage. The French Amiot 140B bomber of 1931 (FIG. 14-35) was an odd transitional model. With a fuselage too shallow to accommodate a conventional cabin, there was a cabin *beneath* the fuselage for the pilots, bombardier, and others. The defensive gunners retained their old positions in traditional open cockpits on top of the fuselage.

Bell Airacuda In 1936 the Bell Aircraft Corporation of Buffalo, New York, entered the high-performance military aircraft field with its innovative XFM-1 Airacuda twin-engine multiplace fighter (FIG. 14-36). Other than having the novelty of a low wing with the engines above it, the XFM-1 went back to the Staaken V.G.O.1 of 1915 for its most unique feature—pusher engine nacelles with gunners in the forward ends.

Other than latter-day structure and streamlining, the major difference from the Staaken was that the gun-

ners in the nacelles were aggressors, not defenders. The Airacudas (the company-originated name verified the offensive nature of the design) were the only airplanes to carry the U.S. Army's Fighter Multiplace (FM) designation.

Armament was a single 37mm cannon in each nacelle, one .50-caliber machine gun in each fuselage side blister, and two .30-caliber machine guns, each in retractable ports above and beneath the fuselage. Powerplants were the then-new 1,150-hp Allison V-1710s. Wing span was 69 feet 10 inches and gross weight of the YFM-1 was 10,000 pounds.

After testing the XFM-1 prototype, the Army ordered 14 service test YFM-1s. In spite of a top speed of 270 mph at 12,600 feet, almost equal to single-engine fighters of the time, no production Airacudas were ordered.

Butterfly-tail Beech Bonanza From the middle 1920s, various designers have introduced original or modified models that utilized what has come to be

Fig. 14-35. The French Amoit 140M (for military) bomber of 1931 was a conventional twin-engine monoplane with a cabin added to the bottom of the fuselage. Open cockpits were retained for topside gunners.

Fig. 14-36. The American Bell XFM-1 Airacuda twin-engine fighter, with armament and wing engines based on the Staaken V.G.O. of 1915, was a sensation when it appeared in 1936.

Fig. 14-37. The Beechcraft Bonanza with its distinctive butterfly tail was introduced in 1947 and remained in production for 38 years.

254

called a "butterfly" tail, which has no traditional vertical fin or rudder. The horizontal stabilizers are angled upward 30 degrees (or even more) in a V-form, and the elevators serve the double function of elevators and rudders—called *ruddevators*.

Claimed advantages are reduced weight and drag, and in some cases, increased control effectiveness. Pilots who fly them claim to detect a small degree of directional instability, or "hunting."

The "butterflies" built to the end of World War II were one-time experimentals. It remained for the four-place American Beechcraft Model 35 Bonanza to make a mass-production item of it in 1947. A few other production models have since appeared, notably in France, but the V-tail and the Bonanza made each other famous (FIG. 14-37).

Other than its tail (a conventional tail version is also available), the Bonanza holds another distinction. The V-tail Model 35 was in continuous production from 1947 to 1985, 38 years.* The equivalent single-tail

Model 33 is still in production, with the end nowhere in sight.

Inverted Gull-wing Vought F4U Corsair One of the most effective U.S. Navy and Marine Corps fighters of World War II was the Vought F4U Corsair often called the "Bent-Wing Bird." Its inverted gull wing was not chosen for aerodynamic reasons, but due to the combination of its 2,000-hp Pratt & Whitney R-2800 Double Wasp engine, which turned a large-diameter propeller, and the design of its landing gear, necessitated by the Navy's requirement for folding wings for storage aboard aircraft carriers.

The landing gear retracted straight aft, and the wheel pivoted 90 degrees on the single strut to lay flat in a well near the trailing edge of the wing. Because of the large propeller diameter, the landing gear would have had to be too long to retract aft on a conventional straight wing. So to shorten the gear and still get the necessary propeller/ground clearance, the wing was bent downward at the center section (FIG. 14-38). This

---

*Some readers might dispute this, citing the famous Cub which has been in production since 1931. However, this was built by two separate companies, first Taylor and then Piper, has gone through several separate model designations, and was out of production for six months when Piper was shut down in 1947. Piper sold the design to another firm in 1982, but the new owner of Piper bought it back a few years later. The Super Cub is still in production in 1990.

Fig. 14-38. The famous Vought F4U Corsair of World War II adopted the distinctive inverted gull wing as a means of shortening the landing gear.

negative dihedral was compensated for by the dihedral of the longer outboard panels.

The XF4U-1 prototype flew on May 29, 1940, and the type was not retired from first line service until 1955; it served in the reserves a few years after that, the only prewar U.S. service type to remain in production after the war. The last one was delivered in December 1952.

Bellanca's Extra Lift An Italian immigrant to the U.S., Guiseppe Bellanca, built his first airplane, a monoplane, in 1911. By 1922 he had developed an advanced cabin monoplane that had two unique features. First, the wing struts were extra-wide and had an airfoil cross-section to act as small wings to provide extra lift (FIG. 14-39). Second, the top line of the fuselage was shaped like an airfoil, supposedly to act like a long narrow wing and also generate extra lift.

The "lifting strut" concept worked well, and was incorporated on later production CH, Pacemaker, and Skyrocket models built from 1927 to the late 1930s in the form of wide fairings over otherwise conventional steel tube struts. Some other Bellanca designs, most notably the P-200 Airbus and Aircruiser series of 1931-35, had the two struts on each side merge at the rear spar and filled in the area between them to create additional wing area that was included in the total for lift calculations (FIG. 14-40).

The airfoil-shaped fuselage was a better advertising gimmick than a practical feature. It didn't stand up very well under analysis as a pure wing. If it were generating effective lift, any center of pressure travel would have a noticeable effect on aircraft balance. Also, such a great length relative to width gave a fractional aspect ratio, with high induced-drag characteristics. Finally, with two "wingtips" (the fuselage sides) so close together, the tip losses would be enormous relative to any lift that was generated.

Approach Parachute; Boeing B-47 The amazing B-47 also had a second parachute that served as an air brake. Early jet engines were notorious for poor acceleration characteristics; if a plane like a B-47 had to abort a landing and go around, the throttled-back engines would not come up to speed soon enough to get the plane flying properly. In order to make landings at higher engine speeds, an "approach parachute" was deployed (FIG. 14-41). This was much smaller than the braking chute used on the ground and provided enough drag to require considerably higher engine speed to maintain the proper airplane approach speed. If the B-47 had to go around, the pilot simply jettisoned the approach chute and advanced the throttles of the engines, which picked up the needed speed quickly.

Beechcraft Staggerwing Biplanes with negative stagger—that is, with the upper wing positioned

255

Fig. 14-39. Wide fairings on the conventional wing struts of the 1926-1939 American Bellanca monoplanes generated a little extra lift.

256

Fig. 14-40. Bellanca filled in the space between two converging wing struts to create additional wing area for the Airbus and Aircruiser models.

Fig. 14-41. To permit early jet engines to remain at fairly high speed during landings, the Boeing B-47 employed an approach parachute to offset the higher thrust of the engines and maintain a normal approach speed.

Fig. 14-42. The Beechcraft Model 17 biplane of 1933-47 had negatively-staggered wings, but became known as the Staggerwing with no indication of positive or negative needed. This is the U.S. Army YC-73 of 1941.

slightly aft of the lower—are relatively rare. Positive stagger is almost universal, and a very few biplanes have no stagger at all.

Walter Beech had two good reasons for using negative stagger in his Model 17 when it was introduced in 1933. The forward location of the lower wing pro-

vided a good support point for the main landing gear (which was fixed on the earlier models and retractable on later), and the rearward location of the upper wing gave the pilot excellent visibility from the front of the four-place cabin (FIG. 14-42).

Since biplanes were still the most common aircraft type at the time, the unofficial name of "Negative-Stagger Beech" was applied by the aviation community to distinguish the new Beech design from other biplanes. In a fine example of changes in the application of language, the "negative" dropped out of the name with repeated use and the plane is now referred to as the Staggerwing Beech or the Beechcraft Staggerwing without any indication of positive or negative. No matter; the words are positive identification for this particular airplane regardless of configuration detail.

The Beech 17 was produced until shortly after World War II and is now a prime status item in the antique airplane movement.

Specifications, D17S model produced for the U.S. Army and Navy as C-43 and GB: Powerplant 450-hp Pratt & Whitney Wasp Jr.; wing span 32 feet; area 296 square feet; gross weight 4,250 pounds; top speed 190 mph.

OTHER UNORTHODOX CONFIGURATIONS

258

Sometimes the overall configuration of an airplane, while still clearly within its recognized type category, differs from the others in more than just detail. Four are described in this section.

Gerhard Cycle Plane Unorthodox in many ways was the Gerhard Cycle Plane of the early 1920s. First, it did not use a conventional powerplant. The propeller was driven by the pilot through bicycle pedals and chains. The fact that such systems had been tried since early in the century did not deter designer Gerhard—he thought he had a way of defeating the poor aerodynamics of the earlier designs. He knew that high aspect ratio wings had less induced drag. However, for a reasonable wing span, high A/R reduced the area, so he increased the number of wings to an unprecedented *seven*, conveniently overlooking the added drag of the necessary struts and wires and the interference drag between adjacent wings that in the past had pretty much limited multiplanes to three wings.

The saving grace of the Cycle Plane was its crude construction, easily noted in FIG. 14-43. During a high-speed taxi run (or possibly an attempted takeoff), the wings collapsed as they began to pick up the load,

thereby ending the experiment.

Gerhard had left out some essential details: flying and landing wires to take the wing loads. All of these were taken by a single diagonal strut on each side of the fuselage running down to the inboard strut of the bottom wing. Why the engineers of the U.S. Army Air Service Engineering Division at McCook Field, Ohio, let him try it will forever be a mystery. The engineers might have figured that it could not go fast enough to hurt him no matter what happened to it.

Dorand Tractor Biplane It is hard to call this 1908 French Dorand (FIG. 14-44) unorthodox as to overall configuration because "orthodoxy" had hardly been established at the time. Actually, Captain Dorand's creation utilized several features common to other designs of the period: pulley drive via V-belts from the 43-hp air-cooled Anzani radial engine to a metal-frame propeller with fabric covering, wheeled landing gear, biplane main wings, and a long wide-span horizontal tail that could almost double as a tandem wing.

The major point of unorthodoxy was the use of perfectly flat wing surfaces, a feature hard to justify at the time in view of plentiful data on the use of cambered, or curved, surfaces by all successful builders and pilots dating back to Lilienthal. Had its wings been cambered, Dorand's contraption might have flown. The designer learned from it, however, and went on to become a very successful designer and builder of thoroughly conventional types to the end of World War I. His unsuccessful 1908 effort had a wing span of 37 feet, 968 square feet of wing area, and weighed 611 pounds.

John's Multiplane Little is known of the background of this seven-winged three-engined 1919 bomber other than the builder's name and the details evident in a few photos (FIG. 14-45).

Although there are three separate sets of wings, the arrangement does not really qualify the design as a tandem-wing. The forward set of biplane wings has its trailing edges slightly overlapping the leading edges of the central set of triplane wings while the rear set of biplane wings has leading edges slightly overlapping the trailing edges of the triplane set. It almost seems that this was an easy way of avoiding the excessive height that would result from a seven-wing design with the wings stacked vertically.

Fig. 14-43. The seven-wing Gerhard Cycle Plane was driven by the pilot pumping on bicycle pedals.

Fig. 14-44. In spite of its unique boxkite-like cells and the flat wing surfaces that kept it from flying, the French Dorand of 1908 can be regarded as a pioneer of the conventional tractor biplane configuration.

A more unconventional feature was the engine arrangement. One 400-hp Liberty engine was in the nose of the conventional fuselage; the two others were installed as pushers in very long side nacelles that crossed all three wing sets and had gunners in the forward ends.

It is perhaps fortunate that the Multiplane was extensively damaged before it actually flew.

Powered Parachute Introduction of the rectangular ram-air parachute in the 1960s revolutionized the sport of skydiving and exhibition parachuting at airshows and other public exhibitions. The new 'chute, while still having a cloth canopy, was now in effect a pendulum-stabilized tailless biplane hang glider with a very narrow gap. Forward motion forces air between the two surfaces, inflating the canopy into a wing-like shape with an airfoil section that permits a glide angle of as much as five to one while being much

more maneuverable than a conventional dome-canopy parachute.

Because the ram-air parachute "flies" like a hang glider, although not well enough to be used for typical slope-soaring, it was inevitable that someone would treat is as some earlier hang gliders had already been treated by putting a small engine on it to make it an ultralight airplane.

This was done in the early 1980s. A small tubular frame for three wheels, the pilot, and a two-stroke-cycle engine driving a pusher propeller (FIG. 14-46) was the only addition necessary. The propeller was surrounded by a tubular metal frame to keep the lines connecting the canopy to the frame from getting tangled in the propeller. With a 35-hp engine, or two 15-hp engines driving contrarotating coaxial propellers, the powered parachute can take off with about a 300-foot run and cruise at 26 mph. At this writing, at least

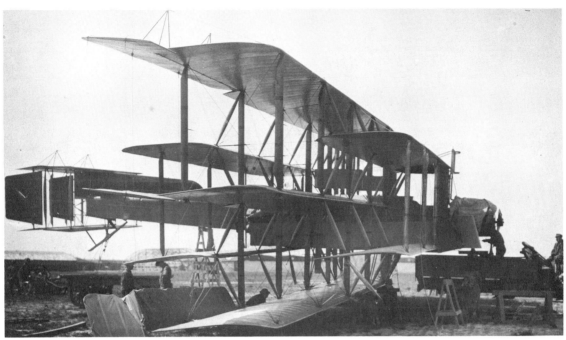

Fig. 14-45. The seven-winged John's Multiplane of 1919 photographed at Langley Field, Virginia, after a mishap knocked off its landing gear and damaged its lowest wing.

Fig. 14-46. Adding an engine, wheels, and supporting framework to a ram-air parachute made an ultralight airplane of it.

two, named Parawing and Paraplane, are on the market as ultralight airplane kits.

Representative specifications: Wing span 36 feet, empty weight 179 pounds, gross weight 379 pounds.

Transavia Skyfarmer The Australian Transavia Skyfarmer T-300 (FIG. 14-47), introduced in 1965 and still in production, has several unorthodox features that were dictated by the special purposes for which the machine was to be used. The T-300 is a tractor sesquiplane (lower wing with less than half the span and area of the upper wing) with twin tail booms where most other twin-boom designs have been pushers. Further, each boom supports a separate set of T-tail surfaces, a reversion to the Fokker K.I of 1915.

The Skyfarmer was designed for agricultural use, and the booms and high tail avoid impingement of dust and spray that is a problem with conventional fuselages. For further corrosion avoidance, the rear portion of the pod-like fuselage is a fiberglass shell.

In a further departure from conventional practice, the pilot sits high and above the payload for maximum visibility and protection from forward movement of

262

Fig. 14-47. The twin-tail arrangement of the unique Australian Transavia Skyfarmer sesquiplane paid off handsomely when a pilot knocked one tail off after hitting high-tension wires. He was able to fly home safely with the remaining tail.

the payload in case of accident. The lower wing, while not contributing significantly to the total lift, uses its turbulent downwash to more effectively distribute the dust/spray.

A variant, designated PL-12U Airtruck, replaces the agricultural hopper/tank with a cabin that can accommodate four passengers, with a fifth riding behind the pilot.

Specifications, Skyfarmer: Powerplant, 300-hp Lycoming IO-540; wing span 39 feet three and one-half inches; gross weight 4,244 pounds; cruising speed 117 mph.

15
CHAPTER

Unconventional Operations

ONCE THE AIRPLANE WAS ESTABLISHED AS A RELIABLE military and commercial vehicle, people began to adapt it to special purposes. In some cases, these required relatively little modification and did not interfere significantly with the overall utility of the plane. Some modifications limited an aircraft's utility severely and permitted it to perform only the one special function.

In many cases, the modifications were reversible; the planes could be restored to their original configurations with relative ease. Some of the changes merely involved bolt-on equipment. In other cases, some special-purpose uses became so commonplace that it made sense to design airplanes specifically for the job rather than modify standard models. The best examples are agricultural planes—crop dusters and sprayers. As factory-designed-and-built types, these date from the middle 1950s when the widely-used war surplus (and therefore cheap) biplane trainers that virtually monopolized the business began to wear out and replacements were no longer available. Such specially designed planes are good for that work only.

In a few extreme cases, standard airplanes have been modified irreversibly for work that made them expendable, such as radio-controlled (drone) targets or guided missiles, and the extreme case that was introduced late in World War II—manned suicide bombers. Again, after a period of adapting obsolete service models for such destructive work, special designs were developed specifically for the purpose of one-time, one-way missions.

A wide selection of unconventional operations, grouped by related activity, is presented in this chapter. Some that were initially novelties are now commonplace but are not familiar to the public because certain operations are conducted in remote areas or at such high altitudes as to be out of sight. Other operations, with no practical application, are conducted purely for entertainment at airshows—aviation show business.

IN-FLIGHT REFUELING

The range of airplanes has always been limited by the amount of fuel they could carry. Maximum range could be achieved in various weight classes, but at the expense of payload. Combining endurance and/or range with practical payloads was dependent upon being able to refuel the aircraft in the air.

Hose Tankers Increasing duration by in-flight refueling was first tried by the U.S. Army Air Service in 1923, using a pair of de Havilland 4B observation planes. The "tanker" lowered a hose to the "receiver." The rear-seat occupant then grasped the end of the hose and put the nozzle in its receptacle. An endurance record of 37 hours 15 minutes was set this way on August 27-28, 1923. Fifteen in-flight refuelings were required.

Little was done with this procedure until January of 1929, when the Army again set a record, this time of 150 hours (FIG. 15-1). This set off a boom in hose-refueled endurance flights that continued into the mid-1930s and raised the record to 653 hours between June 4 and July 1, 1935. Brief commercial use of a revised procedure by the British Flight Refueling Ltd. firm was used for transatlantic airmail just before World War II.

In 1948, the U.S. Air Force used the British system to increase the range of 74 B-29s that were re-designated B-29MR (for receiver) and converted 92 to tankers as B-29M. Fifty-seven improved B-50As (originally B-29D) were also modified as hose receivers, and one made the first nonstop flight around the world in 94 hours between February 26 and March 2, 1949.

Fig. 15-1. The 150-hour air-refueled flight of the U.S. Army Fokker C-2A Question Mark triggered a several-year boom in hose-fueled endurance flights.

This cumbersome hose method was unsuited to new high-performance aircraft, so new methods were soon developed, as shown.

Boeing Flying Boom By 1950, the Boeing Airplane Company came up with an improvement on the hose refueling method. A "flying boom" was fitted to C-97 cargo planes and to obsolescent B-29s (FIGS. 15-2, 15-3). This consisted of a telescoping boom fitted with ruddevators; it could extend and retract and move to a considerable degree in all directions under the control of an operator in the tanker. The nozzle was "flown" into a receptacle on the receiver airplane, which could be a small fighter or a big bomber. The prefix letter K identified boom tankers—KC-97 for various C-97 series (KC-97E, KC-97G, etc.) and the 116 KB-29Ps. The procedure was extended into the jet age with the Boeing KC-135A tanker and has been adapted to other Air Force models such as the Douglas KC-10 adaptation of the DC-10 airliner.

Flying boom refueling was used by three Air Force B-52Bs to fly nonstop around the world in 45 hours 19 minutes in January 1957—just half the time of the B-

50A. A novel use of the boom is in icing tests of other airplanes. To avoid the risk of flying in actual icing conditions, water is sprayed in clear air on only part of the test airplane (FIG. 15-4). The effects of ice on one engine, for example, can be evaluated without risk to the others.

Probe and Drogue Refueling The flying boom system was not suited to U.S. Navy operations, so the Navy standardized on something that the Air Force and the British has already tried—trailing a hose with a funnel-like receptacle on the end. This is engaged by a probe extending from the nose of the receiver airplane. The fixed length of the hose and its lack of directional control puts all the responsibility for maintaining contact on the receiver pilot (FIGS. 15-5, 15-6).

Towed Fuel Tank A glider towed by a bomber would seem to be a routine military operation, but the Cornelius XFG-1 (for Experimental Fuel Glider) was unique on several counts.

Primarily, it was an auxiliary fuel tank to extend the range of the bomber. Although having a cockpit and conventional controls for test and ferry purposes (FIG.

Fig. 15-2. The Boeing flying boom, mounted on a Boeing KB-29P tanker, refueling a North American F-86A jet fighter.

Fig. 15-3. The first Boeing KC-97A, refueling a Boeing B-50D by means of the Boeing flying boom.

Fig. 15-4. One special use of the flying boom was spraying water into one engine of a four-jet Lockheed C-141 transport for an icing test at hight altitude.

Fig. 15-5. One U.S. Marine Corps Douglas A4D-2 refuels from another by means of the probe-and-drogue ''buddy system.''

Fig. 15-6. A Boeing B-50D converted to a KB-50J tanker with the capability of refueling three planes simultaneously: (left to right) USAF North American F-100, Douglas B-66, and Lockheed F-104.

Fig. 15-7. While the concept of towing a glider behind a bomber as an auxiliary fuel tank was novel, the Cornelious XFG-1 Fuel Glider was also unorthodox in being a tailless glider with a forward-swept wing.

15-7), it was to be unmanned for normal missions. An automatic pilot kept it in the high-tow position behind the bomber, from which point its 677-gallon fuel load could be transferred by gravity to the bomber through the hollow towline that doubled as a hose. The glider would then be cut loose.

Another oddity of the XFG-1 was that it was tailless. Again, nothing new, except that the wing was swept forward instead of aft in the traditional pattern. Two XFG-1s were acquired by the U.S. Army Air Forces in 1945. After brief testing, the towed tank concept was abandoned.

EXPENDABLE AiRPLANES

Airplanes are designed for great strength, ease of maintenance, and long service lives. It seems strange that some should be designed for only a single flight. This has been true in some very limited cases, notably the Japanese Kamikazes of late World War II. Most other planes whose final flights were (or are) expected to end in destruction were obsolescent or worn-out service models at the ends of their normal useful service lives.

Antiaircraft Targets

In the 1930s, the British converted some twin-float seaplane trainers into unmanned radio-controlled target planes called Queen Bees. Being seaplanes, these were relatively easy to land by remote control if they were not shot down after they were launched by catapult. In 1940 the U.S. Army Air Corps began to convert numbers of obsolete trainer and observation biplanes to radio-controlled target drones. Because these were landplanes, the tricky landing procedure was simplified by converting them to tricycle landing gear (FIG. 15-8).

This practice continues to present day, using high-performance jets as the targets. In the early WWII years, some planes were built specifically as targets. The first to achieve mass production were simple adaptations of the popular Culver Cadet lightplane (FIG. 15-9). The main change, other than the addition of the radio controls, was conversion to tricycle landing gear. The Army designation was PQ-8. The PQ-8 was followed by a higher-performance Culver model designed from scratch as a target, the PQ-14 (FIG. 15-10). This looked like a conventional airplane due to its enclosed cockpit, but this feature was used only for test or ferry flights with a human pilot. Altogether, 2,571 PQ-14s were built, of which 1,201 were transferred to the Navy as TD2C-1s.

A few PQ-14s and Navy TD2Cs survived the war and were converted to single-seat sportplanes that flew on limited licenses.

One-Way Bombers

The idea of using unmanned airplanes under radio control was logically expanded to make the plane the

Fig. 15-8. An obsolete U.S. Army Douglas BT-2B Basic Trainer modified with tricycle landing gear for use as a pilotless radio-controlled gunnery target in 1941. The revised Army designation was Type A-4 target.

Fig. 15-9. Standard Culver Cadet lightplanes were fitted with tricycle landing gear to become radio-controlled targets in 1941. New U.S. Army designation was PQ-8 in a continuation of the original A-for-target series.

Fig. 15-10. The Culver PQ-14 was designed as a radio-controlled target but was provided with a conventional pilot's cockpit for test and ferry purposes.

weapon itself instead of the weapon carrier. Both sides experimented with this in World War II with only a fair degree of success. It remained for the Japanese to apply the ultimate control to a one-way bomber—human pilotage right into the target.

Radio-Controlled Bombers Some German World War II targets were so extensively protected by heavy concrete that the only way a heavy bomber could destroy them was by getting the whole bomb load onto exactly the right spot. Because this was virtually impossible from 20,000 feet with a conventional bombsight, a novel approach was taken. Instead of hitting the target with free-falling bombs, the idea was to hit it with the airplane itself, which was packed solid with explosives—actually a winged and controllable bomb.

The overloaded bomber, either a Boeing B-17

Fig. 15-11. The pilot's cabin and the upper fuselage structure of war-weary Boeing B-17s were cut away to simplify pilot egress by parachute after they got the BQ-7 radio-controlled flying bomb safely on course.

270

(redesignated BQ-7) (FIG. 15-11) or a ConVair B-24/PB4Y (redesignated BQ-8), was taken off by a two-man crew who departed by parachute once the bomber was on course and under the control of the accompanying control plane. Sighting and the dive into the target were visual by means of a television camera in the bomber. A few of these controlled-bomb attacks on German targets were moderately successful in World War II; others were accomplished by U.S. forces in the Korean War, using Grumman F6F Hellcat fighters.

Pilot-Guided Bombers In 1944 the Germans developed an unmanned bomber program of their own that differed greatly from the U.S. program. From appearances, this system, named *Mistel* (German for mistletoe, a parasite plant), seemed to be a revival of the scheme whereby a large plane carried a small one. Not so; the little one, either a Messerschmitt Me. 109 or Focke-Wulf FW 190 fighter, was mounted on top of an unmanned and explosive-laden Junkers Ju. 88 bomber, but the pilot in the *fighter* controlled the whole operation (FIG. 15-12). His controls were connected to the controls of the bomber, and he flew the combination like a single airplane.

After visually acquiring the target on a relatively low-level mission, he aimed both planes directly at it,

locked the bomber's controls to keep it on course, then released the fighter from its supporting structure and hoped he could escape the defensive fire and get home.

The Germans assembled a fleet of some 60 Mistels in Denmark late in 1944 for a massive raid on the British fleet then anchored at Scapa Flow, Scotland. Continuous bad weather forced cancellation of the mission; most of the Mistels were eventually expended against Russian forces advancing on Germany from the east.

Manned Kamikaze Bombers As a last desperate defense measure, Japanese pilots were organized into a Kamikaze force to destroy Allied ships pressing the attack on the Japanese home islands. This was named for the "Divine Wind" that destroyed an invading enemy fleet in the year 1281; the latter-day Kamikaze pilots were supposed to destroy the threatening ships by guiding their explosive-laden planes right into them. Solemn religious ceremonies were held for the pilots before the start of each mission.

At first, obsolescent service models were used, but they were too easy for the defenders to shoot down. This situation called for the development of something faster and much harder to hit. The result was a rocket-powered single-seat aerial torpedo developed by the Yokosuka Naval Arsenal that was officially named

Fig. 15-12. The German Mistel of late World War II used a manned fighter (here a Focke-Wulf FW 190) atop an unmanned Junkers Ju 88 loaded with explosives to guide it to the target area and aim it before detaching to return home.

Fig. 15-13. The Japanese designed and built special Kamikaze airplanes for suicide bombing missions late in World War II. This is a test model of the Yokosuka Ohka with landing skid and wing flaps.

Ohka, Japanese for "cherry blossom." The technical designation was MXY-7. Not knowing the official designation, the Allies dubbed it *Baka,* Japanese for "fool."

The little Ohka carried 2,645 pounds of explosives in the warhead nose; a 1,765-pound thrust solid-fuel rocket engine was in the tail to bring the straight-down

speed of the Model 11 version of the baby dive bomber to over 600 mph. A smaller Model 22 version had a 1,765-pound warhead and was driven by a 440-pound thrust jet engine.

FIGURES 15-13 shows a special test model with a glider-like landing skid and wing flaps. While it might not seem logical at first to have a recoverable version of a suicide plane, it was necessary to gather data on its performance and handling characteristics so that the data could be passed on to the pilots. Altogether, 775 Ohka 11s and 50 22s were built.

Some Allied ships were hit by the Ohkas that went into action on March 31, 1945, to supplement the converted service planes. They had to be carried to the vicinity of their targets by specially modified twin-engine bombers, and therein lay their vulnerability. The sluggish bombers were easy targets for alerted defensive fighters, so few Ohkas got through; many were forced to release too far from their targets to permit a hit.

Ohka 11 specifications: Wing span 16 feet 5 inches; wing area square feet; gross weight 4,718 pounds; maximum flight speed 535 mph in a 5-degree dive.

Ramming Rocket Interceptor Another one-way manned missile, not quite as extreme as the Kamikaze, was the German Bachem Ba 349 Natter of 1944-45 (FIG. 15-14). This wooden single-seater was propelled by a 4,410-pound thrust Walter liquid rocket motor and was launched vertically from guide rails by four detachable booster rockets. Because of its limited range, with a powered time of only four minutes 20 seconds, the launching sites had to be pretty well under the path of the invading Allied bombers.

At altitude, the pilot had time for one pass through a bomber formation and the opportunity to use his forward-firing armament of 24 73mm rockets. He also had the opportunity—and was expected—to ram a bomber and then take to his parachute. He would have to take to the silk anyhow because there was no provision for landing the one-shot Natter. To eliminate the difficult task of climbing out of a conventional cockpit at high speed, the nose and cockpit were designed to separate from the rest of the airframe with the pilot in it. After this structure was slowed by a drogue parachute, the pilot could evacuate easily.

Approximately 36 Natters were built, but most were expended in test flights. A few were set up on their launchers near Stuttgart in April 1945. However, Allied tanks were getting close to the launch sites, so the unique missiles were destroyed to prevent their capture before they could be used against the bombers.

Specifications: Wing span 13 feet $1\frac{1}{2}$ inches; wing area 50.6 square feet; gross weight 3,900 pounds; climb to 37,400 feet one minute; maximum level-flight speed (estimated) 620 mph at 16,400 feet.

Fieseler Fi.103 Not quite in the same category as the Ohka and the Natter was another unique manned missile, the German Fieseler Fi.103. This was originally the first of the infamous V-weapons introduced late in World War II. The Germans gave it a cover des-

272

Fig. 15-14. The Bachem Natter rocket-powered one-way interceptor, one of the German desperation weapons of late World War II.

Fig. 15-15. The Fieseler F1.103 was a piloted version of the notorious German V-1 Buzz Bomb that was to be launched from a bomber close to the intended target for greater accuracy.

ignation of FZG-76, but designated it V-1 in the V-for-Vengeance weapon series. The Allies soon called it the Buzz Bomb because of the distinctive sound of its 660-pound thrust Argus As.014 pulse-jet engine.

The V-1 was a very ingenious little pilotless airplane, not a true missile, so small that its engine had to be installed on top of the fuselage (FIG. 15-15). It was normally catapulted from an inclined ramp that was pointed toward the distant target area. A pre-set mechanism levelled it off at its cruising altitude of approximately 1,000 feet and a timer matching its cruising speed of 350-400 mph with the distance to a wide-area target like the city of London put the V-1 and its nearly one-ton load of Amatol in a dive into the target area.

Buzz Bomb attacks on Southern England began on June 13, 1944, shortly after the Allied invasion of Europe. Some of the launching sites were soon captured, and British and American fighters, particularly the new Gloster Meteor jet, were able to intercept many V-1s and destroy them before they reached their targets. The Germans soon supplemented ramp launches with air-launches, carrying the V-1s under the wings of Heinkel He.111 bombers and aiming them toward area targets prior to releasing them. Approximately 6,725 V-1s were launched against England between June 13, 1944, and March 29, 1945. Of these, 1,859 were shot down by antiaircraft guns and 1,846 by fighters. Others

were launched against targets in areas of Europe occupied by the Allies.

For more accurate attacks on specific-point targets, a piloted version of the V-1 was developed under its manufacturer's designation of Fi.103. This was simply a quickie modification of the V-1 to accommodate a pilot in an enclosed cockpit just ahead of the pulse-jet. The Fi.103 was air-launched from an He.111, which was to take it relatively close to the target. After release, the Fi.103 pilot was to fly toward the target, get the plane aimed straight at it, lock the controls, and then bail out by parachute to face certain capture. However, getting the canopy open and bailing out in front of the pulse-jet intake proved to be almost impossible; a mission in a piloted Fi.103 was almost certain to become a suicide mission.

As with the Ohkas, some training versions of the piloted Fi.103 were made and 107 V-1s were modified to accommodate pilots. However, the impracticality of the project was soon evident and it was cancelled in October 1944 with no combat missions flown.

AERIAL AIRCRAFT CARRIERS

In contrast to the use of large aircraft as a means of getting others airborne, described in Chapter 13, there have been examples of airplanes not only being

273

launched from mother aircraft, but returning to them after the mission.

Airplanes Carried by Airships

This practice evolved slowly. Late in World War I, the two countries using large rigid airships—Germany and England—both carried single-seat fighters aloft. These were released successfully, but did not return to reattach. The U.S. Navy released a two-seat trainer from a non-rigid airship (blimp) in December 1918, but again as a one-way trip.

Sperry Messenger The U.S. Army began serious experiments in 1923 aimed not only at releasing a small single-seat plane, the 20-foot span 65-hp Sperry Messenger, but at reattaching it in flight (FIGS. 15-16, 15-17). The Messenger was released from the Army blimp TC-7 on October 3, 1924, and released from and returned to the TC-3 on December 15. Although the system, featuring a novel "skyhook" above the nose of the plane, worked, the army did nothing more with it. The Navy, however, picked up the idea and made it world-famous.

Curtiss Sparrowhawk Starting in 1932, eight tiny Curtiss F9C Sparrowhawk fighters with skyhooks (FIG. 15-18) were assigned to the Navy's rigid airships *Akron* and *Macon*. Four of these could be raised on the trapeze into a hangar in the belly of the airship, while a fifth rode on an external perch. Since the Sparrowhawks were fighter planes, it was popularly supposed that they were carried for the defense of the airship. Not so; they were used as scouts to expand the area patrolled by the airships on scouting missions. Very small planes were required because of the limited stowage space available.

Four Sparrowhawks were lost at sea with the *Macon* on February 12, 1935. All but one of the four survivors was scrapped; it is now displayed at the National Air and Space Museum.

Airplanes Carried by Airplanes

In the 1930s, the Russians tried experiments involving the carriage of one or more fighter-type airplanes on top of or under their largest multiengine airplanes, but nothing other than airshow fly-bys seems to

Fig. 15-16. The tiny U.S. Army Sperry Messenger fitted with airship hook-on gear for 1924 experiments.

Fig. 15-17. The Messenger hooked on to the Army blimp TC-7.

Fig. 15-18. A U.S. Navy Curtiss F9C-2 Sparrowhawk engaging the trapeze of the airship Macon in 1933.

have resulted from it, although some fighters converted to dive bombers were carried briefly early in World War II.

XP-85 Goblin   In 1946, with the huge six-engine ConVair B-36 soon to enter service, the idea of a short-range defensive fighter being carried along received favorable consideration by the U.S. Army. A contract was awarded to the McDonnell Aircraft Company for two XP-85 Goblins. These were odd-looking swept-wing jet monoplanes that were short enough (15 feet) to fit most of the way into the big plane's bomb bay (FIG. 15-19).

The Goblins flew, but neither operated with a B-36; the testing was done with a specially-modified Boeing B-29 (FIG. 15-20). The advent of new jet bombers and in-flight refueling for fighters made the idea of a parasite defensive fighter impractical and the idea was then abandoned. Both XP-85s survive today, one in the Air Force Museum at Dayton, Ohio, and the other in

the Strategic Air Command Museum at Offutt Air Force Base, Omaha, Nebraska.

RF-84F FICON   The idea of a parasite airplane for the B-36 did not die with the rejection of the XP-85, however. To extend the reach of reconnaissance versions of the long-range B-36 (RB-36; R-for-Reconnaissance) into heavily defended target areas, a reconnaissance version of the swept-wing Republic F-84 (FIG. 15-21), the RF-84F Thunderflash, was adapted to ride along. This arrangement was code-named FICON, for Fighter CONveyor. Unlike the XP-85, which had to take off and land with the mother ship because it had no landing gear, the hitchhiking Thunderflash took off and landed on its own. Once hooked onto the bomber, it was drawn partway into the bomb bay. In order for the plane to fit, the horizontal tail had to be angled downward, a unique feature of the 25 RF-84Fs that were modified for this mission as GRF-84F (later changed to RF-84K). The bombers became GRB-

276

Fig. 15-19. The tiny McDonnell XF-85 was intended to be carried as a parasite fighter by USAF heavy bombers.

Fig. 15-20. The XF-85 just prior to hooking onto a Boeing B-29 mother ship.

Fig. 15-21. A modified Republic F-84F about to catch a ride on a ConVair GRB-36 bomber.

278

Fig. 15-22. Project Tom Tom was an unsuccessful scheme to enable short-range Republic F-84 jet fighters to accompany long-range Boeing B-29 bombers by being physically attached to the bomber.

36D, F, H, or J, depending on the individual aircraft modified. The FICON system was in use with the Strategic Air Command for about a year during 1955-56.

Towed Fighters A major disadvantage of the XP-86 and FICON projects was that the necessary modifications to the parent airplane's bomb bay ended its effectiveness as a bomber. An attempt to overcome this was Project Tom Tom, initiated after the end of WWII.

In this, two Republic P-84 jet fighters were towed by a Boeing B-29. However, instead of being towed behind at the end of a rope glider-fashion, they were towed by their wingtips, which were attached to wingtips on the B-29 (FIG. 15-22). The three planes would take off separately, then the fighters would pull in and attach themselves to the bomber's wingtips through automatic fittings that were rigid relative to yaw and pitch movement, but were flexible for vertical movement.

The scheme was tried initially with a manned Culver PQ-14 (see FIG. 15-10) and a Douglas C-47. This worked well enough to encourage the use of jet fighters with the B-29, but the program did not go beyond that.

ROLLING TAKEOFFS FROM VERY SHORT RUNWAYS

Because the idea for carrying a fighter plane to the vicinity of patrolling Zeppelins atop a flying boat didn't work out, the Royal Navy tried other ways of taking landplanes to sea other than using actual aircraft carriers. The two methods described required the planes to make uncommonly short rolling takeoffs from uncommonly short runways.

Towed Lighter To bring fighters to the Zeppelins, navalized Sopwith Camels were placed on lighters that had been fitted with 30-foot flat flight decks and were towed behind fast destroyers (FIG. 15-23). The speed of the ship, plus the wind it was headed into, was enough to enable the Camel to take off in a very short distance.

Why use this clumsy method instead of one of the regular carriers that was just coming into use? Tactics. Taking a large ship like a carrier, with its necessary escorts, close to the German coast would bring out German warships and draw widespread attention to the whole operation. The destroyer-barge combination was a low-profile operation more likely to be able to get close to the Zeppelins.

On August 11, 1918, Lt. Stuart Douglas Culley took off from a lighter towed by H.M.S. Redoubt to attack the Zeppelin L-53. Between the ship's speed and the wind, his takeoff roll was a mere five feet. He was able to reach L-53 at the Camel's maximum altitude. One of his two machine guns jammed after only seven rounds, but he managed to destroy the Zep with the other.

Too far from England to make it home, Culley was considering heading for neutral Holland and internment when he luckily spotted his ship through the clouds. He headed for it and ditched in the sea beside it. His Camel was salvaged and is now on display in the Imperial War Museum in London. Culley won the Distinguished Service Order (D.S.O.) for his feat and remained in the service, retiring after World War II.

Battleship Turrets Short-takeoff landplanes also went to sea with the fleet for other than offensive purposes. They served primarily as scouts for capital

Fig. 15-23. A British Sopwith Camel fighter at the aft end of a 30-foot flight deck built on top of a lighter that was towed by a destroyer, and (right) taking off. This system succeeded in shooting down a German Zeppelin in 1918.

ships, taking off from platforms built over the forward turret guns of the battleships (FIG. 15-24). Because of the required short takeoff, the planes were usually single-seaters powered with light rotary engines, such as the British Sopwith Camel and the French Hanriot HD-1. However, some two-seaters were also able to fly from the turret platforms.

This practice was introduced in 1918, and the British, French, American, and Japanese navies all used turret-planes for several years after World War I. The U.S. Navy even designed a single-seater, the TS-1 (for Turret Scout) specifically for the purpose, but by the time it was built in 1922 suitable catapults had been developed and two-seat seaplanes quickly monopolized the battleship and cruiser observation and scouting roles.

Bomber on a Sea Sled While towed barges and battleship turrets could get small airplanes into enemy-controlled skies, the U.S. Navy wanted to put real bombers over enemy territory. As an improvement over the British towed barges, the Navy proposed to put a heavy bomber on a powered sea sled (FIG. 15-25). The

barge was to carry the bomber close to the enemy coast. Then, with its own power plus the power of the bomber, enough speed would be attained to let the bomber take off with a very short run. After reaching its target, the bomber would presumably have enough fuel to make it back to friendly territory.

Late in 1918 the Navy obtained a twin-fuselage Italian Caproni Ca.5 bomber (see Chapter 9) through U.S. Army channels and had the Hickman firm build and enlarged version of its fast sea sled to carry it. Without the bomber aboard, the sled reached a speed of 65 mph in tests. The added thrust of the three airplane engines was expected to more than offset the handicap of the bomber's added weight.

Tests were conducted on Chesapeake Bay on November 15, 1918, but with the war over there was no longer a need for the mission, so further development was abandoned.

SHOW BUSINESS

In the years before WWI, there was no recognized commercial use of airplanes, yet they earned substan-

Fig. 15-24. A French-built Hanriot HD-2 fighter of the U.S. Navy flies from a platform built over the turret guns of the battleship U.S.S. Mississippi in San Francisco Bay in 1920.

Fig. 15-25. An Italian Caproni Ca.5 of the U.S. Navy mounted on a Hickman sea sled, November 1918.

tial sums of money. This was not from commerce, but from "show business." Before the war, practically any local flight was an event, and often the public was charged to come into the field to observe the activity. From 1909 on, major gatherings, called "air meets" at the time, were held. These attracted the outstanding pilots, who competed in events for altitude, endurance, and speed, and drew enormous paying crowds.

As specialized airshow acts became a separate activity from normal operations, some unorthodox one-only airplanes were built for no other purpose than to entertain the public. They were and still are auxiliary acts to the main show, usually air races, and can rightly be called "side show freaks." Two examples are the Twin Ercoupe in Chapter 9 and the Coward Wee Bee in Chapter 14 plus others that are presented here.

In addition to these special creations, there are also unconventional performances by stock model aircraft that are strictly for entertainment and have no military or commercial application whatever.

Upside Down
Takeoffs and Landings

In 1986, an airshow performer named Craig Hoskins treated spectators to something new. He installed a second landing gear on top of his modified Pitts S-2 aerobatic biplane (FIG. 15-26). While the plane

could be flown from either gear, Hoskins chose to make his takeoffs and landings on the "top" gear, with canopied cockpit facing the ground and himself strapped in upside down.

As sensational as the act was, it was not new. It was another of those specialties that was so old that it was forgotten after the novelty of its initial appearance had worn off. It was first seen in Germany in 1912, when a pilot named Fritz Jahn had a special Grade model monoplane modified for the first inverted takeoff airshow act (FIG. 15-27). That one, however, did not simply add wheels to the top of an existing airplane. Because of the need to brace the wire-supported wing from both sides, the upper gear exactly duplicated the lower and had the same flying and control wire attach points. A duplicate of the tailwheel support structure was also built instead of merely adding a wheel to the top of a reinforced rudder as on the Pitts.

A similar act, also largely forgotten, came between Jahn and Hoskins. In 1939, airshow pilot Mike Murphy built another twin landing gear showplane (FIG. 15-28). Like the Grade, it was built up from a wrecked Taylor E-2 Cub specifically for the act, and like Hoskins' Pitts, it was set up with the cockpit on the bottom. However, it was built to operate only that way. The registration numbers were painted on the rudder upside down, but the apparent "normal" landing gear was just a dummy—it was never used.

281

Fig. 15-26. A popular current airshow act is this Pitts S-2 with an additional landing gear built above the upper wing. The pilot takes off and lands upside down on the new gear as shown.

Simulated Curtiss Pushers

Reproductions of 1912 Curtiss Headless pushers began to appear in U.S. airshows in the late 1920s. These did not have the detail accuracy of the meticulous replicas of the 1950s and on, but were quickie assemblies of latter-day thick-section wings, cut-down tail surfaces from other airplanes, steel tubing instead of bamboo for the tailbooms, a modern engine, and modern controls (FIG. 15-29).

These departures from authenticity did not bother the public. A machine with no fuselage, the pilot way out front, a pusher engine between the wings, and a tricycle landing gear was a show all by itself just flying by. If it could do mild aerobatics and low-altitude "crazy flying," so much the better.

After WWII with no 1912-type pusher replicas available, some airshow operators stripped the fuselage fabric from selected 1931 Curtiss CW-1 Junior pusher lightplanes, falsely labelled them as 1912 models, and carried on the same old act with no noticeable decrease in the public's appreciation (FIG. 15-30).

World's Smallest Airport

After production lightplanes in the 40- to 65-hp range, best exemplified by the famous Taylor/Piper Cub* that came on the market in the 1930s, they too joined show business. Their low speed and easy controllability suited them perfectly for a new act—taking off from and landing on a platform on top of a moving car (FIG. 15-31). The act was billed as "The World's Smallest Airport."

The plane would be placed on top of the car, which would then make a run into the wind. When the combination of car and wind velocity reached the flying speed of the plane, the plane lifted off the platform and flew on.

The act was completed in reverse. The car would run at the airplane's landing speed, the plane would set down on the platform, and the car would then slow to a stop. For a while twin-float seaplanes were used for the act; once the plane was down on the platform, it was not apt to slide off. The Cubs and other lightplanes of the time did not have brakes and could easily roll off the

---

*In 1937 the Taylor Aircraft Corporation became the Piper Aircraft Corporation while producing the Model J-2 Cub. Certain J-2s therefore are Taylors while others are Pipers. The J-3 Cub and on are all Pipers.

Fig. 15-27. Topside landing gear for airshow work is not new. This 1912 German Grade monoplane does not have the extra gear as a simple add-on. It forms an essential part of the wing bracing and control system, substituting for the normal topside bracing pylon. Note added topside tail wheel. The two-stroke V-4 engine is installed in the inverted position here.

platform if the speeds were not right. This problem was soon resolved by building wheel wells into the platform that effectively locked the wheels in position when the plane was down.

Pick-a-Back Cubs

One of the truly different airshow acts of the late 1930s was billed as the "Pick-a-Back Cubs." Two Piper J-3 Cubs were fastened together as shown in FIG. 15-32, an arrangement that could almost be called a twin-engine twin-fuselage biplane. The landing gear of the lower unit was reinforced to carry the additional load.

The two would take off together as a stacked pair and go through an aerobatic routine. After awhile, they would break apart, continue aerobatics on their own, and land as two individual airplanes.

Car-to-Plane Pickup

One of the earliest special acts to be seen when airshow business resumed after WWI was the transfer of a daredevil performer from a speeding car to an airplane via a rope ladder suspended from the airplane. This act is still performed today, albeit under "safe" conditions on a long airport runway and mostly into the wind, with plenty of time for the plane and car to match speeds and for the daredevil to make several grabs at the ladder.

It was not so easy in the old days, especially when the show took place on a county-fair racetrack, with a high grandstand, nearby trees, and no proper alignment of the short straightaway with the wind. Making a pickup under such conditions (FIG. 15-33) called for masterful timing and control by all hands, plus a large dose of luck.

A latter-day variation on the same old act has the daredevil, still on the ladder after the pickup, pulled through a lightweight gasoline-soaked framework set up alongside the runway and set afire (FIG. 15-34).

Helicopter Antics

The ability of a helicopter to fly vertically, as well as to hover, fly backward, and sideways, makes it a natural for unusual airshow acts. The two illustrated here are 1956 performances by a special U.S. Army exhibition team. One featured a Bell H-13E with its front-end made up to resemble the head of a clown. After a low-level act in which it picked up hoops with its landing skids, it had a three-foot-diameter yo-yo attached to its external hoisting hook (FIG. 15-35). It then climbed to about 100 feet and, by rapidly flying up and down vertically, it was able to run the yo-yo up and down on its string.

Another spectacular act involved four Sikorsky H-19D helicopters, two dressed as boys and two as girls to make a square dance team (FIG. 15-36). The pilots did a fantastic job of maneuvering in various directions within the square, with couples circling each other while maintaining the same heading, the entire four intermingling, etc., all to the accompaniment of an

283

Fig. 15-28. This double landing gear showplane was built up from a crashed Taylor E-2 Cub in 1939 and took off and landed with the pilot upside down.

Fig. 15-29. This 1929 showplane was built from latter-day parts to generally resemble a 1912 Curtiss Headless pusher. Note thick-section wings, stick control, and fixed radial engine.

Fig. 15-30. After World War II the 1912 Curtiss Pusher act was revived with 1931 Curtiss Junior pushers stripped of fuselage fabric to give them a greater appearance of antiquity.

Fig. 15-31. This 1936 Taylor J-2 Cub is representative of lightplanes flown from and landing on top of moving cars in ''The World's Smallest Airport'' act. Note left wheel of the J-2 in a well, and that the airplane is slightly longer than the platform.

286 **Fig. 15-32.** Two Piper J-3 Cubs made up the ''Pick-a-Back Cubs'' act of the late 1930s. The engine of the upper plane was started by the upper pilot flipping the propeller from behind, seaplane fashion.

Fig. 15-33. A daredevil transfers from a moving car to a rope ladder on the wing of a Curtiss JN-4c Canuck in early 1920s. Note the short remaining straightaway on the racetrack and the car with cameraman ahead of the plane and change car.

287

Fig. 15-34. A latter-day variation on the car-to-plane transfer act with a Piper PA-12 Super Cruiser. The daredevil stays on the rope ladder and is then flown through a burning framework set up alongside the runway.

Fig. 15-35. By rapid up-and-down movement, this Bell H-13E Army helicopter was able to make this oversize yo-yo roll up and down on its string.

Army band playing appropriate music over the public address system.

MISCELLANEOUS OPERATIONS

Unorthodox special uses of conventional or slightly modified aircraft are too numerous to cover in this chapter, but some are presented as being of particular interest. Several are now relatively common practice but are not often seen by the public because of the relative remoteness of the operations.

Fig. 15-36. Four U.S. Army Sikorsky H-19D helicopters made up a square dance team for a 1956 airshow. Facing pairs would advance into the square, pass each other, then slide sideways and back into their original positions after passing the partner on the opposite side.

Towing with Helicopters

Helicopters are well-known for their use in direct lifting operations such as moving heavy objects short distances, placing signboards on the roofs of buildings, etc. (FIG. 15-37). Less known is their use as tugs. They are very effective in moving heavy items on the surface as well as off of it. Examples are naval minesweeping equipment, boats of various sizes, and even large ground-effect craft that have gotten onto terrain or sea ice that is a little too rough for them to traverse successfully (FIG. 15-38).

Fig. 15-37. When a load is too large or heavy for one helicopter, two can be used for the lift, as demonstrated by these U.S. Army Vertol H-21's lifting this large steel framework.

Fig. 15-38. Heavy helicopters are very effective at towing surface vehicles. This Boeing/Vertol 107 is towing a heavy surface skimmer that can't quite move itself over rough ice. Note the flight angle of the helicopter as it converts lift to thrust.

Banner Towing

Practically every American living near an urban area has seen an airplane towing a banner at sometime or other. This practice is too common to be called unorthodox. One country's application of it is, however. Where normal operations call for the banner, consisting of enough block letters to spell out a short message, to be towed behind the airplane, the Russians have sometimes carried the banner on a vertical staff. Such operations are not to spell out messages but to contribute spectacular decoration to parades and large public gatherings. Several planes may fly in formation to pass in review with banners carrying the colors or symbols of various participating organizations.

The airplane shown in FIG. 15-39 is the Polikarpov Po-2, a slow biplane that deserves inclusion in this book on its own merits, not just this one peculiar use. It was designed in 1927 as a trainer by Nikolai Polikarpov

and produced as the U-2. It proved to be thoroughly adaptable to any task that a single-engine airplane could be asked to do, even serve as a nighttime nuisance bomber over the German lines in World War II. Nearly 20,000 were built in Russia until 1952, and others were built in Poland until 1958. Until surpassed by the American Beech Bonanza, the U-2, renamed Po-2 in honor of the designer after his death in 1944, held the record for continuous production of a single airplane model.

Po-2 specifications (1938 model): Powerplant 110-hp M-11; wing span 37 feet 5 inches; gross weight 2,167 pounds; top speed 90.7 mph.

Borate Bombers

A specialized modification of a standard airplane that the public seldom sees in action is the "borate bomber." In operation it is somewhat like a large crop-

Fig. 15-39. This Russian Polikarpov Po-2 is carrying a banner on a pole instead of trailing it behind as is common western practice.

sprayer in that it carries a large cargo of disposable liquid. Unlike crop dusting and spraying, which originated in the mid-1920s, the dropping of a water-borate mixture on forest fires is a post-WWII phenomenon. The first planes used for the job were surplus multiengine bombers or single-engine torpedo planes (FIG. 15-40) in which the existing bomb bay was easily converted to a tank for the fire-fighting liquid. The tank was compartmented to reduce liquid surge and to allow selective or salvo dropping of the load through separate fast-acting doors. Later, post-war surplus bombers were used; more recently, retired four-engine airliner such as the Douglas DC-6 have been used with the liquid carried in a long belly tank.

Fig. 15-40. A World War II surplus TBM (Gerneral Motors-built Grumman TBF) demonstrates how water-borate mixture is dropped on forest fires.

Water Skiing

Alaskan and Canadian bush pilots who operate their airplanes on skis found that the skis would slide easily on smooth mud as well as on snow and ice. It was then a logical move to extend a mud takeoff onto open water. As long as the initial water speed was enough to keep the plane "up" on the skis in the manner of a water-skier, the procedure worked and the plane could take off.

Water landings can be made, too, but are a bit more tricky (FIG. 15-41). Getting ashore before the plane sinks from too little forward speed is the problem. With a muddy beach, the plane can hit it head-on at taxiing speed and slide clear of the water. On gravelly or sandy beaches where the skis cannot slide, the approach has to be made at a shallow angle nearly parallel to the beach. The shoreward ski may stop right at water's edge or even slightly ashore while the seaward ski sinks. In such cases the water should be shallow enough so that the wing of the plane does not reach the water. Even in shallow water, if the plane is stopped head-on to the beach, the tail will sink into the water.

Airplanes Converted to Gliders

When the U.S. Army got interested in military gliders after the German successes in 1940, it ordered several hundred minor adaptations of established civil sailplanes, plus new designs as trainers (TG for Training Glider). These soon proved unsuitable because their relatively high performance resulted in handling characteristics vastly different from the clumsy cargo gliders the pilots would later be flying. As a result, a new type of low-performance training glider was developed.

TG-5, -6, -8 These were standard 65-hp lightplanes (FIG. 15-42), specifically the Aeronca Defender (L-3), the tandem Taylorcraft (L-2), and the Piper J-3 Cub (L-4) with their engines removed and a third seat added in a new nose structure bolted onto the original firewall through the engine mount attach points (FIG. 15-43). With no propeller to be held clear of the ground, a new short landing gear was installed. These former lightplanes were designated TG-5, TG-6, and TG-8, respectively.

Most survived the war, but none joined the postwar glider movement, which was equipped mainly with the earlier and higher-performance surplus TGs. The former lightplanes were easily reconverted to airplanes by reinstallation of standard engines and landing gear and removal of the special glider spoilers on the wings.

TG-5 specifications: Wing span 35 feet; area 169 square feet; gross weight 1,260 pounds; best gliding speed 55 mph; stalling speed 46 mph; maximum towing speed 129 mph.

291

Fig. 15-41. A Bellanca 14-19 Cruisaire fitted with extra-width skis under its wheels about to touch down on water for a hydro-ski run to shore. Note that there is no ski on the tail wheel.

Fig. 15-42. In 1941, the U.S. Army adapted some civil lightplanes like this Aeronca Defender to light observation/liaison planes. The Aeronca became the O-58, later L-3.

Fig. 15-43. Some of the militarized lightplanes had their engines removed and a third seat installed in the nose. The Aeronca O-58/L-3 is seen here after conversion to the TG-5 training glider.

Douglas XCG-17 One of the handicaps of the big cargo and troop-carrying gliders was their slow speed on tow, which caused engine overheating problems on the transport-type airplanes used to tow them. Rather than design a fast glider from scratch, the Army decided to make a cargo glider, the XCG-17, out of a Douglas C-47 transport plane, the military version of the famous DC-3 airliner (FIG. 15-44).

With the engines removed (but the nacelle structure retained by a requirement that the airframe be

Fig. 15-44. A standard U.S. Army Douglas C-47, itself a variant of the famous DC-3 airliner, after conversion to the XCG-17 cargo glider.

reconvertible to power), the XCG-17 had the desired towing speed and—because of its clean lines—the flattest glide angle of any Army cargo glider of the time. However, the war was too far along, with thousands of Waco CG-4As on hand, to justify setting up a C-47/ CG-17 conversion program. The single prototype was reconverted to a C-47 and found a new civil owner on the postwar surplus market.

Specifications: Wing span 95 feet; area 987 square feet; gross weight 26,000 pounds; maximum towing speed 255 mph.

Gliders Converted to Airplanes

While some airplanes were converted to gliders, the opposite was also true. Some of the conversions were of a temporary nature, such as adding bolt-on power packages to established gliders to ferry them from one point to another. Self-launching sailplanes are a separate story entirely; their engines are designed-in but the aircraft themselves remain high-performance sailplanes and operate as such.

In other cases, the design started as a glider, power was added, and the new combination was sufficiently

desirable to justify continued production as a powered aircraft. Three examples follow.

Northwestern XPG-1* With thousands of the U.S. Army's 15-place Waco CG-4A troop gliders being used in World War II, there was a considerable problem involved in retrieving them. One idea was to attach a pair of small standard airplane engines (when the supply services could reach the landing zone) and fly the now-powered gliders out (FIG. 15-45). An alternative was to build engines into the gliders in the first place. Such designs could be towed into the air and to the landing zone as gliders, then use their power to select the most desirable landing area, and fly out later. Supposedly, they could also take off and fly the whole mission on their own as low-speed airplanes.

Several different engines were tried on the CG-4A and the CG-15A (a clipped-wing version of the CG-14A with a much higher towing speed). Some of the additions, as on the Northwestern conversion of the CG-4A, which was designated XPG-1 for Experimental Powered Glider and fitted with two 175-hp Franklin O-300-5 engines, were relatively easy on-off arrangements. The Ridgefield XPG-2,* another CG-4A conversion, had two 200-hp Ranger engines in nacelles

293

---

*Northwestern Aeronautical Corporation of St. Paul, Minnesota, was one of 16 firms that built the Waco CG-4A cargo glider under license.

*Ridgefield Manufacturing Company was another CG-4A licensee.

Fig. 15-45. U.S. Army Waco CG-4A cargo gliders were tested with different airplane engines during World War II. This conversion by Northwestern was designated XPG-1 for Experimental Powered Glider.

built into the underside of the wing. The Waco XPG-3 conversion of a CG-15 had a pair of 245-hp Jacobs R-755-9 radial engines in nacelles built onto the leading edge of the wing like a bomber or transport plane. On the XPG-2 and -3, the powerplant installations were permanent.

Nothing came of the bolt-on concept, but work continued after the war on adding permanent power to designs that started as gliders. The main postwar change was much higher power on much faster designs. Takeoff performance of the 175- to 200-hp CG-4A conversions was very poor; even JATO didn't help much.

XPG-1 specifications: Wing span 83 feet 8 inches; wing area 852 square feet; gross weight 7,500 pounds; speed under power 80 mph.

Chase C-123 Series In the public's mind, jet propulsion is associated with high-speed flight while gliders are considered to be at the low end of the speed scale. It might come as a surprise, then to realize that the first jet transport airplane built in the U.S. was a converted glider!

The Chase Aircraft Company of Trenton, New Jersey, built two 62-seat all-metal G-20 assault gliders. With their modern structure, clean lines, and retractable landing gear, they were like a large transport airplane except for the lack of engines. When the U.S. Air Force decided to do away with gliders altogether in the late 1940s, Chase converted the two G-20s (the old prefix letters, C for Cargo, T for Training, etc., were deleted in 1948) to powered designs. When fitted with a pair of 1,900-hp Pratt & Whitney R-2000-CB15 engines in leading edge nacelles in 1949, the first G-20

became the XC-123 in the C-for-Cargo plane series (FIG. 15-46).

The new combination was very successful. The Air Force wanted C-123s in quantity, but little Chase had no production facilities. The design was licensed to Fairchild, and over 300 were built, starting with 2,300-hp engines in the C-123B of 1955 and ending with 2,850-hp units in the C-123Ks.

The second G-20 was fitted with four 5,200-pound thrust General Electric J-47 turbojets in the unique strut-mounted two-engine inboard pods of the Boeing B-47 jet bomber to become the XC-123A in 1951 (FIG. 15-47). This combination did not work as well as the XC-123, so was dropped.

C-123B specifications: Powerplant two 2,300-hp Pratt & Whitney R-2000-99W; otherwise as XC-123A except gross weight 60,000 pounds; top speed 245 mph; range 1,470 miles.

Volmer VJ-23E Powered Hang Glider The now-booming ultralight aircraft movement got under way in the mid-1970s when some designers and fliers began adding small two-stroke cycle engines to their established hang gliders. These were not particularly efficient, because they turned small propellers at very high engine speeds and were fitted onto the airframe at sometimes very inconvenient locations. The early powerplants were primarily aids to launching, or a means for ferrying a short distance from level ground to a good slope-soaring site. The Volmer VJ-23E (E for Engine added to the standard rigid-wing Volmer VJ-23 Swingwing hang glider of 1971) is representative of the earliest conversions (FIG. 15-48).

Fig. 15-46. The first of two Chase G-20 assault gliders was fitted with reciprocating engines and became the XC-123.

Fig. 15-47. The second G-20 was fitted with four jet engines to become the XC-123A, the first American jet transport.

The success of the small engines in the lightweight glider airframes made them appealing to people other than glider pilots—those who wanted to fly locally, at minimum cost, and free of regulation. These people started the booming ultralight movement.

Major improvements were soon made in the powerplants, and power was increased from chain saw and go-cart engines to specially modified 20- to 30-hp snowmobile units. Propellers became much more efficient, being of larger diameter and turning slower as a result of gear, chain, or belt-drive reduction. Many established hang gliders were quickly adapted by developing new substructures (it is hard to call them fuselages) for pilot, engine, and landing gear. Other designs were developed from scratch as ultralight powered types, but they still owe much to previous hang glider technology.

VJ-23E specifications: Powerplant 12-hp McCullough Mc 101; wing span 32 feet 7 inches; length 17 feet 5 inches; area 179 square feet; gross weight 340 pounds; top speed 30 mph.

Fig. 15-48. The Volmer VJ-23 Swingwing rigid-wing hang glider fitted with a 12-hp two-stroke-cycle engine above the wing.

Curtiss Flying Lifeboat

Airplanes have been used extensively in air-sea rescue operations since World War I, but the operation has always been strictly airplane—set down at sea, pick up the victims, then take off and fly home. The Curtiss Model BT triplane flying boat of early 1917 (FIG. 15-49) took a different approach. It could perform the first part of the mission as an airplane and then, if necessary, complete it as a boat.

This was achieved through the use of a very short hull on the flying boat, with the tail surfaces supported by booms. The single 200-hp Curtiss V-2-3 engine was installed in the hull ahead of the wings and drove two oppositely-rotating propellers via shafts and gears. If the airplane was unable to take off after making the rescue, it could jettison the wings and tail as shown in FIG. 15-50 and proceed as a boat driven by the airplane propellers.

Fig. 15-49. Original form of the Curtiss Model BT flying lifeboat of 1917.

Fig. 15-50. Curtiss drawing of how the flying lifeboat could shed its wings at sea and proceed as a boat driven by the airplane propellers.

The airplane-to-boat conversion was never tried. In its initial configuration, the airplane couldn't fly; the power transmission system was unworkable from the start. The BT was modified to conventional configuration with the engine mounted on the center wing and driving a tractor propeller before turned over to the U.S. Navy.

Rohrbach Flying Sailboat

One of the touted safety advantages of the flying boat was its ability to set down on the water in the event of a power failure or other reasons. Once down, however, it was usually helpless, able only to drift with the wind. There have been some notable historic exceptions, such as the U.S. Navy NC-3 being forced down 205 miles short of the Azores Islands on its transatlantic flight attempt of May 1919 after which it was able to taxi to the islands. Another was the U.S. Navy PN-9 attempting a non-stop flight from San Francisco to Hawaii in August 1925. It came down 450 miles short; the resourceful crew removed some wing fabric and used it as sails to reach the islands.

The German designer Rohrbach, a pioneer in all-metal stressed-skin aircraft structures, developed several large flying boats after World War I but had to build them in Denmark because of the weight limits imposed on German-built aircraft at the time by the

Allied Control Commission. The R.II of 1924 was an all-metal flying boat with a difference—it could also function as a sailboat (FIG. 15-51). Rohrbach fitted one Ro.II with two demountable masts and sails, one installed on the bow and the other near the trailing edge of the wing, this before the PN-9 misadventure. However, in spite of a demonstrated need, the feature was not adopted as standard.

Dry Seaplane Operations

Practically since the advent of pontoon seaplanes, pilots have had occasion to put them down on dry ground, usually without damage. Putting a light seaplane down on grass, and sometimes getting it to take off again, became an airshow act in the 1930s. It was old stuff to the seaplane pilots, but a new thrill for the spectators.

Another old seaplane trick seen occasionally at airshows is a seaplane takeoff from a wheeled dolly (FIG. 15-52). Often, landplanes are put on floats at an airport shop that is not conveniently close to water, where the plane can be launched from a dolly or other shop equipment. The plane is put on a dolly, uses its own power to roll down the runway until flying speed is attained, then simply flies off while the dolly rolls to a stop.

A minor air show variation to landing a seaplane

Fig. 15-51. This German-designed Rohrbach R.II, built in Denmark, was fitted with two masts and sails for emergency use after a forced landing at sea.

298

Fig. 15-52. Flying seaplanes from a wheeled dolly after the floats have been installed away from suitable water is common practice. It also makes a good airshow act that usually follows a "dry" landing.

on the ground is to do the same with a retractable-landing-gear airplane when the wheels are up. The engine is stopped in flight, the propeller is nudged to a horizontal position with the starter, and the plane makes a wheels-up "Dead Stick" landing. For this act, the airplane is usually modified to the extent of having small skids attached to the underside to keep the belly skin from contacting the ground. After landing, the plane is hoisted by a crane, the landing gear is lowered, the engine started, and the plane taxis to the grandstand for its acclamation. That's *Aviation Show Business!*

Manned Glider Intercepter

The mission description of the Blohm & Voss Bv.40 is a contradiction in terms. Gliders are associated with low-speed flight while intercepters are associated with high speeds, yet the Bv.40 (FIG. 15-53) was both.

It was another of the German defensive weapons of desperation developed late in World War II. In concept, it was an armed interceptor glider, intended to be towed at over 300 mph behind a conventional fighter plane to the vicinity of an Allied bomber stream. With no bulky engine, it offered an extremely small target to the Allied gunners, thereby giving it a better chance to make a safe pass. Released above and ahead of the bombers, the Bv.40 was to make a diving attack at a closing speed in excess of 500 mph. This allowed time for only one burst from its pair of 30mm cannon. The pilot, who lay prone on his stomach, was protected by a 120mm armor glass windshield, 20mm steel armor in front of him, and 8mm armor at his sides. An early additional weapon concept was to unreel a steel cable with a small explosive charge at the end of it and hope that it would hit a bomber during the pass through the formation. This was not adopted.

The Bv.40 was an extremely simple design, with an almost crude wood-and-steel structure that could be built quickly by relatively unskilled labor. Like many gliders of the time, takeoff was made on a wheeled dolly that was dropped after the glider was airborne. In spite of its small wing area and generally ungliderlike characteristics, the Bv.40 could be spot-landed with precision thanks to the use of special flaps.

Only seven prototypes of the Bv.40 were completed between May and August 1944 out of 19 ordered. A production order for 200 was cancelled.

Specifications: Wing span 25 feet 11 inches; length 18 feet 8½ inches; wing area 93.6 sq. feet; gross weight 2,094 pounds; calculated diving speed 560 mph.

299

Fig. 15-53. The German Blohm & Voss Bv.40 of 1944 was an interceptor glider that was to be towed in the vicinity of Allied bomber streams and then released to dive through them while firing 20mm cannon.

Turboprop Test Beds

Turbine powerplants, both pure jets and those driving propellers, turboprops, were something new to the aircraft industry at the end of World War II, and many experiments were conducted in order to adapt them to existing aircraft and to determine their characteristics and performance for new designs.

One simple way to test these engines under flight conditions was to carry them on a test-bed airplane. For small-diameter pure jets this was easily accomplished by carrying the jet on a retracting mechanism in the bomb bay of a standard bombing plane. The jet could be extended into the airstream and its centerline location had no effect on the flying characteristics of the host airplane.

One turboprop installation that did give trouble, however, was that of the Curtiss XC-113 in October 1946. This was a standard C-46G Commando cargoplane given a later designation in the Army's C-for-Cargo series because of its modifications. In the interest of economy and time-saving, and to avoid trusting the safety of the airplane to two untried engines at once, only one 2,200 equivalent shaft horsepower (ESHP, plus 600 pounds of jet thrust) General Electric TG-100 was installed in place of the 2,000-hp Pratt & Whitney R-2800 piston engine on the right wing of the plane. The left-side R-2800 was retained (FIG. 15-54). It was believed that the nearly-equal power of the two dissimilar engines would not cause significant trim problems, but it did.

While the power was nearly equal, the acceleration characteristics and response to throttle movement of the two engines were not, and the XC-113 was almost completely unmanageable. The pilot lost control on a takeoff run, veered off the runway, and hit some parked ground equipment. The project was cancelled.

A much more logical way of testing large turboprop engines was to add the test engine to the nose of a modified four-engine bomber, for centerline operation. In 1947 Boeing did this with two B-17Gs, modifying one for the 5,000-hp Pratt & Whitney XT-34 turboprop (FIG. 15-55) and one for the competing 5,500-hp Wright XT-35. Seven years later General Motors modified another B-17G as a test bed for the 3,750-hp Allison T-56.

A notable feature of all these turboprop installations was the ability of the test turboprop engine alone to fly the airplane when all four piston engines were shut down.

Three-engine Lockheed Constellation

The Lockheed Constellation was a popular four-engine airliner in wide use from the end of World War II until replaced by jet airliners in the late 1950s. One, however, flew briefly as a trimotor (FIG. 15-56).

It lost No. 4 engine, the right outboard, on a return flight to the U.S. from Europe. "Lost engine" in this case did not carry the usual meaning of one engine that shut down—it actually departed the airplane. Because

300

Fig. 15-54. The one-only and unsuccessful Curtiss XC-113, a standard C-46G Commando cargoplane fitted with an experimental 2,200-hp General Electric TG-100 turboprop engine in place of the right-side 200-hp Pratt & Whitney R-2800 piston engine.

Fig. 15-55. A more successful approach to testing large turboprop engines was made by installing a 5,000-hp Pratt & Whitney XT-34 in the nose of the B-17G that retained all of its original engines, which are feathered in this photograph.

Fig. 15-56. A Lockheed Constellation, normally a four-engine airliner, landing at the factory with only three aboard after the No. 4 engine fell off the airplane over the Atlantic.

there was no structural damage to the wing, and it would be inconvenient to rebuild the damaged nacelle and replace the missing engine on the East Coast, it was decided to fly the three-engined Connie to the Lockheed factory in Burbank, California, for the major repair.

The remains of the damaged nacelle were removed and the leading edge of the wing at that point was covered with sheet aluminum. The asymmetrical trimotor then made an uneventful transcontinental flight at a takeoff gross weight of 74,000 pounds instead of its normal 105,000 pounds.

16
CHAPTER

What Is It?

MANY SO-CALLED (AND SOME ACTUAL) AIRCRAFT DEFY classification by the commonly recognized configuration standards. Many were developed with intelligent application of the laws of aerodynamics and did manage to fly—whether well or just barely is beside the point. Others have been the product of far-out inventors who maintained that everyone from the Wright Brothers on had been going at the problem of flight the wrong way.

This concluding chapter presents a collection, in approximate chronological order, of some of these hard-to-classify designs. Some can be considered successful in that they did fly; others obviously had no chance except in the dreams of their well-meaning but misguided inventors.

The French Guiser Cyclo-Plane of approximately 1909 (FIG. 16-1) is representative of early attempts to fly fixed-wing aircraft by human muscle power, a feat that

Fig. 16-1. Guiser Cycle-Plane.

was over half a century in the future. This bicycle, with its hard-to-define aerodynamic attachment, used belt or chain drive from the rear wheel to turn the propeller.

Another French experiment was the two-seat Domingo Aeraptere built approximately 1910 (FIG. 16-2). Except for the configuration of the wing, it has much in common with the Rogallo-winged Ryan Flex-Wing introduced half a century later.

The French Vedo Velli of 1911 (FIG. 16-3) had a collection of relatively conventional wings in an unconventional arrangement. The rudder was up front, and a pusher engine was at the rear of the cabin, which was itself an innovation at the time. The rear wing was supported by two deep but thin booms.

The Russian Bessa-Brasov of World War I (FIG. 16-4) can be regarded either as a triple tandem monoplane design with the wings at different levels or as a straight-wing tailless triplane with an extreme degree of stagger. Elevators were on the rear wing, ailerons on the center wing, and either elevators or ailerons on the forward wing.

The details of the engine and the over-all style of the apparition shown in FIG. 16-5, plus a 48-star American flag, indicate that it was built after 1912. Because the unidentified negative was acquired with some others verified in the 1915-16 range, that period is logical. It is interesting to note that the shape of the topmost surface approximates the "flying saucers" so widely reported in the early post-World War II years.

The oddity in FIG. 16-6 with the high dihedral angle on its streamer-covered wings was built in Colorado in the late 1920s. The fuselage and landing gear were relatively conventional and the engine was a war-surplus 80-hp Le Rhone rotary.

The American McClarey Model 1A of the late 1920s (FIG. 16-7) was powered by a 90-hp Curtiss OX-5 engine and seated the pilot in a streamlined pod below the longitudinally-aligned wing, which was slotted to accommodate the propeller. Note the projecting ailerons and the damage farther aft.

C.E. Brooks of Pattonville, Missouri, is reported to have worked 30 years—from 1910 to 1940—on the

304

Fig. 16-2. Domingo Aeraptere.

Fig. 16-3. Vedo Villi. Is it a canard or a tandem-wing?

Fig. 16-4. Is this Russian Bessa-Brasov a triple-tandem monoplane or a heavily staggered tailless triplane?

Fig. 16-5. Unidentified "flying saucer."

hard-to-describe paddle-propelled design shown in FIG. 16-8. The welded steel tube fuselage construction is mid-1920s or later in style. The paddles come close to categorizing Mr. Brooks' effort as a Cyclogyro, but the presence of supports for a beam-type engine mount ahead of the cross-mounted engine shown would indicate that another engine with conventional propeller was to be used for propulsion.

Two brothers, Ervin and Lyle Joy, built the unique twin shown in FIG. 16-9, powered by 40-hp Salmson radial engines, in Portland, Oregon, in the early 1930s. It can best be classified as a reverse-delta with conventional horizontal tail surfaces, but because of the extra lifting surface between the engines it might also qualify as a sesquiplane. Note the use of fins and rudders both fore and aft.

Another openwork design of indeterminate configuration (FIG. 16-10) was built in Denver, Colorado, in 1931 by an organization known as Gray Goose Airways. No details of its powerplant or means of operation are known today, but the original caption accompanying the photo stated that it had reached a height of 14 inches during a 1932 test. It would be interesting to know just how this precise measurement was obtained.

Charles Rocheville, then chief engineer of the Emsco Aircraft Corporation (Emsco was an acronym for E.M. Smith Co.) of Downey, California, created an interesting amphibian that is difficult to identify as to type (FIG. 16-11). Built quickly (for arctic exploration) from the wing and tail of a Lockheed Altair monoplane, the unique amphibian used other Lockheed parts

Fig. 16-6. Unidentified streamer-covered design of the 1920s.

Fig. 16-7. McClarey Model IA.

Fig. 16-8. Paddle-propelled design of C. E. Brooks.

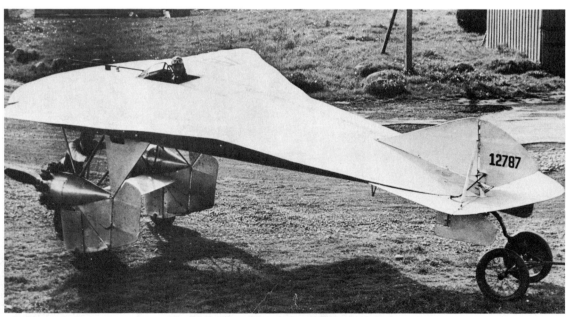

Fig. 16-9. Twin-engine design of Ervin and Lyle Joy.

Fig. 16-10. The Gray Goose of 1931. The two walking beams on the body appear to transmit alternating opening and closing motion to the 10 slats in each of the four tandem sections that make up the single upper wing.

Fig. 16-11. Because of the filled-in spaces between the amphibious pontoons and the wing, Charles Rocheville's Arctic Tern can be regarded as twin-hull flying boat rather than a twin-pontoon seaplane.

while including many odd features. A short pod contained an open cockpit and a small cabin, plus a 420-hp Pratt & Whitney Wasp engine that might also have come from the Lockheed.

The tail surfaces were supported by four booms, two from the wing and two from the rear of the floats. The spaces that would normally be between the floats and the wings were filled in to make two cabins, complete with side windows and forward windshield. This filling-in of the space would seem to qualify the Arctic Tern, as the amphibian was named, as a twin-hull flying boat rather than a pontoon seaplane.

The Arctic Tern was sponsored by the Shell Oil Company for exploration in the Canadian north. It flew successfully for a month in the early 1930s, but experienced engine failure during the flight on which the photo was taken, and was destroyed in the subsequent forced landing.

Built by a gentleman named Ben Brown, an interesting pusher, with propeller at the rear of the fuselage and driven by an extension shaft, was photographed in Kansas City in 1932 (FIGS. 16-12, 16-13). Is it a tandem wing design with wingtips joined to form a diamond wing, or is it a tailless monoplane with a big cutout in

310

Fig. 16-12. Is Ben Brown's unconventional flying machine a tandem-wing . . .

Fig. 16-13. . . . or a tapered-wing tailless monoplane with the center cutout?

the center of a single wing? The ailerons are at the tips of the rear portion of the wing and the elevators are next to the fuselage on the "forward" portion. The struts contribute to the total lift in the style of the Bellancas.

The French Payenne Pa 22 of 1939-41 (FIG. 16-14) can be regarded either as an early delta wing design with a canard, as a tandem with a large rear wing, or a conventional tractor with an oversized horizontal tail. The invading Germans found it in the full-scale wind tunnel at Chalais-Meudon, put Luftwaffe markings on it, and took it to Villacoublay in 1941 for flight testing. With 180 hp, it had a front-wing span of 15 feet 9 inches, total area of 107 square feet, and a gross weight of 1,894 pounds. Top speed was reported to be 242 mph.

The Horten Model HW-X-26-52 Wingless (FIGS. 16-15 through 16-17) built in Santa Ana, California, in 1954, was misnamed in that it did have wings. These

Fig. 16-14. Payenne pa 22.

311

Fig. 16-15. Horten HW-X-26-52 Wingless.

Fig. 16-16. Horten Wingless.

Fig. 16-17. Horten Wingless.

were semiretractable and contained ailerons for control during low-speed flight. Major components of the unique rectangular airframe, such as wings, landing gear, engine mounts, and some fuselage structure were adapted from a twin-engine Cessna T-50. The Wingless, with 450-hp Pratt & Whitney Wasp Jr. engines, flew very briefly.

The Advance Jeep-O-Plane of the 1950s comes close to standard classification as a biplane with heavy stagger (FIGS. 16-18, 16-19). The horizontal tail was on a boom while the fins and rudders boxed the ends of the wings in a style reminiscent of some pre-World War I designs. Additional fin area was placed above the engine.

The Hiller Flying Platform (FIG. 16-20) is another hard-to-classify flying machine. It is not an airplane, and although capable of vertical flight, is neither a helicopter nor a convertaplane. It was developed in 1954 for the U.S. Office of Naval Research without an official naval designation and the U.S. Army followed up with an order for two under the designation of VZ-1 in the VTOL research series.

The one-man platform followed the concept of the De Lackner Aerocycle (see Chapter 5) in that after vertical lift-off, it was steered by the pilot leaning in the desired direction.

Actually, the platform was the first vehicle driven by a ducted fan to lift a man into free flight. In this

Fig. 16-18. Advance Jeep-O-Plane.

Fig. 16-19. Advance Jeep-O-Plane.

Fig. 16-20. The Hiller Flying Platform developed for the U.S. Army and Navy was steered by the pilot leaning in the desired direction.

respect it was different from a conventional surface-skimming hovercraft in that it could reach a considerably higher altitude. Power was provided by two 40-hp Nelson air-cooled engines driving a pair of coaxial and contrarotating fans inside a six-foot-diameter duct. The shrouding gave the fans the efficiency of unshrouded

propellers having 40 percent greater diameter. The only control that the pilot had was a hand throttle with which to control power and altitude. The first flight was made on February 4, 1955, but like the Aerocycle, the successful experiment was not followed by production orders.

In 1963 the Bell Helicopter Company of Fort Worth, Texas, added a conventional monoplane wing, complete with ailerons, flaps, and tip-mounted fuel tanks, plus a small horizontal tail, to a standard Bell Model 47 helicopter (FIG. 16-21). The result was a hybrid aircraft that could operate either as an airplane or as a helicopter without actually being a convertaplane.

The purpose of the experiment was to develop an aircraft that could carry a payload in excess of the helicopter's hover capacity by utilizing the additional wing lift provided by running takeoffs. The four-wheeled landing gear was readopted from early Bell 47s built before the company standardized on skid gear.

In addition to the normal practice of tilting the rotor for forward thrust, Bell tilted the rotor mast on its

Fig. 16-21. A wing was added to a Bell Model 47 helicopter to give it greater lifting capability from wing lift generated by running instead of vertical takeoffs.

winged helicopter, which retained all its normal helicopter capability in spite of the addition of wings and tail. No production aircraft resulted from this experiment.

The closest thing to a real "flying saucer" was the Canadian Avro Avrocar built on a U.S. Army/Air Force experimental contract as the VZ-9V in 1955 (FIG. 16-22). Direct lift from three internal jet engines enabled it to rise vertically, after which vectored thrust gave it forward motion. Stability problems prevented it from reaching its planned top speed of 260 mph. Diameter was 18 feet and gross weight 5,650 pounds.

Fig. 16-22. Avro VZ-9Z Avrocar.

Index

316

317

318

Other Bestsellers of Related Interest

THE BLOND KNIGHT OF GERMANY
—Raymond F. Toliver and Trevor J. Constable

The fascinating biography of the most successful fighter ace in the history of aerial warfare—Erich Hartmann whose 352 victories amounted to more than six times those of the top U.S. ace! You'll relive Hartmann's extraordinaryaerial achievements, the ordeals suffered during 10 years of post-war imprisonment by the Soviet Union, and his role in the new West German Air Force. 352 pages, 166 illustrations. Book No. 24189, $16.95 paperback, $21.95 Hardcover

HALF A WING, THREE ENGINES AND A PRAYER: B-17s Over Germany—Brian D. O'Neill

Historians consider the Eighth as the air force responsible for breaking the back of the German Luftwaffe in April 1944. This book is a stirring account of one B-17 bomber crew's experiences, and an accurate report of this war period. Through *Half a Wing*, you will learn firsthand—or perhaps relive—what it was like to fly a B-17 into combat during the worst period of America's air war against the Germans. 304 pages, Illustrated. Book No. 22385, $16.95 paperback only

THE LUFTWAFFE: A Photographic Record 1919-1945—Karl Ries
Written by Germany's premier Luftwaffe historian!

This book is a behind-the-scenes look at the Luftwaffe from a noted author who has studied and written about the subject for more than 20 years. Author Karl Ries provides an actual account of the German Air Force. Hundreds of previously unpublished photographs and accompanying text chronologically tell the Luftwaffe's origins, rise, combat, and ultimate decline. 240 pages, 450 Illustration. Book No. 22384, $24.95 hardcover only

YOUR PILOT'S LICENSE—4th Edition—Joe Christy

"A valuable reference manual during training" *(ALA Booklist)*. "A book you should not only read but have as a permanent part of your bookshelf" *(Colorado CAP Flyer)*. 176 pages, 73 illustrations. Book No. 2477, $12.95 paperback only

ACES OVER THE OCEANS—The Great Pilots of World War II—Edward H. Sims

This exceptional account gives you detailed and colorful coverage of 12 dramatic naval air battles that took place over the seas during WWII. Ed Sims compiled these stories as a legacy to the heroism of the naval pilots of the United States, Germany, and Great Britain. Personal interviews with the pilots who flew these missions set the stage for accounts of these historic battles. 192 pages, 10 Illustrations. Book No. 22392, $14.95 paperback only

AMERICAN AIR POWER: The First 75 Years—Joe Christy

From the earliest days when the Wright Brothers delivered the first plane for military use, to the very latest decisions being made about the cruise missile and the stealth bomber, the MX, and the B1, you'll benefit from the meticulous research that went into this book. Includes rare photographs from private archives, glimpses of secret strategy sessions, and the men, the machines, the tactics, the politics and the technology that made American air power. 208 pages, 254 Illustrations. Book No. 2327, $21.95 hardcover only

THE MUNSTER RAID: Bloody Skies Over Germany—Ian Hawkins *"Few books tell the glory of war so well . . . or its horror."* **—100the Bomb Group Newsletter**
". . . recalls, far better than anything else I have read, that which I term the 'flavor' of a combat mission." — **Colonel Joseph Moller, 8the Air Force, Bombardment Group Commander**

The Munster Raid over Germany is considered to be one of the most vicious and destructive air battles of World War II. Author Ian Hawkins has compiled firsthand accounts of more than 200 battle participants, both American and German, and has pieced them together with official reports to produce this fascinating historical narrative. 448 pages, Illustrated. Book No. 20001, $17.95 paperback only

AMERICAN AVIATION: An Illustrated History—
Joe Christy with contributions by
Alexander T. Wells, Ed. D.

Here, in a comprehensive, well-researched sourcebook, Christy and Wells have taken the history of American aviation and transformed it into a fascinating story of people, machines, and accomplishments that is as entertaining as it is informative. With its hundreds of excellent photographs, this is a book that every aviation enthusiast will want to red and reread! 440 pages, 486 Illustrations. Book No. 2497, $24.95 hardcover only

THE ILLUSTRATED HANDBOOK OF AVIATION AND AEROSPACE FACTS—Joe Christy

A complete book at American aviation—civil and military. All the political, social, economic, and personality factors that have influenced the state of U.S. military airpower, the boom-and-bust cycles in Civil aviation, America's manned and unmanned space flights—including little-known facts on the flights—and information on the birth of modem rocketry, is all covered here in this complete sourcebook! 480 pages, 486 Illustrations. Book No. 2397, $28.95 paperback only

1001 FLYING FACTS AND FIRSTS—Joe Christy

Here are the who, what, where, when, and why of significant aviation events from World War I to the present. Here are the significant airplanes, civil and military. Here are the current official record flights—all arranged so that this book may be used as a quick reference, or as a just-for-fun quiz book! More than 150n photographs illustrate the points of history, aircraft, facts, and trivia that are included in this aviation sourcebook. 224 pages, 161 Illustrations. Book No. 2428, $15.95 paperback only

THE MCDONNELL DOUGLAS APACHE (Aero Series, Vol. 33)—Frank Colucci

A concise, illustrated look at the history, design, and mission of the world's most advanced attack helicopter. ''I believe this book will give . . . a full appreciation of the Apache program—how it evolved, what it is today and the difference it will make should we have to go to war in the future'' (Major General Edward M. Browne, USA [Ret'd], Manager of the Apache Program, 4/76-12/82). 112 pages, 104 illustrations. Book No. 20614, $10.95 paperback only

---

Look for These and Other TAB Books at Your Local Bookstore

To Order Call Toll Free 1-800-822-8158
(in PA and AK call 717-794-2191)

or write to TAB BOOKS Inc., Blue Ridge Summit, PA 17294-0840.

Title	Product No.	Quantity	Price

☐ Check or money order made payable to TAB BOOKS Inc.

Charge my ☐ VISA ☐ MasterCard ☐ American Express

Acct. No. _____ Exp. _____

Signature: _____

Name: _____

City: _____

State: _____ Zip: _____

Subtotal $ _____

Postage and Handling
($3.00 in U.S., $5.00 outside U.S.) $ _____

In PA, NY, & ME add
applicable sales tax $ _____

TAB BOOKS catalog free with purchase; otherwise send $1.00 in check or money order and receive a $1.00 credit on your next purchase.

Orders outside U.S. must pay with international money order in U.S. dollars.

TAB Guarantee: If for any reason you are not satisfied with the book(s) you order, simply return it (them) within 15 days and receive a full refund. **BC**